Michelle Grattan has been a political journalist in Canberra since 1971. She has written for the *Age*, the *Sydney Morning Herald*, and the *Australian Financial Review* and was editor of the *Canberra Times*. She is currently political editor at the *Age* and does commentary for the ABC's Radio National.

For Ron Younger

Back on the
Wool Track

Michelle Grattan

VINTAGE

A Vintage Book
Published by
Random House Australia Pty Ltd
20 Alfred Street, Milsons Point, NSW 2061
http://www.randomhouse.com.au

Sydney New York Toronto
London Auckland Johannesburg

First published in Australia by Vintage
Copyright © Michelle Grattan 2004

Picture sections: unless otherwise stated, photographs are
by Michelle Grattan.

National Library of Australia
Cataloguing-in-Publication Entry

Grattan, Michelle.
Back on the wool track.

Bibliography
ISBN 1 74051 167 0

1. Sheep industry – New South Wales – History 21st century.
2. Rural conditions – New South Wales – History – 21st
century. 3. Sheep shearers (Persons) – New South Wales –
Social conditions – 21st century. I. Title.

338.76314509944

Cover design by Darian Causby/Highway 61
Typeset in 11/14 Sabon by Midland Typesetters, Maryborough, Victoria
Printed and bound by Griffin Press, Netley, South Australia

10 9 8 7 6 5 4 3 2 1

Table of Contents

PROLOGUE: In Search of a Lost Empire   ix

PART ONE: A BIOGRAPHICAL SKETCH

  1.   'The Finest Selector'   3
  2.   The Making of an Australian   8
  3.   Becoming a Journalist   17
  4.   Birth and Baptism of the Anzac Legend   31

PART TWO: THE WEST – THEN AND NOW

  5.   'The Land That Never Leaves You'   45
  6.   Adaptation and Change   60
  7.   Fighting the Elements   72
  8.   Women of the West   88
  9.   Falling off the Sheep's Back   100
10.   The New Merino   109
11.   The Old Trade in a New World   119

PART THREE: BACK ON THE TRACK

12. The Start of Bean's Wool Track 131
13. The Town with Iron Windows 139
14. A New Industry and a New 'Church' 153
15. The *Jandra* Sails Again 163
16. The Once Great *Dunlop* 173
17. The T on the Gum Tree 182
18. The Shearing at *Toorale* 187
19. Modern Bards Celebrate an Old Romance 200
20. Sale of a Bride 211
21. A Garden in Need of Watering 217
22. 'The Farthest Town' 230
23. 'A City Girl in Central Australia' 236
24. Mining the Art Market 244
25. The Maidens of Menindee 257
26. The Secret of *Kilfera* 264
27. Hospitality in a Western Town 271
28. The Mystery of Mossgiel 286
29. The End of the Line 295

PART FOUR: THE FUTURE

30. The Future of the Darling and its Land 305

EPILOGUE 316

NOTES ON SOURCES 318

ACKNOWLEDGEMENTS 334

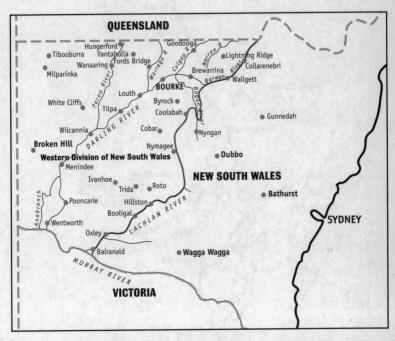

The Western Division of New South Wales

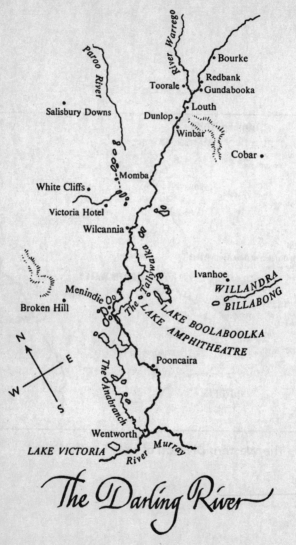

The Darling River

Map from C.E.W. Bean, *The Dreadnought of the Darling*, 1956 edition.

— Prologue —
In Search of a Lost Empire

It is almost a century since Charles Bean, a young Sydney-based journalist later to become the nation's famous chronicler of World War I, set out on his journey of discovery along the Darling River in the far West of New South Wales, where vast pastoral holdings were producing a significant part of the great annual wool clip and were home to a distinctive type of Australian.

In introducing his resulting pen picture of the far West, *On the Wool Track*, Bean gave his own summation of what he found in the little-known region that could prove so deceptive to the uninitiated visitor.

> The truth is that a great part of New South Wales outback there – though it is marked off into little squares on the map and has well-known names written over it and even roads drawn through it, and therefore is never dreamed of by us city folk as being any different from other civilised lands – is not really as yet a country in which a man can be sure of keeping his life . . . [To the first white men] the countryside looked like a beautiful

open park, with gentle slopes and soft grey tree clumps
. . . There might have been a pool of cool water behind
any one of those tree clumps; only – there was not . . .
It is precisely the same beautiful, endless, pitiless
country that it was when [the explorers] found it – with
one exception. Sheep have come there.

Bean felt that 'someone ought to write a book about the
West' – and he did just that. Two books, in fact: first *On
the Wool Track* (published 1910), and then *Dreadnought
of the Darling* (1911) in which he explained the crucial role
played by the paddle-steamers plying the long and tortuous
inland waterway.

Bean first travelled to the back country to report for the
Sydney Morning Herald on alternative routes for the extension of the railway. That was in 1908, before his 1909
assignment for that paper to investigate the wool industry,
which produced *On the Wool Track*, a book described at
the time by London's *Evening Standard* as a 'narrative as
brisk and bright as a May morning'. It went on to become
a minor Australian classic.

Bean later confessed to an English audience that in spite
of his deep involvement he was in no sense an expert on the
wool trade. 'I have followed it from the centre of Australia
to the Bradford looms [in Britain] merely as an outside
journalist & the small books which I wrote "On the Wool
Track" & the "Darling River" were simply an endeavour to
give a picture of the Romance of life out-back in Australia,'
he said. And it is the 'Romance' that gives the charm to
his account.

Bean travelled a settlement frontier, and it had a frontier's characters, so wonderful tales leap from his pages. Just two give a flavour. One is the story he heard of the station hand known as 'Slimy Sam' – because of his personal habits.

> He lived in a hut near the track. One day he came back to his hut, and found writing on the door of it. It struck Sam that it might be an important message. Unfortunately, he could not read. So Sam took the door off its hinges, carried it five miles to an hotel along the road, and had the message read. It was: 'Slimy Sam, of Mumblebone, was the dirtiest beggar ever known.'

I particularly like his personal encounter with a man lighting up the publication for which he (and later I) worked. Bean was travelling on a train with three shearers who were holding forth on wet sheep. One of them, 'a hard little nut of a Cornishman', began to tear off the corner of the daily paper. He borrowed tobacco from another in the carriage, and started to roll it. 'Finally he roughly squared off a piece of newspaper the size of his hand, wrapped it cigarette-wise round the tobacco, licked it to make it stick, put it in his mouth, and began to smoke the *Sydney Morning Herald*.'

Bean's approach brought a fresh eye to the strangeness and challenge of the outback, on which Henry Lawson and Banjo Paterson were the more famous writers.

The best part of a hundred years later my cousin Margaret Cerabona and I revisited the places to which Bean had gone. We were in search of both the old West and the new West, and some of the links between the two.

We also visited Gunnedah, the area to which Bean went in 1909 to familiarise himself with the wool industry. This country on the Namoi, one of NSW's northern rivers and a tributory of the Darling, enjoys a relatively benign climate and is scarcely a foretaste of the country along the Darling River, the harsh, unrelenting West. In following Bean's track to Bourke, a pivot of the old wool track, we moved towards the inner part of the continent, across a significant shadow-line into the Western Division, passing through first the 15-inch average rainfall line, an early prelude to the even more stringent 10-inch isohyet, beyond which we were in the true West. Here is the 'outside' country.

How did I come to be interested in the pastoral wanderings of a man who became famous for his other writings? I first read *On the Wool Track* many years ago. It was one of those books that lingers in the mind. Bean was also writing about a part of the country in which I had some special interest. My cousin Bill Younger, Margaret's brother, had (and still has) a property, *Gladstone*, near Ivanhoe. Over a long time I heard tales, some of them tall ones, about this area, although it was years later that I actually visited his property.

Bill and other members of the family were always talking about Loma Marshall, a remarkable bush woman, who lived near *Gladstone*. She caught my imagination and in 1990 I went to Mossgiel, a one-woman town, to interview Loma for the *Age*. Her home was the old, long-defrocked post office, the sole building surviving from what, when Bean had passed through the general area, was still a viable town.

The idea came of journeying 'in the steps of Bean', perhaps for a series of newspaper articles. As it happened, the opportunity to retrace Bean's travels of 1908–09 arose when a book publisher showed interest.

Prologue

After I began work on the project, I became more and more fascinated by the story of Charles Bean himself, one of the key forgers of the Anzac legend. Hence this book attempts to give a feel for the man as well as for his outback writings, and for the country now.

I soon found that going 'in the footsteps' turns into a journey into the mind and skin of the earlier traveller. We have his writing about what he saw, but inevitably it can be only partial, leaving the imagination to roam free.

As Bean jolted over the plains in buggy or coach, was the still-young journalist dreaming of a famous future? Did the words come easily or with difficulty? What would the men he describes so vividly have said about this English-educated observer, if they had been doing the writing? And later, as he shared the agonies of Gallipoli with the soldiers, did he think back to the shearing shed and the stone store at *Dunlop* station on the Darling?

As I've worked on this book, I've found myself seeking out writings by others who've followed 'in the steps'. Some have done it with extraordinary dedication to exactly replicating the travels of their models.

Kieran Kelly, a Sydney stockbroker who had been captivated since a boy by the exploits of Australian explorer Augustus Charles Gregory, decided to follow his tracks through northern Australia.

The title of Kelly's book, *Hard Country, Hard Men* is an understatement. His project required a decade of planning, training and fund-raising, and replicated conditions of the original trek as men from diverse backgrounds were thrown 'into a struggle to survive in the wilderness'.

On a less ambitious but still testing scale, Richard Holmes

in *Footsteps* recounts a character-forming journey through France, following the walk Robert Louis Stevenson took with Modestine, an animal he made famous in a wonderful little book called *Travels with a Donkey in the Cevennes*.

Needless to say, Margaret and I took a less literal approach to our travelling than these authors. Indeed, our enthusiasm might have waned had someone offered a horse and buggy or a replica of one of the brightly painted old coaches that traversed the West.

As a book, *On the Wool Track* is both poetic and practically descriptive. It has lasted because of the lyricism, the 'feel' it gives for the Australia of its day, or at least the way that Australians liked to think of their country and themselves.

Much of the *On the Wool Track* is thematic, dealing with categories of bush people. Some of these, such as the shepherds, had already disappeared before Bean's time; some, like the bullocky, were there then but are gone now. Others, notably the shearers, continue doing the old job in a new world.

We travelled between 2001 to 2003 (mostly together, but I did a couple of extra forays), seeking out particular towns and stations Bean mentioned from his two journeys.

Margaret, who lives in Wagga Wagga, in the 'inside' country of NSW, has a network of contacts that led to many of our encounters. As I became increasingly intrigued to track down descendents of those Bean encountered, she showed exceptional detective skills.

And as I'm not a driver, she also had the burden of being behind the wheel throughout our several trips, which added up to quite a few weeks.

Just before Christmas of 2001 found us in what Bean calls

'the Old Port'. In his day Bourke was a thriving river centre to which wool of the Darling area was brought for transporting by the riverboats when the water was high enough.

The town has long since ceased to be a port, although it is striving to be reborn as a tourist centre. A modern *Jandra*, the name of the paddle-steamer on which Bean went down the river to the great sheep property *Dunlop*, has recently been built; one hopes it might become the symbol of Bourke's 21st-century aspirations.

As well as visiting *Dunlop*, we went to nearby *Toorale*, also on the Darling, which Bean passed. In those days it had one of the grandest houses of the West. Later – because *Dunlop*'s great shearing days are over – I returned to watch the shearing at *Toorale*.

Early in 2002, we travelled to Ivanhoe, which Bean went to in 1908; among our stops was *Kilfera*, a property that he stayed at overnight. A third trip took us to White Cliffs and the sheep stations beyond.

In other excursions we returned to Bourke; we caught up with Loma Marshall in Mossgiel; and we explored Broken Hill, its numbers much shrunken compared with Bean's era and facing the prospect (as it had, that time on a false alarm, even in his day) of being a mining town with little mining. A special visit to Louth for its much-anticipated annual race meeting gives me one up on Mr Bean! In writing, I have taken the liberty that Bean took of not reporting our travels chronologically.

Having the comfort, speed and flexibility of a car for the modern wool track increases one's admiration for how Bean covered this ground by buggy, coach and rail, observing so much, so acutely.

A few years after Bean set down the special qualities of the far West and its changing fortunes, he himself went on to his great defining role: as the Anzacs' war historian he established the place of the nation's fighting men in the Australian identity.

Significant as his work as a war historian was, also enduring (albeit much less known) has been the image created in his books of the relentless forces and dauntless characters shaping the back country and carried down from Australia's great – but now vanished – pastoral age.

When we follow in Bean's footsteps we find the wool empire a shadow of its former self, but the people who choose to remain in the West adapting to their new world.

1

A Biographical Sketch

1

'The Finest Selector'

On the road to White Cliffs, in the far back country of New South Wales, is a station with an elegant, rather prim name. Since the 19th century *The Avenue* has been home to the Leckie family.

On Graham Leckie's bookshelves is a well-worn copy of *On the Wool Track*. One page has become detached, so often was it proudly displayed to visitors in his grandfather's time. Golly Leckie liked to say, '*The Avenue* is in print.'

Bean names few individuals – although he vividly sketches the character types – in his stories of the outback. But he lionises Graham's great-grandfather Robert, a bullock driver who had taken up land.

The finest selector of all that we met across the Darling, Mr Leckie of *The Avenue*, a magnificently made, keen, kindly, intelligent giant of a pastoralist, is no longer a selector. He has gradually increased his holding to 109,627 acres. That is not a big station as yet. It is only one of the small blocks into which *Momba* (once 2,000,000 acres – the biggest single holding in New South Wales) has lately been cut up.

But it is a splendidly improved little property. And any man who understands the West and has improved his piece of it and shown what can be done with it in the way in which this selector has done, deserves every encouragement the Government can give him to come to and remain in the West.

At *The Avenue* in Bean's time, 93 acres were irrigated, and the hayshed was as big and the chaff as good 'as any in Australia'. The old homestead is long gone, but Graham tells us the irrigation area is still visible.

And not far from the house still stands the old kitchen of the Victoria Hotel which Bean, years before arriving there, had often noticed as 'a name on the map, in the middle of a big blank in the West'. The Leckies take us to what's left of the wooden building, surrounded by scrub; we imagine Bean arriving by buggy around sundown to see 'a long low verandah half entrenched behind a rampart of sand dropped by the wind in the shelter of the trees. A long dining-room behind the verandah; a few bedrooms; stable-yard and some dogs at the back; the whole overhung by a dense clump of pepper trees . . .'.

Several years after Bean's visit, three of Robert Leckie's sons – Robert, Jack, and Will – enlisted for World War I. They fought on the Western Front; Robert, who sailed in February 1917, was killed in November that year, in Belgium.

There is no evidence Bean encountered any of the Leckie boys as he covered the action, compiling newspaper reports and collecting material for future books. They were, however, the sort of country-bred soldiers of whom he made heroes in his war history.

The CEW Bean Foundation was launched in 2001 in Canberra to commemorate journalists who have reported on wars in which Australians have fought. The name was chosen because Bean was a great war chronicler, some would say Australia's greatest – though Alan Moorehead would also have claim to this fame – and its most prodigious.

As official war correspondent, Bean saw most of the Gallipoli campaign, landing on April 25 and leaving in the December evacuation, with only a few weeks away. Later he moved to the Western Front. His reports were available to all the newspapers. After he returned to Australia in 1919 he wrote six volumes of the huge official history, supervising the rest in detail.

Hardly any Australians today read those volumes, and modern experts dispute his interpretations. But the Anzac legend that he helped forge not only lives but blooms anew. Young people flock in large numbers to Gallipoli each year, and remembrance services at home are well attended. More than 800,000 annually visit the Australian War Memorial in Canberra. Bean was a moving spirit behind the great monument, and closely connected with its construction and development.

The Memorial contains many relics he collected from the battlefields. It also has his typewriter, uniform, library, and some 300 war notebooks and diaries which he filled, and from which much of the history came.

There are too, notebooks from his 1908 and 1909 trips. His hand is fairly legible, but there are also pages of shorthand. He'd done some scissors and pasting, organising material into subjects. One notebook contains a meticulous record of expenses for the 1908 trip, including rail tickets, hotels, the cost of telegraphing his material back to the *Herald*, his purchase of fruit (especially apples, on which he would spend sixpence) and often a shilling for unspecified 'sundries'.

Out in the Western country, quite a few people have read or heard of *On the Wool Track*. Often they don't connect the author with Australia's Anzac tradition. The link, however, is strong.

Bean's outback experiences made a huge impression on him, shaping the view he brought to observing his countrymen in war. The qualities he saw in the country people also fitted with the English public school spirit he valued highly.

In his pre-war writing Bean, recently returned to Australia after an English education, interpreted the Australian bush to the city reader – and, with the publication of the books in London, to the British reader as well. Later, in his war volumes, he would interpret the nation to itself through the Anzac legend. And he would see the bush ethos as central in moulding the character of the Australian soldiers.

In his preface to later editions of *On the Wool Track* he wrote that 'men from this life and industry, together with similar folk from New Zealand, formed a considerable fraction of the "Anzac" forces in the First World War; and – as probably also in the Second World War – the traditions of the back country weighed far more heavily than the mere number of its representatives among the influences that moulded the Australian and New Zealand soldier.'

Military historian Denis Winter, in his edited collection of Bean's war writings, asks: '[W]hat turned an unpromising journalist into a distinguished military historian?' Winter is

wrong to call Bean unpromising; in fact, it was the percep-
tiveness and promise of the journalist which matured into the
extraordinary reportage and rural-oriented analysis of the
historian.

— 2 —
The Making of an Australian

One surprise about Charles Bean is that he became so Australian. His early life was much more likely to have bred an Englishman.

He was, in the words of historian Ken Inglis, from 'an imperial family'. His grandfather was a surgeon-major in the East India Company; his father Edwin aspired, but failed, to enter the Indian Civil Service. Edwin, who arrived in Australia in 1874, never lost his Englishness.

Charles had his most formative school years in Britain, and all his university education. He keenly embraced his heritage, and he had a strong commitment to Empire. Yet in both his bush and war writing he speaks with a strongly Australian voice, although the eye of the Englishman is also clearly there in the bush books.

Born in the NSW town of Bathurst on November 18, 1879, Charles Edwin Woodrow Bean was the first son of Edwin, a school headmaster, and his wife Lucy. Edwin, educated in the classics, and Lucy, who came from a legal family, had met in Hobart, immediately after Edwin landed in Australia to become tutor to two local boys. He had fled to the colonies after suffering a double setback, scoring only a third-class degree at Oxford as well as flunking the Indian Civil Service place.

After teaching posts at Geelong Grammar and Sydney Grammar, Edwin was appointed headmaster of All Saints, Bathurst, an Anglican school opened only several years before.

Edwin did not have a fixed salary, but received his income from the proceeds of the school. Much of his energies would have to be directed to attracting pupils. The education offered was in the English public school tradition, adapted to local Australian conditions, the mix that imbued his son.

'We arrived in Bathurst on a hot day in January, when my husband was twenty-six years old, and I twenty-five, young people for such a responsible task!', Lucy wrote later. 'In those days Bathurst was very primitive . . .'

The town was well past its gold-rush days. Its fortunes relied primarily on the surrounding pastoral district, reflecting the ups and downs of the seasons. One year Lucy recorded they had enough drinking water to last six weeks but they would soon have to buy bath water.

Bathurst was a railway centre and a gateway to the West that Bean would later travel and describe so vividly. Cobb and Co. had its headquarters for the central West there.

The young boy learned about rural life in his earliest formative years. Bean was not the only famous Bathurst son of his generation; future Labor prime minister Ben Chifley was born there a few years later.

Charles was the eldest of three boys: Jack followed in 1881 and Montague in 1884. A first-born daughter had died in infancy, and his mother worried about the health and suspected asthma of the red-headed Charles. He was never strong, and repeatedly in later years had bouts of ill-health. They did not deter him, or limit his ambitions or achievements.

Charlie was intelligent and a fast learner, helped by having a scholastic father, and living at the school, which had attracted some impressive teachers.

In an account of his early life written for his wife Effie, Bean recalled learning at three-and-a-half to say the ABC backwards. 'Your husband was fairly quick at his lessons . . . but not in any way a marvel of learning or industry.' Before he was seven, he had begun to write poetry; according to his mother, he turned the story of the Prodigal Son 'into a kind of verse'.

All Saints' prospered through the 1880s becoming, its history says, the 'best known Anglican school in the West', with its influence extending 'to the Queensland border, and to the north-west and west, beyond Bourke', as well as having 'a very large Sydney connexion'.

But the struggle to keep up the school continued to take its toll on its headmaster. Edwin threw his whole energy into whatever he did, sometimes to the point of exhaustion. In the late 1880s he decided to leave Bathurst because, according to his son later, he was 'overworked'. An inheritance from his father had also given him modest financial independence.

Both Edwin and Charles Bean, however, would retain their links with All Saints'. When Edwin and Lucy followed their three sons back to Australia many years later, they immediately visited the school. Charles was generous with gifts, and in 1954 became Patron of the Old Boys' Union.

The family sailed for Britain in early 1889. 'I loved the journey,' Bean recalled. 'I was passionately fond of children, & most of the people on the ship who had children allowed me to nurse them.'

Learning became, for the boys, an adventure. For two years, the family divided its time between England and the Continent. 'Father decided to live during the summers at Oxford & during the winters in Belgium, in order to educate us boys in what he considered the best surroundings.' Edwin taught his sons himself.

They went rowing on the river at Oxford. They took lodgings in Brussels, where Charles and Jack learned French. They saw at firsthand the battlefield of Waterloo. In London Charles was 'deeply impressed' by the Nelson relics. He had begun his lifelong fascination with things military – in the early days, he was particularly interested in the navy. His brother recalled how he enjoyed drawing battle pictures.

When Edwin's fortunes declined in the Australian 1890s bank crash, he looked for a headmaster's job sooner than he'd intended. There were attractions, too, in a position being advertised – for headmaster of Brentwood Grammar School. Edwin's grandfather had been a warden there; his father had attended it. Edwin took the job; the family moved in.

As at Bathurst, the boys found themselves pupils in a school at which their father was principal.

Brentwood was then a small school of 42 boys, & there Jack and I were for the next 3 years as boys in our father's school. We lived in the private part of the school house, but counted – and were treated as – boarders.

Father was very fair, & necessarily strict in dealing with us – & so our time at Brentwood was happier than that of many schoolmasters' sons; for never for a moment did any boy accuse us of being favoured.

His father changed the 'tone' of the school from 'snobbish & not very good' to 'splendid & gentlemanly'. His mother made her home there 'an Australian centre overseas'.

The way Bean later synthesised his British background and experience and his Australian nationalism shows in the dedication of *The Dreadnought of the Darling*:

To the boys of Brentwood school in Essex, where, with several other young Australians, he first made the acquaintance of the English boy and many a lifelong friendship, the author affectionately dedicates this book – in the hope that many more of them may some day help to fill in the borders of the wide country with which it deals.

The family visited Germany for holidays, and Charlie learned the language. Biographer Dudley McCarthy writes that he developed 'a great affection for the ordinary German people. He would never lose that, even during the years to come of war with Germany with which he would be so intimately involved'.

In 1894, aged 14, he sat for a scholarship to Clifton College, which his father had attended, but he failed to get it. However, he and Jack were sent to the school anyway.

His attachment to Clifton, as to his other schools, became strong; years later he named his several houses in Sydney *Clifton*. The red nameplate is still there at his last house, in the Sydney suburb of Collaroy, which overlooks the sea.

He entered Clifton 'on the Classical Side', with his colonial origins apparently showing.

> I must have had an Australian accent at that time, for the boys used to chaff me about it. I don't know when I lost it – gradually, somehow, I suppose . . . I never consciously tried to pick up any English accent; as kiddies Jack & I used to think it was affected . . .

He remembered later, in a passage that also set out one of his tenets of a good writing style, that: 'I was fond of "essay" work at school . . . apt to imitate the style of the fiction I read – J.K. Jerome, Stevenson, Kipling.

> I admired the Greek method of moderation & understatement; but the only real style I ever acquired originated at Oxford when, partly in rebellion against some of the philosophers whose works we read, & partly because the practice interested me, I determined never, if possible, to write a sentence which could not be understood by, say, a house maid of average intelligence.

It was an admirable aim, although some of his writings, particularly his war work, did not live up to it.

Bean combined modesty with a keen awareness of how he compared with others. 'I was only 7th in the School; father in his day was 2nd'. His family instilled in him strong notions of duty. When an early school report from Clifton was poor, Edwin Bean wrote to his son: 'remember that you must live a life of *duty*. If your new Study life produces results like this – it cannot be good.' It was an aberration in successful school years.

The family was never poor but finances were stretched. It was a relief when Bean won a five-year scholarship to Oxford worth one hundred pounds annually. He studied 'Greats' – the classics – and then law. But he had doubts about what career he wanted, flirting with the idea of an army life, applying in vain for a position in the Civil Service of the Transvaal and the Orange Free State, and then unsuccessfully sitting for the Indian Civil Service examination.

Although ill just before his exam for 'Greats', he didn't think it affected his performance. Indeed, he rather fancied his ability to match examiners: '. . . from the time I was a small boy I always knew what the examiners wanted; I could always, on a minimum of work, pass a good examination – it was a sort of a game which I always enjoyed.'

He did better than expected in the written exam, but in the 'oral' grilling he had to admit he had derived some of his knowledge from a secondary source rather than the original Greek. He was awarded second-class honours, which he judged 'undoubtedly all that I was worth'.

Unlike his father, who had been devastated by falling short, Charles saw a bright side.

I have been exceedingly thankful for it since, for if I had obtained a first in Greats . . . I should probably have become a don or a schoolmaster & stayed in England

& never have met my wife or taken up journalism or wandered around the world as I have done or settled in Australia. For the same reason I have been glad that I failed in the India Civil Service Examination.

Throughout his life, Bean's character appealed to most who knew him. In an assessment reprised by many who met him, his tutor in ancient history wrote: 'He is a man of wide interests and general culture, and his manners are such as to ensure him friendly relations with those with whom he is brought into contact'.

Bean went to help his father at Brentwood; he became a tutor to a boy sent because of ill health to winter in the Canary Islands. After finishing legal studies at Oxford, he was called to the Bar in June 1904.

Then came the choice that would shape the rest of his life. In 1904, 'father & I decided that I should go to Australia & try my luck at the bar in Sydney'.

As McCarthy says, 'Suddenly there was little doubt in Charles Bean's mind where he was now headed. He was headed for home.'

The young man of 25 who sailed in SS *Ophir* for the country he had left as a nine-year-old was adventurous and optimistic. He had had a happy childhood, and a fortunate youth. He would always remain close to his parents, whatever distance separated him from them. He dedicated his first book, 'To the most capable Man and most gracious Woman he is ever likely to know.'

He loved learning, and had acquired a broad education through travel as well as formal study. In a quiet, understated way, he was a bold character and an enthusiast in spirit, although he was, all his life, in McCarthy's words 'an unsophisticated and unassuming man'. A keen and frequent letter-writer, it was already clear he had a facility with the pen; as well, he often illustrated his accounts with sketches. One of his Brentwood school prizes, which his granddaughter Anne now has, was for drawing. Later he would become deft with a camera – an early 'photo-journalist' – taking pictures in the West and at Gallipoli.

His values were set and strong, moulded by the English public school but tempered with a democratic flavour that reflected his father's views. These strands would run through his life and his writings.

He was a man of continuities, whether in friendships, beliefs, or the way he saw national character. By nature reserved but sociable, he was able to relate to people, although his shyness prevented him becoming matey (apparently to his regret). He enjoyed tennis and loved cricket with a passion, despite being only an average player. Some of the serious interests that would consume his life were evident, such as his fascination for things military. And, despite all those years in Britain, he was taken by the Australian countryside of which he had only a distant memory. He was so excited at the prospect of catching his first glimpse of the Australian shore that 'on this night of all nights, I slept on deck.'

— 3 —
Becoming a Journalist

In Sydney Bean obtained some teaching at Sydney Grammar School while he prepared for his legal career. After being admitted to the NSW Bar, he became associate to Mr Justice William Owen who was inquiring into 'some scandals connected with the Lands Department'.

Bean was 'lent' to other judges when they were on circuit. This took him in 1906 to Wagga Wagga and Deniliquin; the following year, he travelled with Justice Owen to Newcastle and Tamworth. 'One saw thus a good deal of the country – perhaps the worst side of it.'

He then went into chambers for himself. The hoped-for briefs, however, did not appear. As on other occasions in his life, Bean frankly identified his own limitations. He felt he was temperamentally ill-suited to be a barrister: 'I was a nervous, self-conscious speaker, very liable to break down, or anyway to do injustice to my subject through extreme nervousness.' Nor did he believe he was cut out to be a schoolmaster: 'My school-discipline was not good. I was too soft with the boys – or, rather, too anxious to please & be popular with them.'

Another calling had started to attract his interest early on: 'I amused myself writing articles ready for publication when I should give up the associateship.'

He had already contributed to the *Sydney Morning Herald* and written 'a few articles' for the *Evening News*, of which A.B. (Banjo) Paterson was editor.

Paterson was the great bush balladist whose cheerful and romantic view of the outback was at odds with the darker, more socially critical and sceptical interpretation of Henry Lawson. In the next few years, Bean's writings, with their optimistic view of country life, would be firmly in the Paterson camp. It was little wonder the men became friends. Paterson had already trodden a similar path to the one Bean would embark on, working first in the law and then moving to journalism.

In 1909, Bean contributed to the *Spectator* in London a defence of the White Australia Policy, conventional for his time, arguing that 'for the good of either Australia or England, a Western and an Oriental race cannot live together in Australia'. He was to modify this view many years later, although he urged only a small number of Asians be allowed in.

He 'loved writing', preparing and illustrating a book about Australia called *The Impressions of a New Chum*. But when he tried to get it published the reader 'slated it, on the whole very justly. It was a rather crude & somewhat priggish production'. However the *Sydney Morning Herald* printed some of the chapters in 1907.

The articles are an early flowering of the romanticisation of the bush people that characterises his outback books and the war history.

'Your first shock when you find the Australian native is to discover that he is not a black man; your second to discover that he is not an Englishman . . . Australian country life . . . has hammered out of the old stock a new man,' Bean wrote.

The man he describes could be out of *Crocodile Dundee*.

The Australian is a tall, spare man, clean and wiry . . . of a certain refined ascetic strength. You would expect him tanned, but he is often fair . . . His character is the simplest imaginable. The key to it is just this – that he takes everything on its merits, and nothing on authority. Perhaps he goes further, and takes everything on its merits except for a bias against authority.

This was the 'genius of Australia', to look the 'facts in the face . . . taking nothing on authority. The Australian is a deduction from it – in his virtue, his vice, manners, dress, customs; in his politics, in the elections, in the elected; in the problems he tackles, and the way he tackles them.'

Men were accepted on their worth, with little or no class distinction; it all added up to a very 'square' man. 'In the country especially frankness is written largely across his face'. Bush life was producing 'a type of man of immense value to this country . . . It does not take one long to realise that somewhere over the hills there, over that faint blue line of the dividing range, which you can see almost any day from your back windows, there must all this time be a very extraordinary set of circumstances at work in the building up of this man.'

Life in the bush was the life of an adventurer, 'not so very different in a way from that of the searovers of Queen Elizabeth's time, who found the new world . . .' The Australian was 'always fighting something'. In the bush it was 'drought, fires, unbroken horses, wild cattle; and not unfrequently strong men'. In Sydney, 'you will see more fighting . . . in a week than in London in a year'.

All this battle with men and nature, 'fierce as any warfare', Bean concluded prophetically, made the Australian 'as fine a fighting man as exists'. There was one qualification – the hatred of authority that would 'make it hard for him to submit to any irksome command.'

Here already was the Anzac-in-waiting.

The flip-side of Bean's elevation of bush virtues and people was his distrust of cities. He saw in big cities hectic cleverness and an 'almost unnatural sharpening of the wits in the furious race for wealth', an 'itching for excitement and amusement and change for its own sake', as shown in 'the Londoner of to-day, fast turning into the Parisian of the future'. He believed the result was demoralising.

Australia was going the same way; it had to avoid this senile decay. This meant making 'the life in the cities as near as possible to life in the country . . . to preserve the country in the town, where it exists, as in Sydney; and to import it where it has been lost'. There was also a 'special chance' for Anglo-Saxons; properly encouraged, their 'devotion to sport and athletics will save the Anglo-Saxon people.'

Looking ahead to Sydney in 2000, he predicted '6,000,000 in the State [of NSW] at the very least.' This would require a minimum of 1,500,000 in Sydney; '2,500,000 will be nearer the mark.' He was almost right about NSW, which had nearly 6.4 million in the 2001 census. But the flight to the cities would have horrified him – Sydney had almost 4 million in 2001.

The young Bean railed against the loss of many 'priceless sites'; in Sydney, he urged planning. As things were going, 'the Sydneian of 2000' would inherit a 'magnificent city. It will be all there, far finer than at present; and he and his visitors will be able to see about as much of it as you can from Mark Foy's pavement'.

Journalism strengthened its grip on him. 'I took a delight in writing, &, after thinking it over & over, decided that before I went into some profession – such as teaching – which I did not greatly like, I would make an attempt to succeed in one that I knew I should love.'

He was advised to see the Fairfaxes of the *Herald*.

'I went to Geoffrey Fairfax. He told me that there was only one way to enter the profession in Australia – & that was from the bottom.' The initial step was to learn shorthand, which he did – eight hours a day for four months.

In 1908 he was put on as junior reporter at £4 a week. He didn't like, at the start, having to go to the law courts and public meetings and sit 'at the feet of people of whom I had been the friend a few months before'. But the strangeness wore off, and he delighted in the comradeship of colleagues.

'I spent one of the happiest times of my life in the old *Herald* office', which was a 'big family' from office boy to editor and even the proprietors.

He was liked in turn. Charles Brunsdon Fletcher, who was associate editor and later editor (1918–37) of the *Herald*, wrote of those early days, '[n]o one was more popular in the office or better qualified to help the paper in every call made upon him.'

Bean's first job was to report on a deputation asking the NSW minister for works to build a bridge. He made a paragraph of it, which the sub-editor liked.

The taut style of modern journalism is a world away from the extended and often rambling articles found in the newspapers of the early 1900s, and today's sub-editor would be horrified at some of Bean's newspaper copy. Nevertheless, his description of how he approached his journalist's craft could usefully be given to the modern young trainee.

> I always looked on the reader as a fish, to be hooked, if possible, in the first sentence & then 'played' (or kept tight on the hook) until the article was finished. You should never relax your hold on him – if you put in one uninteresting sentence (for example, if you repeat yourself) he will get away & wriggle off and dash away to some other article. Books are like that, too. You cannot, in a history, catch your reader for good & all in quite the first sentence; but you must get him soon (if you want the book to be read) & then try not to let him go.

At the *Herald* he was put on 'rounds' – ringing the police, hospitals and fire station. He was also on 'Trades & Labour', covering a substantial wharf strike, 'an extraordinarily involved strike over a simple quarrel'. He would appear at the Trades Hall in his Clifton boater.

In May 1908 he was sent to report on two rival routes for the railway to Broken Hill – one from Cobar via Wilcannia and the other from Condobolin via Menindee. He travelled by train to Cobar and then by coach to Wilcannia. From Wilcannia he was driven by buggy to White Cliffs and back by Mr William Morrison, 'one of the grand men of the Darling country', who owned local coaches as well as *Bulla* station.

He set out from Wilcannia for Broken Hill, then went to Menindee by coach, and made the next leg of his journey, which took him to Ivanhoe, by a buggy which he hired. After that he travelled to Condobolin, and back to Sydney. (He decided the southern route would be preferable for the railway.) The long trip 'was my first view of the West, & I was intensely interested in the people, the country, the grasses, the animals, the trees & the life.'

When he got back he was sent in July by the *Herald* to meet the American fleet at Auckland, travelling for several weeks in the British flagship HMS *Powerful*. The trip was via Norfolk Island and Fiji. 'I was by then one of the recognised descriptive writers of the *Herald*'; he decided a book would help his reputation and published privately his collected articles as *With the Flagship in the South*, illustrated with his drawings and a watercolour he painted.

With the Flagship in the South showed many of the characteristics of Bean's outback books, and some that his war writings displayed. His descriptions – including of the 'ship's heart', sea life, and Suva (he predicted racial troubles in Fiji) – were colourful and evocative although at times considerably overdone, as was his excessive admiration in the book for all things British.

Powerful was 'a great grey warhorse, brave and big and fast, and full of the gentleness of all big things.' The ship was furnished as a 'comfortable home'; the officers' accommodation resembled a London club, and Bean dressed for dinner. The men had 'the cleanest of clean quarters, with rows of spotless mess tables – which for some reason reminded one of the shearers' hut on a well-kept western run . . .'

In *With the Flagship in the South* Bean ranged, in anecdotes and observations, well beyond what he actually observed on the trip. Here we see his military interests and his nationalism. He made a strong plea for the fledgling Australian nation to have its own navy. 'The task is enormous, but England can manage it; and what England does one will not put beyond Australia.'

Bean thought the £100 publication cost worthwhile: the *Argus* and *Daily Telegraph* offered him jobs. But the *Herald* twice raised his salary and he stayed.

The *Herald* editor was Thomas Heney who, *Herald* historian Gavin Souter records, was 'the first *Herald* editor to face the world completely without a beard'. A one-time editor of a Wilcannia paper who also published poetry and fiction, Heney had a deep admiration for the resilience and grace of the people of the West. In 'A Darling Squatter', written while editor, he described them as 'ready day and night for any move on fortune's chess-board of drought or rain, rising or falling prices, strikes, rabbits, land laws, Governments, money panics', the wives 'the ladies bountiful of the stations . . .'

Heney assigned Bean in 1909 to write about the wool industry, believing its reporting neglected. Bean felt it a dreary subject, and his chief of staff would have preferred him around chasing 'scoops' in Sydney.

Still it had to be done, & one day it struck me – the industry can be described by describing the processes, which is dull; but it can surely also be described by telling of the life's work of the men who are engaged in the processes – the boss of the sheep-station; the shearer; the boundary-rider . . . It came home to me that a description of these men & their work had never yet been given in any book that I knew of . . . It was an extraordinarily fine chance . . .

He began with a week at *Kurrumbede*, near Gunnedah, to get to know a sheep station; he observed shearing at nearby *Gunnible* station. *Kurrumbede* was owned by Charles Mackellar, a leading Sydney doctor and father of budding poet Dorothea, although she and her parents lived in Sydney.

In the year before Bean's visit Dorothea started her road to fame, publishing her evocative poem, eventually called 'My Country' – 'I love a sunburnt country/ a land of sweeping plains'. This poem would become immensely popular during and after World War I. For many years every Australian school child knew it.

Bean and Dorothea, who was several years younger, were friends. She mentions him in her diary: in 1910 they were both part of a theatre party when 'two rats made a diversion in the gallery'. He suggested she compile a poetry anthology, and in 1911 he was acting as 'agent' for her with his London publisher.

Like Bean and Paterson, Mackellar (whose reputation came to rest on 'My Country' and who has now fallen out of fashion) was in the genre of Australian writers who dwelt on the best face of the outback.

After the *Kurrumbede* familiarisation tour, Bean travelled to the town of Bourke and took 'an old river steamer', the Brown brothers' *Jandra*, down the Darling for four days to *Dunlop* station, where he stayed with the manager (T.W. Vincent) and his wife, before returning on the boat. The trip took about a fortnight. In Sydney he went to the Vicars woollen mills at Marrickville, to observe the end of the process.

A visiting English journalist asked if he could take the articles – which appeared as a series titled 'The Wool Land' – back to Britain for publication. They came out in 1910 as *On the Wool Track*.

The *Herald* appointed its by now well-established feature writer to London as correspondent, and he sailed to Britain via America. The work was easy compared with the *Herald*'s Sydney office and Bean had 'three lovely years', happily slipping back into English – and school – life. He stayed at Brentwood with his parents, 'living the life of the old school' with masters who had been there years before, and helping with cricket.

'I always sent the *Herald* more good stuff than they could print', he complained – his comparison of the East End slums with those of Sydney never appeared. While in Britain he put together the Dreadnought book, using the leftover material from his outback journeys that covered general life and country in the West. This had already appeared in article form in the *Sydney Mail*, the *Herald*'s sister paper.

The construction of the first ships for the Australian navy dominated his reporting from Britain, and he gathered this and his earlier Flagship book into *Flagships Three*. The book commenced with 'The First Flagship', a description of an old Norwegian galley from the Vikings' time which he and his father had seen in Norway when they were on holiday in 1912. *Powerful* was the second flagship, while *Australia*, being constructed for the new Australian navy, was the third.

Meanwhile he was 'in danger of becoming accepted as an authority on wool', thanks to good reviews for *On the Wool Track*. Students wrote asking what they should read. The London School of Economics had him do a series of lectures on the wool industry and the Royal Society of Arts asked him to speak on the wool trade of the Empire.

Bean and other Australian journalists would meet, as a dining club, at the Connaught Restaurant; there was also an Australian section of the Colonial Institute, including much the same group. This formed a body to celebrate Australia Day in London.

Bean suggested a feature should be a display of wattle, which in England was called mimosa. He wrote an article saying the mimosa of the Riviera was really wattle imported from Australia. He and H.C. Smart, who was on the staff of the Australian High Commission in London, had it published in about 30 papers. 'The result was on Jan 26 Selfridges was decorated with wattle & most Australians appeared wearing it.'

Bean returned to Australia in 1913; his parents followed soon after. He was set to writing *Herald* leaders. But he did not like the job, feeling he could do much better by going into the country as a roving correspondent.

In May 1914 he was sent with a South Australian commission which was inquiring into the desirability of locking the Murray, Darling and Murrumbidgee. He motored through the Riverina, from Burrinjuck to Wentworth, and on to the mouth of the Murray, and Adelaide.

There he took leave from the paper, and accompanied another commission which was inquiring into the education of the Aborigines, going up to Kilalpaninna on the Cooper.

He also went to the transcontinental railway under construction near Tarcoola. He had in mind a book about 'the underground & overground waters in that part of Australia'. But war was looming when he got back to Sydney, and he was put on to compiling 'War Notes'. 'The war broke out & the work became important.'

His brother Jack had enlisted the first day and Bean asked him to inquire of Colonel McLaurin (later an early Gallipoli casualty) whether he should enlist; he was told 'not yet'. Meanwhile he was writing Saturday leaders for the paper, and wondering how best to see the action.

The Australian Government got an offer from the British to send an official Australian war correspondent to the front. Bean had already been attempting to get there. 'I had been trying before to get an appointment as "Eyewitness" – a sort of official recorder under that name having been appointed for the British Army.'

The Labor Government asked the Australian Journalists' Association to choose a candidate. In the ballot, Bean was up against Keith Murdoch – later father of Rupert.

Murdoch, in Melbourne, nearly got in; but Archie Whyte [the *Sydney Morning Herald*'s Melbourne correspondent] down there kindly acted as a press agent for me (all his own idea for I knew nothing of what he was doing) & I received most votes. Murdoch came next, & sent me a generous telegram.

It is interesting to speculate what would have happened if the result had been the other way round. Murdoch became a distinguished and controversial war correspondent, embroiled in the political intrigue over the disastrous Gallipoli campaign. It is impossible, however, to imagine the man who later built the *Herald & Weekly Times* empire forgoing a business career to undertake the war history, which was part of the official correspondent's brief.

Bean left the *Sydney Morning Herald* at once, 'though I always look on myself in a way as a *Herald* man'.

Conley [the paper's manager], I remember, told me I was foolish: 'You don't think the Australians will ever be used at the front, do you?' he said. 'They will never be further than the lines of communications – they won't use these troops when they have disciplined regiments to employ; & if they did they would never let you get near the front any way.'

Both prophecies turned out untrue, for the Australians were continually in the thick of it, & I obtained a chance such as no journalist in this war, or probably any other, has had of going absolutely where I liked, in the line (or indeed in front of the line, if I had wanted) without any restriction so long as I was with our own troops.

In farewelling Bean at a dinner put on by the Victorian district of the AJA at Melbourne's Cafe Français on

October 3, 1914, Defence Minister Pearce stressed his role as historian.

> We hope that Mr Bean may go to the front. But he may not be allowed to do so. He will have something more to do than to write reports from day to day. He will have to write part of the history of Australia. That history will be written on French or German soil. It will be written in blood. But it will be as much our history as if it were written in the Australian backblocks or on the mining fields or in the cities of Australia.

— 4 —
Birth and Baptism of the Anzac Legend

Describing the Gallipoli landing, Bean would reach for a country memory. On the deck of a troop ship, watching and listening as dawn came, he heard a distant knocking, 'like the sound of an axlebox heard far off in the wood when the cart's coming along a rough bush road'. It was rifle fire. This was his initiation into war.

In the history of war reporting, few other Australian correspondents have undergone such intense, sustained rigors. At Gallipoli, Bean was ashore within hours of the troops; despite the horrors and the hardship, by the time 80,000 Allied troops were evacuated in December, it had become a strange sort of home.

'So I have left old Anzac', he wrote in his diary. 'In a way I was really fond of the place. I have certainly had some quite enjoyable times there in my old dug-out, yarning to friends or going round the lines.'

Accompanying the troops to the Western Front, he wrote during the battle of the Somme, 'I always feel surprised when I get alive out of Pozieres. I don't pretend to be very brave.'

After the war he got a letter from Nellie Simmons, from

Lower Lia station, near Bourke. She wrote that she had seen in the *Town and Country Weekly* that he had watched the Australians in the fight for Passchendaele on October 12, 1917. Her husband had been killed on that day, and she asked 'if you would be so kind and let me know something of that battle'.

'I remember the day very well,' Bean replied, following with a detailed account. 'When my little sons are old enough to understand and read your letter, how proud they will be of their daddy . . .'. Nellie wrote in thanks.

Bean chose to be in the thick of the conflict. He coped with the unspeakable horror, month on month, year on year, working indefatigably, surviving emotionally. His physical strength was remarkable; yet his health had been questioned when he was selected as correspondent.

McCarthy describes him on the Western Front as

this lanky, red-haired Australian, spectacles perched precariously on his nose, making his way, unassuming and courteous, among the fighting up in the front line, portable typewriter in one hand, a small suitcase in the other. He is hung about with his telescope in its case and other accoutrements. Over his uniform he wears his old leather coat', warmly lined, to which, in his letters home, he attributes his freedom during that terrible winter on the Somme from the pneumonic infections to which he has been prone for so long. As always, he is completely unarmed. This curiously unmilitary figure shows no signs of perturbation among bursting shells and all the other hazards of the greatest battlefield the world has ever seen. He is completely

Bean passionately loved cricket but his ability was well behind his enthusiasm.
Courtesy of the Australian War Memorial, Neg. A5390.

With brothers Monty (left) and Jack (right). Jack, a doctor, was at the Gallipoli landing.
Courtesy of the Society of Australian Genealogists.

Bean seemed a confirmed bachelor until he met Effie (sitting to his right) during a stay at Queanbeyan hospital.
Courtesy of the Australian War Memorial, Neg. P02751.569.

With Joyce, Effie and Violet Gibbins, headmistress of Osborne Ladies College in the Blue Mountains. Joyce boarded at Osborne, which was run on naval lines and had a sick-bay known as HMS *Dreadnought*.
Courtesy of the Australian War Memorial, Neg. P03788.002.

Bean watching the Australians on the Western Front, 1917. He was a meticulous chaser of detail for his reports and in preparation for later writing the history.
Courtesy of the Australian War Memorial, Neg. E00246.

A country homestead at the site of the future national capital was where the writing of the war history started in earnest. In between a rigorous work schedule, there was time for cricket, and a horse ride in the morning.
Courtesy of the National Library of Australia.

The history occupied
more than two decades.
*Courtesy of the Australian War
Memorial, Neg. P02751.459.*

Bean was a moving spirit
behind the War Memorial
and collected many relics
for it when he returned to
Gallipoli at the end of the
war. In turn, it has
become something of a
shrine to him.
*Courtesy of the Australian
War Memorial, Neg. 042411.*

The windows of the houses are like black sockets whose eyes have perished with despair.

In 1944, *Sydney Morning Herald* special reporter Keith Newman roamed the drought areas, accompanied by artist Russell Drysdale, whose drawings sparked bitter controversy because of their harsh edge.

Images courtesy of the National Library of Australia and captions from the Sydney Morning Herald articles.

Kitchen of a country pub.

Left: *Its roots bared by eroding winds, a dying tree raises supplicating arms to rainless skies.*

Centre: *From among the rotting carcases of sheep rise the dry skeletons of trees that died in an agony of thirst.*

Bottom: *Dead animal, drying stream: carcase of a bullock trapped by drying mud in the Great Anabranch of the Darling.*

The original edition of *On the Wool Track* was illustrated with photographs by George Bell of the *Sydney Mail*.

The shearers' cook: some might say the most important member of the team.

A backbreaking job then – and only marginally easier now.

A shearer travelling. This part of the shearer's life has transformed.

Mr Leckie of *The Avenue*: 'The finest selector of all that we met across the Darling.'

'The finest selector's' great-grandson, Graham Leckie, and his wife Julie, who now live at *The Avenue*.

absorbed in his observations and his conversations and note-taking.

The war history must have a 'front line view', Bean said – it had to be written from 'the point of view of the front line soldier as well as of the Commander-in-Chief'.

His was to be a long war, but at the start, as the *Orvieto* left Melbourne in October 1914, he worried about missing the action: 'we were . . . rather afraid that the war might be over before we got there'.

The 34-year-old reporter, a civilian but given the title of Captain, was accompanied by a batman, young Arthur Bazley. Though 18, Bazley posed as 19 to meet the army's requirements. Whyte had suggested Bazley, a junior clerk at the *Argus*.

Nearly half a century later Bazley remembered vividly that first meeting with Bean, in Melbourne late on a Friday night in October 1914. It began a lifetime association. After Whyte fired questions (already knowing the answers) at Bazley, 'Bean – who was wearing pince-nez and a straw hat, but I forget now whether the hat-band or his tie were the colours of his old school, Clifton College, Bristol – thereupon asked me quietly whether I would like to go away with him.'

Being 'the man that he was', Bean was troubled by the lie about Bazley's age, but he went along with it. Although Bazley did not know what was meant by 'batman', 'I soon learnt; but my duties, far from being those of an officer's servant, were largely those of a clerk and typist.' After the war Bazley became librarian, custodian of records and 'deviller' on the history team, and later acting director of the Australian War Memorial from 1942 to 1946.

From the start, Bean saw himself as historian as much as journalist. As the war went on, this role would increasingly become the one of greater importance to him. The priority Bean gave the history – although he pictured it as 'a small one-volume work' rather than a project stretching from 1919 to 1942 – determined how he tackled his tasks.

'News was not his main object', according to Bazley. Nor was his writing as dramatic as that of some competitors. As well as the history coming to dominate his thinking, he also unabashedly saw himself as part of the force rather than an outsider looking on. Bean was not uncritical, but a big part of why he was there was to record the heroism of Australia's manhood. His patriotism, discretion and trust-worthiness helped win the confidence of the Australian military hierarchy. But his natural cautiousness as a reporter, combined with a subtle shift to the 'historian' mindset, gave a tinge of officialese to his despatches.

His reports had their critics. While he was at Gallipoli the *Age* and the *Argus* said they would stop taking his articles. Bean, with a rare touch of bitterness, blamed the desire for sensationalism, resenting that material was being taken from men well away from the action while he risked his life.

He even copped criticism for contributing to falling enlist-ments. The *Bulletin* declared: 'The communications from the official correspondent have been colourless and no waverer's pulse has been quickened by them.'

Because of what Bazley denounced as an 'iniquitious decision', Bean was scooped on the biggest story of the young nation's history – the Gallipoli landing. And this despite being the first correspondent ashore at Gallipoli, landing about 9.30 am. His accreditation had not come through. The

British Admiralty had only let him sail from Egypt with the Australian force after he promised in writing he would not send despatches until it did (about a fortnight later).

So English journalist Ellis Ashmead-Bartlett had the first account of that dramatic day in the Australian papers. Bean's, placed much less prominently, appeared several days later. This, Bazley said, led some editors and the Australian public to ask, 'Where was Bean?'.

In fact, he was as busy as if deadline was upon him, inspecting the area, taking notes, talking to the men, photographing, with the shells whizzing overhead. 'I can't say I like shrapnel although it seemed to be quite familiar by this time,' says his diary of the 25th.

He searched for brother Jack, a doctor with the medical corp, only to discover he had been wounded. Like the soldiers, that first night Bean had to prepare his own dugout, accommodation that was 'something between a grave and a cave'. 'I found a vacant corner . . . I started to dig. The man in the dug out next door strongly objected . . . "What do you want to keep a man awake with that damned digging for?" he asked. "Haven't you got any bloody consideration?"' Bean continued, but then moved to a better spot.

His days were spent around the trenches; at night he wrote up his notes. Often he survived on as little as three hours sleep; sometimes he would be out all night. As he went among the troops he carried water and cigarettes, and helped where he could.

After he went to the rescue of a wounded man, he was recommended for the Military Cross. But, despite his honorary military title, he was ineligible because he was not a soldier. Instead he was mentioned in despatches.

In August, he was shot in the leg. He had the wound dressed, then struggled back to his dug-out. He didn't wake Bazley; only telling him in the morning.

He rested for three days, the *Age* reporter, Phillip Schuler keeping him posted on the news. The bullet was never removed.

Bean was passionate about finding the facts, the right ones and as many as possible, sometimes to the detriment of his writing. Les Carlyon, in his highly acclaimed modern *Gallipoli*, describes Bean as 'a clerk of facts; he didn't understand what to leave out'. A journalist contemporary summed up the strengths and weaknesses of Bean's approach succinctly, saying he always wanted to count the bullets.

During the war years he was often rechecking past material, while observing the present. He attached to each volume of his war diaries a warning; they should be used with 'great caution, as relating only what their author, at the time of writing, believed'.

Bean had additional skills besides those of a reporter: he sketched and at Gallipoli he photographed extensively. As he had done in describing the wool industry, Bean humanised and romanticised the characters of his story. He saw and portrayed heroes, making them grander by making them ordinary.

> . . . the Australian soldiers were not . . . titans – demi-gods or supermen . . . but just average Australian citizens, perhaps a little higher-spirited than the average, who in a frightfully severe test proved to have qualities of decision, unselfishness, and self-control that most of us perhaps would not have suspected but which

probably exist in 90 out of 100 Australian boys and girls today . . .

Extraordinarily, given the demands and the difficult conditions under which he worked, Bean managed a number of other activities. He edited a 1916 Anzac book of contributions by Australian soldiers. He also conceived the idea of a permanent war memorial, and began assembling what he termed 'relics' (disliking the triumphalist word 'trophies').

In 1919, before returning home, Bean went back to Gallipoli with a historical team. This was a remarkable journey. He tells the story of it many years later in a riveting account, *Gallipoli Mission* (1948).

Imagine it: walking again those battlefields, not picturesque and ordered, as they are for today's numerous tourists, but still grimly littered with skeletons. Bean wanted to fill in details for the history; the team also inspected war graves, and collected relics. They spent an invaluable week with a Turkish officer, Zeki Bey, seeing 'the other side of the hills'. Zeki Bey was extremely helpful, but it sounds as though he was drained by Bean's forensic intensity. Bean would have liked to probe him further, 'but something caused me to sense that he was wondering why I was keeping him so long under the cross-examination to which he so generously submitted'. The two kept in touch later.

When Bean got back to Australia, he and his research team began work in Melbourne, but soon moved to the site of the national capital (yet to be built). Bean believed it the appropriate place for the writing; the country setting also provided the needed peace and quiet.

The little group took over the rambling *Tuggeranong*

homestead, which the Commonwealth owned. Hoping (unrealistically) the project could be finished in five years, they worked as Bean had in wartime – each night, and through weekends. Still, life was rustic and pleasant, and there was some relaxation.

'We have bought a few horses, a cow and some sheep, and have acquired a tin Lizzie, a billiard table and a pianola. The Government supplied a tennis court (or rather fenced in the old one)', Bean wrote.

They had a morning gallop, cricket matches, and in summer 'we arranged our own daylight saving scheme, and had tennis every evening'. The cricket pitch is still there; the homestead, which now houses a restaurant, has a room and a small outside building dedicated to Beanabilia. It was during this time that Bean courted and married Effie; he met her when he was hospitalised in the nearby NSW town of Queanbeyan.

Later, because of Bean's poor health, the history project shifted to Sydney. Hours were more routine, but Bean did not lose his old wartime habits. He would research in the afternoons, work through the night, and sleep in the early part of the day. His self-discipline was relentless, as he kept at the history for two decades. He had a reading stand to use while dressing and Effie told people that he brought a book to the table at dinner.

Bazley's son Peter recalls as a boy visiting Bean at Victoria Barracks in Sydney. 'He had an eye on me as I pulled out various books.' Later he helped the young Bazley get an interview with Angus McLachlan, of the *Sydney Morning Herald*, who was one of Bean's closest friends.

The detail of Bean's writings on the war is outside our

scope. What is relevant is the link between Bean's pre-war bush travel, and how he sees the Australian soldiers. He draws on the bush time and again. For instance, in *Anzac to Amiens*, written in the 1940s, he recalls how close the Australia of 1914 was to its first settlement.

> Even among the men who went to the First World War not a few had childish recollections of some old shepherd seen sleeping off his liquor outside a country town. . .

And describing the motive moving the Australian people as they faced war in 1914, he finds it in mingling with British standards those of the pioneers,

> the backwoodsmen, and the men of the great runs and the mining fields. It was to these last that Australians owed their resourcefulness and readiness to grapple with their objectives even against authority, and also their basic creed, in industry as in war, that a man must at all costs stand by his mate.

In telling the story of Gallipoli, he noted that it was 'deliberate policy' that Australian officers should live mostly among their men, observing that they 'conversed with them as freely as a manager with the old hands on an Australian sheep-station'.

The link between the bush spirit and the character of the Anzacs suffuses his writing. It is particularly sharply spelled out in a 1927 paper, 'Sidelights of the War on Australian Character'.

At the war, he said, one saw men in their thousands with

their 'innermost nature exposed as it were by the surgeon's knife'. When searching for what made one regiment better than another, the quality of the leader was decisive. Besides that, 'there was one main factor, and only one, that was responsible for any slight difference' between Australian regiments. That was 'the difference between what we may roughly term the bush-bred and town-bred Australian'.

In general, Bean insisted, it was beyond doubt that country-bred men were, other things being equal, better soldiers than city men, although this was not so obvious in Australia as in other national armies. Conditions in Australian cities had not yet produced noticeably smaller or physically weaker types compared with the men from the country. So there were not the contrasts of the British army.

Rather, in the Australian force the edge lay

in the country man having been bred to a habit of decision, whereas the mind of the city man was more dependent on the wills of those about him . . . It seems probable that among our country people the proportion of those who think and act for themselves is considerably higher than in the towns.

Whatever the cause, all the data go to prove this result: that, other things being equal, our generals tended to rely most strongly upon those units which contained most country-bred troops – that is to say, generally speaking, on those from some of our least populated States.

He concluded that 'the old Anzac type' could not be preserved by the control of immigration alone.

[U]nless we in due time, while we have still the power, take steps to preserve the conditions by which the life in our cities still approximates to that in our countryside, no power on earth can prevent the Australian city population from going the way of the city peoples all over the world where those conditions have not been preserved, and the Anzac standards will in our next generation remain only as a memory.

There was an echo of his theme in the 'New Chum' articles of many years before.

By the time Bean published his last volume in 1942, the emphasis had subtly changed. He had to admit that 'the percentage of Australian soldiers who had acquired their powers of determination, endurance, and improvisation from country occupations was probably not much more than a quarter'.

Nevertheless differences between country and city troops were perceptible: 'They were country boys from around Shepparton' might be the comment when there had been some remarkable feat. In acts of heroic leadership, clergymen or their sons figured noticeably, Bean said, but farmers and other country men were also outstanding.

He still held that brigades or battalions from the agricultural or pastoral states were likely to be thrown into the fray first. And if differences were not great – well, many city Australians holidayed in the bush or had been brought up there.

Particularly important in Australian troops effectiveness, Bean argued, was the Australian atmosphere of democracy. The efficacy of the AIF was not in spite of the Australian

Jack's being as good as his master but because of it – or more accurately because Jack and his masters were the same. Social equality in civil life had produced men with the habit of thinking for themselves and acting on their own decision. The Australian soldier had been bred to freedom.

Later historians have pointed out that his claims about the rural origins of the troops did not stand up to closer scrutiny, while E.M. Andrews in *The Anzac Illusion* claims Bean's class background, education, rank and position 'created an unbridgeable gulf between him and the ordinary soldiers' and he 'inevitably sympathised with the world view of the senior officers'. Bean himself acknowledged the truth in a critic's charge that he had not written up the soldiers' lives. 'It has never been written up because I don't know the life,' he confided to his diary in 1918. 'I have been shy of those men – have done my work from outside as a staff officer, as it were . . . I am too self-conscious to mix well with a great mass of men.'

It has been argued by Martin Ball in his thesis on the story of Anzac that Bean's Anzac was based not on what he saw on the battlefields, but rather he 'appropriates the new figure of the Anzac to embody his already established ideal Australian'.

Certainly, one way or another, Bean's Anzac had been in embryo since his first descriptions of the men of the bush as early as 1907 in the 'New Chum' articles and expanded in *On the Wool Track* and *The Dreadnought of the Darling*.

2

The West –
Then and Now

— 5 —
'The Land that Never Leaves You'

The Western Division fits all the stereotypes of Australia's outback: a huge area, relatively empty, and people with a strong sense of belonging there. It contains more than two-fifths of New South Wales – some 32.5 million hectares of arid and semi-arid land. As a booklet from the Western Lands Commission – which administers the Lands Act – explains, with wry understatement: that 'means it either doesn't rain very often, or hardly at all'.

In this country, drought is never a matter of if, but when, and you never know the 'when'. Often it has not been drought alone, but failure to understand that drought's the norm, that has led to the disasters the people and land have suffered.

The *Sydney Morning Herald* has regularly chronicled the West in big series, among which were those by Bean. A decade before Bean, it ran articles by journalist and politician Edward Davis Millen, who travelled round inspecting land ravaged by drought, pests and misuse. Millen knew this country; he was editor of the *Western Herald* which he also part-owned.

The normal condition of the West, Millen wrote, 'is one of drought – drought punctuated with occasional moist seasons. The fundamental error has been in regarding the nominal [sic] condition as one of the fair seasons punctuated with occasional drought'.

Bean goes directly to the heart of the West.

[O]ut here you have reached the core of Australia – the real red Australia of the ages, which, though the rivers have worn their channels through it, and spewed out their black silt in narrow ribbons across it, hems in this flat modern river-soil to the flood lands, so that if you drive only a few miles from the river bank you will always come out in the end upon red land, a slightly higher land rising sharply from the grey plain; a land which stretches away and away and away across the heart of Australia, with the history of the oldest continent on earth lying in interesting little patches – ironstone pebbles, and river-worn quartz, and stony deserts, and a thousand other relics – across the whole face of it.

Dissecting the West, and giving it both nourishment and identity, is the great Darling, which rises in a network of rivers and streams in Queensland and flows down to the Murray.

The Darling, Henry Lawson wrote, 'is either a muddy gutter or a second Mississippi'. This is a river that doesn't live by half measures. People who depend on it – and the wider public that tries to understand it – must grasp this fact: the Darling is a river of extremes.

Although its dries and its highs bring both hardships and challenges, the Darling helps tame this back country. Inevitably we hear mostly about the bad times, but the Darling can also be a bountiful provider when it spills over its floodplains, bringing them richly to life, or rises high enough for the irrigators to be allowed to pump.

For thousands of years before the white men came, Aboriginal tribes found a haven in the softer areas near its banks. Inevitably, they were more in tune with the land and understood the river's moods a lot better than the first, and often naive, European settlers.

The wider Murray-Darling basin is huge – about a seventh of the whole of Australia. The dual-river system is a blood stream for three states: NSW, South Australia and Victoria. Once it was also a long and busy water highway, with steamers plying their trade, collecting wool from the stations and taking to them food and other supplies, including equipment for their 'wool factories'.

The Darling became famous for its 'ports'; goods came this way to what were 'townships' on the properties, as well as to the towns of the districts. Its riverboat captains had great stories to tell; in Bourke Bean interviewed the retired Captain Pickhills, and heard the tale of 'how the *Gemini* relieved Bourke' – from an extended grog 'drought', brought about by a flood cutting off the town.

Today the riverbanks are quiet, the station communities often just a nuclear family, and only a few fishermen, tourists and joy seekers venture onto the water.

While the river itself, like the country around it, is at the whim of the seasons, it is also fragile, and at the mercy of the decisions of those who fight over its precious water.

The Darling is always at the centre of whatever is the current story of the West. Today there is a fierce argument about the allocation of water, between those who use a lot of it and those who say too much pressure is being put upon a scarce resource. In the debate, some graziers are at odds with the cotton growers, and the agriculturalists at the throats of government.

Around 60,000 people live in this country, that remains relatively little-known to those further in, especially Sydneysiders. The Western Division 'is still a *terra incognita* to the great majority of the people of New South Wales', Millen wrote in 1899; the Western Lands Commission echoed the same sentiment nearly a century later.

Comparing the region between the 1996 and 2001 censuses (see table), the picture is of a population down overall. When you look at places individually, things are slightly more mixed. The region's biggest town, the once-great mining centre of Broken Hill, lost more than 1000 people, falling under 21,000 – two thirds of what it was in Bean's time. But Hillston, on the border of the Western Division and in an irrigation area, had a modest increase.

Regardless of numbers, some of the smallest places have a wonderful spark of life about them. The picturesque Tilpa, on the Darling between Bourke and Wilcannia, is way too small to get a separate census entry. It was always tiny but once it had a post office, a police station, a school, a store, and probably six or eight houses.

Now, apart from a little and historic hotel (with an old grave in its front garden), there are two houses in Tilpa. One of them is also a store, opened by the Williams family a few years ago. 'It's the first store in Tilpa in 65 years,' says Carolyn Williams proudly, as she shows us round.

Population counts from Western New South Wales

Statistical Local Area	1996 population	2001 population	ANNUAL GROWTH RATE
UNINCORP FAR WEST	1069	1041	-0.5%
BOURKE	4039	3899	-0.7%
BREWARRINA	2192	2058	-1.3%
WALGETT	8505	8279	-0.5%
BROKEN HILL	21,313	20,274	-1.0%
CENTRAL DARLING	2644	2678	0.3%
COBAR	5668	5144	-1.9%
WENTWORTH	7238	6972	-0.8%
BALRANALD	2961	2763	-1.4%
CARRATHOOL	3151	3302	0.9%
HAY	3818	3562	-1.4%
WAKOOL	4926	4793	-0.6%

Notes: Data extracted from *CData 2001*. Some areas extend beyond
        Western Division

When the Williams – who previously owned a property –
took over the building it was derelict. Two rooms in its
middle had once been part of a hotel, and later part of the
postmaster's residence.

Tilpa might have seen livelier times but it is still very
much a community, with tennis courts, a cricket ground, a
community hall and a regular flying doctor clinic. It is also
one of the many towns of the West turning on a smile for
the tourist. Visitors can see one of Australia's most unusual
war memorials here. Bean would have loved it, so let's
linger on the tale for a moment.

Tilpa only got round to putting up its memorial a few years ago, and the story of it comes from Michael McInerney, a grazier and local historian.

After World War I, a local committee applied to the powers-that-be for something to form the basis of a memorial. In due course a machine gun was dispatched from Melbourne to Sydney, and then sent by rail to Bourke.

It reached Tilpa but, for reasons long forgotten, it wasn't erected. Instead it was stowed under the verandah of the post office; many years later the post mistress had it thrown into the river (despite searches by the historically-minded, it has never been found).

Several wars on, Tilpa decided to make good its gap. When it did so, it adoped an extremely inclusive approach to the stone and brick memorial, which has names from the two World Wars, and also from the Boer War, Korea and Vietnam.

It includes a man killed in a car accident the day he was due to embark, and another who would have gone overseas if he hadn't caught his foot and broken his ankle as he marched up the gangway onto the ship. A driver who spent the war ferrying VIPs gets a guernsey. So do people who didn't enlist from the area but drew soldier settlement blocks there later. And there's the famous Breaker Morant – executed for killing Boer War prisoners – who once worked in the locality.

Today's tourism promoters like to talk about the West as 'the accessible outback'. But however 'accessible', this 'outback' remains 'out back'; it leaves its indelible and special imprint on its people.

'[D]espite modern transport and the aeroplane, for so far

as one can see ahead the people there must always be pioneers in many respects – and probably, therefore, a source of strength for their nation,' Bean predicted in the preface to the 1963 edition of the *On the Wool Track*. His observation stands today. People out here are resilient as ever, because they still have to be. For all advances in modern farm management, they remain as much at the whim of the elements as a century ago. They're individual-istic and resourceful; they also have a strong feeling of community, and being part of the West.

As Wilkie Davis, one of the rich line of bush balladists of the West, wrote in his poem 'Western Qualities':

> There's a kinship in this western land,
> Beyond all human ken,
> For who could know the bonds and ties
> That knit the western men.
> There are women in this western land,
> Who answer trouble's call,
> Should an SOS flare in the night,
> There's a hand held out for all . . .
> There's a welcome in this western land,
> Of forest plain and loam,
> For the lonely stranger within the gates,
> And the wanderer coming home.

Tom Griffiths, in a recent essay on 'The Outside Country' contrasts it with a very different American West. It could be

> heroic and colourful and character-forming like
> America's West . . . it could generate distinctive national

stereotypes like America's West . . . But the westering in Australian history was not nearly as sustained or progressive as America's; settlement ebbed and flowed and regularly confronted its limits. The Australian frontier could never be said to have 'closed' as America's was declared to be in 1890: the Never-Never never ended. The American dream was the Australian nightmare.

In all the Western Division, there are now only about 1500 grazing properties, and almost all the land is Western lands leasehold.

The planners could never make up their minds about whether the region's pastoral properties should be big or small. The 1884 legislation that created the Western Division was designed, unsuccessfully, to get closer settlement. With the great drought that brought in the new century, opinion shifted away from thinking the land suitable for smaller properties, but following World War I, and the desire to settle ex-servicemen on the land, it shifted again, in favour of cutting down the big runs. In the 1980s graziers were allowed to amalgamate once more, as it was realised it was neither economic nor ecologically sound to try to operate limited areas.

At various times in the last century and a half, the Western land was treated appallingly by man and his animals. Bean headed one chapter (in a later edition) 'The Rape of the West', and told the story of the mismanagement and devastation in the 1890s.

He wrote that when the Western Lands Commission at the end of the century inquired into this, 'the story it heard

. . . was as bad and black and hopeless as it could be. The country had been made a desert' – although by the time Bean travelled there, it was reviving again.

Today's West has significant environmental challenges. One often mentioned is that large areas are covered by the scrubby 'woody weed' (shrubs and low trees) that has spread since the 1890s. They became most apparent following the wet years in the 1950s, driving out other vegetation and harbouring feral animals. However, we found there are two sides to the 'woody weed' story – some environmentalists see this growth as a healing scab on the wounded land.

Like other parts of the country, salinity has leached the soil in places. Profligate use of underground water has wasted much of the Great Artesian Basin. And the rivers' problems have become a major national issue.

But there is also active conservation in the West. A new pilot program, launched late last year by federal and state governments, pays landholders to stop grazing a part of their property and manage it for conservation gains. Significant parts of the West have become national parks. The first of these, called Kinchega, was established as late as the 1960s, and the process has been going on ever since. The Paroo–Darling National Park was gazetted recently, and more added to it since. Mungo National Park, World Heritage listed, with its remarkable Aboriginal sites, has been doubled in size.

Apart from attracting tourists, the parks preserve areas that, if they were grazed, would often simply blow away. Indeed, you'll find the occasional person who believes that much of the West would be better as one vast park, because the country is simply too borderline to cope, whether the measure is environment or economics. A livestock trader in Bourke tells us, 'The country should go to national parks. You're just wasting money on it. We don't need the [wool] production – you don't see a lot of people knocking themselves down to buy wool. Apart from the set [wool] price period – it was like Brigadoon – you have to go back to the '50s to have made money.' But the view that the pastoralists might as well abandon the West is not a general one.

Of course the parks themselves could become problems if weeds, vermin and feral animals are not rigorously kept down. The rabbits and the dingoes (interbred with domestic dogs that have gone wild), scourges of the West a century ago, are now under control, although rabbit warrens have to be ripped and the dingo fence along the state borders with Queensland and South Australia must be maintained.

On his journeying Bean saw comparatively few rabbits. They'd been devastatingly prolific before, and would be later; the counter attack, including poisoning (Bean tells the story of three million dead around a watering spot), shooting and even the release of cats, would not permanently get on top of the problem until the development of modern viruses.

At one homestead that Bean visited, a sheep had been bitten to death by a dingo or other wild dog.

There had been a dismal howling round the place the night before, and someone spoke of having seen a white animal, almost the size of a young calf, slinking round the house . . . something waked me in the small hours. And from close outside the windows came the most

> blood-chilling, dismal howling it has ever been one's
> fate to listen to. It was the wild dog come out of the
> bush again.

While many of the modern dingoes are interbred with
domestic dogs, DNA testing has proved that full-blood
dingoes still exist in the 'corner country' which is where
the NSW, Queensland and South Australian borders meet.

The wild pig was around a century ago but it was later
that the pigs became pest to everybody but the enthusiastic
shooters.

In Broken Hill we meet Kerry Holmes, a pest management
officer, whose daily work is battling rabbits, foxes, pigs,
goats, and cats. The practicalities and diplomacies of his job
are more complex than they might seem at first glance.

The goats that can be a boon to graziers are *personae
non grata* in the parks. But if they're shot, the pastoralists
get uptight about the 'waste'; they prefer the parks' authorities to issue contracts for harvesting.

Sometimes the parks' efforts to control 'ferals' of one kind
or another are undone by neighbouring properties not
doing enough. On the other hand, often the properties can't
afford to keep up their end.

The cats are cunning and an 'unknown quantity', Kerry
says. 'They're very hard to deal with. It's difficult to know
how many there are; they're difficult to shoot because they're
difficult to find. And you can't poison them because they
don't take baits.'

There's another problem. The cats are a pest to wildlife
but less of one for the pastoralists, so combating them
doesn't get the priority accorded to some other ferals. In

general, Kerry says, the numbers of feral animals are declining in the parks, and the news is reasonable on the weeds' front too. 'We're holding environmental and agricultural weeds where they are,' Kerry says. But what about the woody weed? Ah, here's the other story. 'We don't consider it a problem on parks – it's generally thought of as a way the country repairs itself.

'When the grass cover gets to a certain low level, the shrubs out-compete the grass. They're native species. In an environmental sense, they are holding the country together.' Anyway, 'we've had the technology to work on woody weed for the last 15 years – but it's not economic [for the pastoralist]'.

Then there are the kangaroos. If you're on the Western roads around dusk, you'll be amazed how thick the kangaroos are in many places. When a local drives me from a property near Cobar into town, soon after dark, there are several sickening thuds as the four-wheel drive vehicle hits them. Here's a hazard for the unwary tourist: an ordinary sedan travelling fast can easily be rolled by the impact.

The kangaroos are seen as a mixed blessing in the West. They're officially described as a 'sustainable, renewable resource', and they're a profitable grazing and meat industry in their own right. But the drought-stricken pastoralist curses them, as they take the last stock feed, break fences and seem to arrive in larger than usual numbers, although many starve in drought times too.

A member of the NSW parliament said in 2003 that before the drought the Western Division had an estimated two million sheep and 1.6 million kangaroos, but possibly hundreds of thousands of kangaroos and wallabies had starved. 'Wallabies starving to death were lined up along the road', he said. He was arguing for the ban to be lifted on culling kangaroos for skins (as distinct from meat).

One story we heard about kangaroos is a sort of metaphor for the harshness of this country. A White Cliffs man recounted how he'd once seen two wedge-tailed eagles (birds that thrive out there) hound a kangaroo to exhaustion and kill it. 'It was a hot day and they chased it for a kilometre at least. The kangaroo hid in the bushes – one of the eagles went in and flushed it out.'

Besides wool, the other industry that's historically shaped the West is mining. And, like sheep, the West's mining is part of the Australian legend. Broken Hill, 'an ash-heap or a green oasis according as you look at it', Bean wrote, had one of the world's largest concentrations of silver-lead-zinc, and it was here that BHP – the Big Australian – started in 1885. But 'the Hill', too, is transforming and adapting.

The Western Lands Commission a few years ago had a touch of defensiveness as it extolled the West. 'The simplistic description, all too commonly heard, gives scant recognition of the climate, landforms, soils and vegetation of the Western Division. The region is predominantly flat. It is hot and it can be dusty. But it can be mild and lush and there is natural beauty in the rolling plains of Mitchell grass in the harsh ridge country or among the Red Gum forests which flank the major rivers.'

The West is what people want to make of it, but it is also a matter of what they can put up with. While many in the West are finding new ways to make livings, others are leaving.

When they are graziers, they often depart only with great

reluctance and a good deal of personal trauma. In 2002 a study was published of Western Division grazing families who were either still on their properties but had suffered financial difficulties, or had left them.

The research (done in 2000, before the 2001–03 drought hit) by the federal government's Bureau of Rural Sciences concludes there is a 'pastoralist identity' that helps the back country people cope with adversity, but also makes it harder for them to quit unviable properties.

The graziers were strongly attached to pastoralism as an occupation and also had a deeply held feeling of 'place' about their properties. They'd held them a long time and a significant proportion had been reared on them.

They valued the independence of being their own bosses; they saw the 'bush' as superior to the towns, and some were keen to pass on their property to the next generation. Those struggling on remained optimistic they'd survive through perseverance and hard work.

For them their properties were 'imbued with individuality, socially and culturally relevant meanings and symbols'. Often particular spots were seen as special, associated with sad or happy memories, such as a death or a shared activity. For these people, leaving pastoralism 'was not just about leaving a place of employment, but also leaving a place of residence, and in many cases it also involved leaving a place upon which they were reared'.

A majority of people who had left – to go into retirement or other jobs – felt their quality of life had improved, but the break with their properties had not been without trauma and 'grief'.

The departure of young people in search of services,

opportunities and income is a recurring theme in the West. 'Mainly education takes the young off the properties', Jan McClure, of *Kallara* station, near Tilpa, says. 'It's just too hard to educate your children.'

Some want a predictable income. The son of the Bourke livestock trader was about to become a teacher. 'A lot of young people are going to Sydney, or to uni to study. Why flog your guts out when you can go and do something like teaching and you know where the next cheque is coming from?' he says.

But for many older people, it's another story. 'I'd find it hard to leave [this land]', one tells us. 'Even if you left it, it would never leave you.'

— 6 —
Adaptation and Change

Almost certainly the West will remain forever relatively empty, although the growth of tourism will mean more people make its acquaintance.

The explorers feasted their eyes on magnificent grasslands. Only later, after huge damage had been done, did white people understand (but not always accept) that this is fragile and marginal land, which can neither be overused (by the greedy) nor oversettled (by struggling small-timers) without disaster.

In the West the towns, like the people, struggle with elemental issues of survival. Many have declined; some have disappeared; quite a few are reinventing themselves. Those that are predominantly indigenous face some special problems.

The biggest story of the West is that the sheep has lost his dominance. The wool track has become a more diverse road.

In the late 1880s sheep numbers here reached more than 15 million. Throughout the 20th century they never got above 10 million, with the average around six million. The numbers are slashed in the droughts; by 2003 there were only two million.

The sheep have not been displaced by cattle. As far as stock goes, this was and remains sheep country. But agriculture has drawn ahead of wool as an income producer. This includes citrus and grapes near the Victorian border, wheat and other dry crops, and the controversial – because it gulps so much valuable and scarce water – cotton. The debate about cotton in the West is a bit like the one about cattle in the High Country in Victoria.

The sheep industry, as well as shrinking, is transforming. 'From the moment he is lambed a sheep is either so much wool or so much meat; and wool or meat he remains until he dies, unless he strikes very evil days and becomes tallow', Bean wrote.

Then, the 'outside' country was unsuited to meat raising. 'It is one thing to take a fat lamb from his mother in a paddock alongside the railway line and truck him in a day to Sydney', Bean observed, 'and quite another to drive him, half-weaned, from the Paroo over a hundred miles of drought-stricken stock-route on the chance that he will survive it and die in a railway truck.'

Sheep travelling from the 'outside' country still have a harder time of it than their 'inside' counterparts. But trucks, fast roads, regional abattoirs, and the combination of dicey wool returns and good lamb prices have moved many Western graziers into sheep that produce better meat.

Marketing goats and kangaroo-shooting have become significant industries. In one case a feral animal has proved a life-saver for many a struggling pastoralist; in the other, we're becoming accustomed to dining out on the national emblem.

Grazing has reached its limit; and, with the controversy over water, agriculture may soon do so. The sunrise industry in the West is tourism; the hope is that it will become a staple.

The wool track has become the tourist route.

Wherever you go, whether in the towns or outside them, they're looking optimistically to the visitors to supplement the old industries of wool and mining. A mega shearing shed north of the remote opal centre of White Cliffs has become an attraction. White Cliffs itself – where few opals are mined these days – entertains foreign as well as local visitors at an unusual underground motel and a B&B 'dug-out'.

Broken Hill is seeing the slow death of mining but a rebirth through the colony of artists whose dramatic representation of the country's landscape has become internationally famous and draws visitors to the town.

Some of the pastoral stations are in the business of 'home stays' where travellers can experience a few days of station life. Once the West was dotted with little hotels which were coach changes for travellers (though hardly, in those days, 'tourists'). In recent years, this new sort of tiny 'hotel' has sprung up. Visitors are put up in the station's house or in newly built cabins, and entertaining them is woven around the property's other activities.

This gives the often financially-pressed graziers some extra income, and is part of the trend for these properties to look for as many strings to their bows as possible.

Jan McClure, a widow who runs *Kallara* with her son Justin and daughter-in-law Julie, moved into tourism in 1991 to supplement finances. Now the family has added the nearby Tilpa hotel to its operations, which include grazing sheep and growing organic crops on *Kallara* (117,000 acres; people in these parts still talk acres rather than hectares) and the other family properties.

Adaptation and Change

In her spare time Jan is researching the history of *Kallara*, where NSW's first artesian water was tapped in 1878. She describes *On the Wool Track* as 'one of my bibles.' Bean carefully recorded in one of his tables that in 1907 *Kallara* was 998,514 acres with 81,581 sheep and 1196 cattle. But it is his column headed 'Sheep carried before the Drought (roughly)' that would strike a special chord with Jan, who's been struggling with the dry when we visit the station; the figure for *Kallara* was 120,000.

Jan's story is like that of many others. *Kallara* in 1896 had 53 people, including several families of Chinese. In 2003 the McClure family, who share staff among properties that add up to 400,000 acres, have only three permanent station hands. Jan says eight are needed to do the work properly. When we visit *Kallara*, she's looking forward to a couple of middle-aged women coming to the station under a new scheme for tradespeople and other volunteers to spend some time in the outback and help out. There's painting and gardening to catch up on.

Some of the 'home stays' have a special twist. Out of Bourke there is a camel farm called *Comeroo*, belonging to Bruce Sharpe, who has about twenty camels. He preferred to get animals that had come from the desert 'and to learn with them'. They're mustered in helicopters and arrive 'pretty wild. I hand-feed them and they get quiet'. He puts them in wagons, but doesn't let visitors ride them. The public liability insurance has become too expensive.

The camels, with their Afghan cameleers (at least they were called Afghans but many were from India's north-west frontier, now Pakistan) used to be transportation vehicles on legs. Now they're a curiosity for the tourists.

It's all part of diversification – or call it survival – in the West today.

With high-powered vehicles and sealed highways, this vast area is a thousand times easier to travel than in the early 1900s. The retired couples from the city in their four-wheel drives or sedan-and-caravan can enjoy a bush holiday and hospitality in air-conditioned comfort. Out here people talk about the 'grey nomads' who are helping buttress the local economy.

Even so, distances are formidable and backroads dusty and corrugated or slippery and boggy, according to season. A brief heavy shower can make driving hazardous (or maybe adventurous, for the more daring of the nomads), while bringing no relief to the drought-stricken farmer.

There are paradoxes in the communications revolution for those who live in the West. Bean observed, while staying at a remote property, how those in the outback were already enthusiastic users of the telephone. He told of arriving at a back station of a big Darling run, and encountering the owner of the main station, who was making a round trip.

> At the end of dinner the boss pushed back his chair and then carried it to the telephone on the wall at his back. He . . . proceeded to have an after-dinner yarn – across a hundred and thirty miles of telephone wires – with his sister, who was at another of his stations somewhere down the river. It was not a mere dialogue. The boss owned some five stations, this side of the Darling, and the other, and at one or two at least, of these, somebody else was joining in the chat.

A century later television, radio, email and internet have brought the global village even to the endless outback, albeit not as quickly or extensively as to city-dwellers. In 2001, 46 per cent of Sydneysiders used a computer at home, and 43 per cent used the internet, but for the far West the figures were 31 per cent and 25 per cent. The lowest use of home computer and the internet was in the largely Aboriginal town of Brewarrina, near Bourke (17 per cent and 13 per cent, respectively).

Despite communications advances, educating children is a real challenge: in the remotest parts, children still must be taught at home, driven long distances to meet a school bus, or sent away to board.

Most Australians in the cities would think 'governesses' went out with the 19th-century novel. But young women, and retired school teachers, are still to be found on some properties out near the Darling, supervising lessons that are co-ordinated centrally through the iconic 'School of the Air'. With times tough recently, the governesses have become rarer, and the visiting retired school teachers more common.

The teachers, whether professionals or parents, have the benefit of computers and other educational mod-cons.

In Broken Hill we call in on the School of the Air, where the first thing they tell you is to forget that old image of the kid with the radio. I can't vouch for its accuracy but the story we were told was that an education minister went to a School of the Air session, couldn't understand what the children had to say, and after that, the transition to satellite equipment came quite fast.

Now the station family plugged into the School of the Air

has in their school room more equipment than most of their city cousins – a computer, a digital camera, a colour printer, a scanner and a graphics template.

Even with these aids, however, families who can't afford to buy in professional teaching help face a struggle tutoring children at home, especially if this has to be fitted around station jobs that the parent–teacher must do. Often the children, too, have to help out with the station work. They learn practical skills early; School of the Air teachers, who regularly visit their remote charges, can find themselves whizzed around the property by a driver aged eight.

Needs breed initiative. Jan McClure and a neighbour, Anna Middleton, began the NSW Volunteers for Isolated Students Education Scheme for retired teachers and health professionals to work on properties for a couple of months to help mothers. There are echoes of the travelling 'schoolie' who went to the stations around Ivanhoe many years ago, staying a while at each – although he was a full-time teacher.

Jan explains how the plan started. 'Anna's daughter has special needs, and I have a Down's Syndrome child. We talked about it in 1991 and had it up and running in '92 in New South Wales. We had 400 people on the national database at the end of the first year. It's still going, administered from Canberra.'

Rural health services have improved, as they've become a political issue. But there are towns without medical facilities that have to rely on the flying doctor for GP, specialist or emergency treatment. The Royal Flying Doctor Service has been written about so much there's almost nothing new left to say about a service that imparts a special feeling of confidence to these far-flung households and communities; their praise and special stories about the service are endless.

One bit of trivia however: have you ever noticed that apart from the Flynn of the Inland portrait, our $20 note also carries an image of the sectioned 'body map' supplied to stations to help people accurately inform the doctor or nurse where a pain or wound is?

While people on remote properties in the West are closer to civilisation, services and help than in the past, they can be more alone than a century ago.

Then the stations, much bigger than they are now, were communities in their own right, with 50, even 100 people living on them. Living was tougher, but there were more people to share the toil. Today, they might be just a not-so-young couple like Barry and Virginia Angell, on *Mt Jack*, out of the opal town of White Cliffs.

To spend a morning with the Angells, we have to scout around White Cliffs to find someone to take us in a four-wheel drive. The road is unmade and the tracks through the paddocks can be death to a car.

A few hours at *Mt Jack* gives you the feel of today and yesterday on one of these stations. In the early 1890s this was a backstation of *Momba*, one of the great runs. In *The Dreadnought of the Darling* Bean tells how the opal town was born of *Momba* land.

Twenty-two years ago a kangaroo-shooter on Momba run wounded a kangaroo in the White Cliffs paddock. As he ran it down, something sparkled on the hillside. He turned, and found a stone with the most beautiful glass in the world sandwiched through it.

Barry has *On the Wool Track*; he read it 40 years ago. With his land so poor, it's not surprising he especially recalls the reference to grass as high as a fence, although that was mostly a memory even in Bean's day.

On the wall of the homestead verandah, where we chat over coffee, the Angells have a 1913 poster advertising the forthcoming auction of *Momba*, in July of that year. *Momba* in those days was 1.6 million acres, with 55,000 grown sheep, plus lambs; the buyer would also get 124 mules and donkeys, 150 horses and 70 camels (but only 44 cattle). The property had a frontage of 30 miles to the Darling 'in a direct line' (equal to about 100 miles actual frontage), and two woolsheds. One was already fitted with 30 stands of shearing machinery, while the Mt Jack shed was ready for machines. The shearing, the poster said, was due to begin on July 24 and last until late August or early September. The *Momba* sheep 'are noted for their excellent frames, splendid constitutions, and are profitable wool producers and heavy cutters'.

After morning tea, we go over to the ruins of the old stone shed. While the typically Australian iron sheds were all round the country in the 19th century, some properties – where material had been locally available – shore in sheds of stone. This one must have been grand – a great baronial hall of the outback, if you let your imagination run – with its 58 stands and sandstone floor. The remnants of its wool press are there; nearby are the stone huts for the men.

Momba in 1913 boasted telephone links between the head station and the outstation of *Mt Murchison*, as well as the town of Wilcannia. And – in a portent of the change soon to transform the back country – the 'Station Motor car' was being offered to take round prospective buyers on their inspection tours.

Despite the convenience of the modern motor, the Angells tell us they shop only about once a month. 'You become an expert at cooking without things,' Virginia says. And adept at doing everything. Before we arrive Virginia has already been out mustering cattle, while Barry was giving a pump a once over. They say they're doing work that previously would have been done by nine people.

Part of the problem is getting reliable workers, even though Wilcannia isn't so far away. Despite high unemployment in parts of the West, there can be a real disconnect out here between the people available for work and the employers, and anyway, it's usually hard to find money for anything but limited extra help.

More tasks and fewer hands on these properties can often mean little time and even less energy for socialising, at least for the older people. (Mind you, when some families decide to kick their heels up, it's with style. The Browns, who also live out of White Cliffs, fly their light plane to outings.)

'We don't really have a social life here,' Virginia says, and Barry chimes in, 'too busy, too damn tired'. The Angells are sceptical about the conventional wisdom that better communications bring people closer together. They claim the opposite has happened – that community life in the bush has been killed.

In the days of primitive communal telephones the women had a gossip session in the morning and the men at night. Party lines might have been intrusive but they brought the district into a general conversation.

'You knew what people were doing,' Virginia recalls.

Automatic phones came in around their district from about 1981 and continued to improve. At the same time, 'the West stopped communicating' in the last couple of decades, Barry says. Just yesterday he'd talked to neighbours on *Mt Jack*'s eastern side – he reckons for the first time in two years.

After leaving the Angells, we bump along tracks to the old *Momba* homestead. The *Momba* run was among the West's big wool properties when Sidney Kidman added it to the string of cattle stations he had established through South Australia, Queensland and NSW. *Momba* even had its own camel team to carry wool south to the rail links.

From the time he was a boy Kidman came to know the land west of the Darling well, and he believed that cattle would be more profitable than sheep. When his early horse trading and butchering enterprises carried him to a level of wealth where he could join the big landowners, it was not as a sheep man but as a cattle man.

Many despised Kidman's approach, considering his methods as less than admirable – particularly his treatment of sheep stations, which he stripped of materials, like the iron on woolsheds, which were not needed for cattle runs. Wire was taken from *Momba* fences and sent away for sale, and the workforce of about sixty slashed, because fewer men were needed for cattle.

While his changes were resented in the area by those who saw them as a backward step, Kidman persisted with his grand plan of having a chain of stations through which he could send cattle all the way from Queensland to southern markets.

Kidman was a risktaker, acquiring properties at crisis prices in the extremities of drought, a process that led to his owning more cattle than any man at that time, earning him the title of Cattle King.

Walter and Maxine Dell, who have what's left of *Momba*, live in a modern house which has been built right up against the old, like neighbours in a suburban street. The old *Momba* homestead is well past its hundredth birthday, and showing the ravages this country brings to many of its pioneer buildings. Some of its windows have found their way into White Cliffs to live a new life, adding to the charm of a beautifully restored old house that once was the police residence.

Although he died in 1935, around here they talk of Kidman as though he had lived in the near past. 'My grandmother came to cook in Kidman's day. He was a tough old codger, but he had to be,' Maxine says. 'He was a man to be admired for what he set out to do and achieved. No man today will ever achieve what Sir Sidney did in his lifetime.'

Maxine has a copy of *On the Wool Track*. 'We trawled Sydney for it. Someone lent us one, and we thought we'd get it. Dad had one – he lent it and didn't get it back.'

We think, how remarkable so many people know about this book, and what a pity it's out of print.

— 7 —

Fighting the Elements

Chapter one of *On the Wool Track* opens with a 'death in the paddock'. It is a tragedy typical of its time in this country.

The West of the early 20th century was harsh and intimidating, ready to best those who did not understand it. Out here, many perished in often horrible deaths. Others were crushed not physically but financially or in spirit, by drought and distance.

> For nine days the police had followed a man's footsteps. Now and again the footmarks would turn back upon themselves. Now they would lead round and round a tree. Now they would shoot off at right angles.
>
> At long intervals they had found depressions and scratches in the surface which showed where he had gone down on his hands and knees to lap the dregs of last month's rain still lying in some claypan.
>
> And now, at last, after nine days' hard following, they found towards the evening that the footmarks began to drag.

They could see clearly the long scrape of the toe before each heel-mark. They hurried on, following for all they were worth. Presently they came to his hat. There the dark closed in upon them. It was too black to follow, and they had to camp.

That night down came the rain. And in the morning every trace of the tracks they were following was sponged away as from a slate.

All day they searched – both the trooper and the black tracker. Months later, a boundary rider came upon his coat. There were letters in it from some man in Scotland. And from that day to this those were all the traces that they found of him.

Long afterwards a letter came back from the man in Scotland to whom the police had written. He was a doctor there, and the dead man's brother.

The dead man had been working his way through the far West from station to station on foot. He had suddenly announced that he meant to walk to Sydney. Probably he drank. Certainly he went mad.

Now, the paddock where that man was lost was not 20 miles out of Menindie [sic]. He never got out of the one paddock.

It was no bigger than most other western paddocks – ten miles by ten miles. And yet either in that paddock or in the one which we drove through next to it, the boundary riders have ridden across, at one time or another, the skeletons of three men, with their swags scattered near them, just as they lay down when they came to the end of their strength.

Bean heard many such stories, like that of the man who had started to drive a 'dry' stage of 70 miles, from near Bourke to Wanaaring, to collect arrears on sewing machines.

> They picked him up alone two mornings later two and a half miles out of Wanaaring waving a handkerchief on a stick, and whispering, 'Water – back there!' They took water back there for four miles and found his mate and the two horses collapsed. Some twig had scratched their water-bag. That was all.

Among the remarkable rescue stories was one a policeman told him, about three children who wandered from a central West homestead into long grass. They were found 'collapsed, but alive' after a nine-day hunt. He heard another tale of two small children who were found alive an astonishing 38 miles from their Bourke home, four days after they walked off.

In today's West, people still sometimes get lost in inhospitable country; they are often the old and frail. John Blair, Broken Hill's Uniting Church flying padre, says that in separate instances in recent times, a man and a woman, both elderly, have walked out into the desert and not been found.

Blair was personally involved in a dramatic rescue of a woman who had been lost for six days. Before we get to that, a little about the padre and his wife Becky, who make an interesting story in themselves.

Both Americans, they first came to Australia in the 1970s, living in Melbourne; John was a chaplain trainee at the Austin Hospital and then a teacher at St Leonard's College in Brighton and Becky worked for Trans Australia Airlines.

They enjoyed Australia but returned to the US because, as John puts it, they wanted to 'raise our son a Yankee,' as well as having him grow up near his grandparents.

Then a few years ago, they visited country NSW to see friends they'd met at John's parish near Boston. John, whose life dream was to combine his hobby of flying with his job of ministering, heard the job of flying padre, based at Broken Hill, was vacant. 'I had three questions. What's a flying padre? Who broke Broken Hill? And where do I apply?'

Since he started in mid-2002, nothing has equalled the joy of the remarkable rescue of Janette Luscombe, an elderly Broken Hill woman suffering from dementia.

Mrs Luscombe disappeared on a cold and very windy Sunday in September 2003 while walking her blue heeler cross dog Dazzie.

John takes up the story. 'On the Monday I dropped Becky off at work. (She's the supervisor of the Royal Flying Doctor Service's tourist centre.) I'd heard of the search and went over to where it was being co-ordinated and offered my 182 Cessna that the church has had since 1974.' Mrs Luscombe was wearing a medical alert necklace and John took up a two-person team to try to pick up a signal. But they got no response.

On the Friday, as the search was about to be called off, John got a call from one of the policemen. 'He said, "The family's clinging to their hope, but we can't go on forever – would you take one last crack for the sake of the family?"

'I went out and got the plane ready. It was a blustery day. It made me a little nervous, because I was trying to go at a slow speed so we could do a visual search. I flew in an

ever-widening spiral from the airport at about 1500 feet.'
He had with him two emergency service volunteers. Sitting
behind him in the aircraft was Lesley, holding an antenna;
Josh sat beside him, with a meter that would register any
signal from the woman's necklace.

Suddenly, as they flew over two dams about 10 miles out
of town, Josh tapped John's leg and said 'turn left'. They'd
picked up the signal. They flew in ever-tighter circles,
making contact with the signal four times. Lesley marked
the co-ordinates; John radioed in, and they returned to the
airport to distribute maps to the ground searchers.

When they took off again to help guide searchers to the
spot, they knew Mrs Luscombe was there but they didn't
know whether she was alive or dead. John spotted something pink floating in one of the dams and suppressed the
obvious thought.

Searchers in place, the plane returned again to the airport.
'We were tying the plane down when "Flies" – the fellow
who does the [airport] roo runs, the mechanical checking,
and is always there when you need him – jumped out of his
truck. His voice broke. He said, "They've found her – and
she's alive". We were so happy.'

Dazzie, who was sitting by the side of the semi-conscious
woman, became a hero. The dog, which would have led her
to water and given her warmth, was credited with helping
keep her alive. But it was modern technology – the medical
alert and the aeroplane – that located and saved her.

Light planes have been a boon to the big properties. They
reduce isolation, shrink the vastness, make running stations
easier and more efficient, and remove some of the fear from
illness.

Several years after Bean's travels a pilot from Britain's Royal Aero Club promoted the virtue of planes for the Australian outback in *The Pastoralists' Review*. Now that reliable machines were available, Australia should take her share in the evolution of flying by providing the first real work to which the aeroplane might be put – this work 'is to be found on the large sheep and cattle stations'. The writer went so far as to claim that nearly all the large stations were 'superior to the finest aerodromes of Europe, and provide the safest possible ground over which to fly'.

The stations did, over the years, take up the use of the aeroplanes. But despite their relative safety they also bring their share of accidents.

A few years ago, two separate air crashes near the small town of Ivanhoe claimed four lives within weeks.

When we were out at *Kilfera* station, we saw where a light plane carrying two South Australians to the station's field day crashed near the old homestead that Bean stayed in.

It had come in to land with a tail wind. When the pilot found it was travelling too fast to pull up on the strip, he tried to climb again, but could not get high enough in time.

The second crash was on *Whyba*, just north of Ivanhoe. The family had sold the place; they were having a clearing sale. One of the family, a 20-year-old university student, came home for the weekend. He wanted to have a joy ride before the ultralight went under the auctioneer's hammer. He and his passenger died when the plane just seemed to fall out of the sky.

Bean made his journeys only several decades after the sheep and the men who went with them spread out through land that could look deceptively benign. But the country's smiling face often turned angry and threatening.

Sometimes the change was capricious, when drought or fire came. Other times, it was retribution for the men's maltreatment of the land, as in ignorance or greed they overstocked and wore it out.

A few years before Bean's journey, the West had been devastated by over-grazing, the invasion of rabbits (which had crossed the Murray by 1880 and soon spread over the Western country) and drought lasting from the mid-1890s into the new century.

The toll was huge. Many owners lost properties; leases were abandoned; stock perished in vast numbers. In 1900 a Royal Commission was set up to inquire into conditions.

These memories were fresh when Bean went through.

Indeed, out West the rule has been disaster – typically Australian disaster, because nothing happened, but it simply did not rain. The stock went on feeding, and the grass went on dying, and the stock routes became dustier and dustier, until one critical day came.

You could not always tell when it came, often not till after it had gone, but it came and went all the same – the day when the stock route was passable for the last time, and the sheep had still strength to get away if the boss so chose.

The boss can hardly be blamed for not choosing. It was a big expense and a big risk. Big ragged clouds were flying low down over the country, and it might rain tomorrow. So the chance went by. The sheep stayed. And presently grass ran out. The boss bought feed for his horses and paid men to cut scrub for his sheep. Then the money ran out too.

It was no good ruining himself to keep the sheep alive and then letting them die when they were his only asset. It might rain to-morrow. So the boss borrowed and went on. In the end, when the stock had trampled out the roots of most of the grass, and then had mostly died, the mortgagees came in and took the station.

Sometimes they left the boss as manager. But the men who owned 'outside' runs before the drought, and who own the same runs still, may almost be counted on the fingers.

In the 21st century, drought can be almost as devastating.

Admittedly, there are crutches that used not be there. Instead of having to be walked to better country, stock can be trucked away, so decisions can be made later and the animals travel with much less wear and tear. Against that, in a big drought, agistment can be hard to find, and the timing of that decision to cut your losses is still crucial. I heard of one Western pastoralist who, after the latest drought, mustered only 800 of what had been a flock of about 25,000.

Government help and social welfare provide cushions for those finding themselves with no income but continuing costs – indeed, if they are trying to feed breeding stock, costs that could be bigger than ever.

Regardless of help, the agony of drought still tears at people trying to make a living from this country.

In 2002 I fly with deputy prime minister John Anderson to *Keewong*, Rob and Robyn Francisco's 136,000 acre property, 132 kilometres out of Cobar. More than 60 people have come from up to 200 kilometres away for a meeting on drought assistance.

As the sun is setting, the small crowd gathers in a circle in the homestead garden to tell their stories.

'When it rains it sings,' says one man, but the country isn't singing now: 'everyone is doing it hard.'

One family bought their property three years before; they've had two years of drought. The man had saved all his life for the place. 'We have sold all the stock. We have no agistment, no feed, no income, no hope. Every day is an eternity. What do we do – walk away?

'We're out fencing, contracting tanks. All the small bills come in. We're on our knees.' He's 33, but he says many of the property owners are in their 60s.

As the dusk deepens, Rob Francisco recounts how he's a fifth generation grazier who's been 43 years on *Keewong*. 'My son and daughter were partners for seven years. My son said, "Dad, sell the place – as soon as you die we'll sell it."' Nearly a year later *Keewong* is still in a drought-stricken pocket. 'We haven't had any stock here for two and a half years,' Rob tells me when I call him back to see how he and wife Robyn are faring. 'But we're not living on government assistance.' How do they exist then? 'We're living on goats. We probably truck away about 2000 a year. They're not fat, but they're saleable.'

The goats get by where another animal would starve; they scavenge and move in from other areas. They're rounded up like sheep, with sheepdogs, and make $22 a head for the struggling pastoralist.

Rob and Robyn are not eating the goats, because of their

poor condition, although 'we have eaten them over the years – they're as good as sheep,' Rob says.

The humble goat is around the West in very large numbers today. Even in earlier times, while he was less numerous, he was there to meet necessity, albeit sometimes as an imposter.

When the coaches on which Bean travelled stopped for meals the meat was 'always nominally mutton. Looking through the window one could often not help suspecting that one saw the venturesome leader of a herd of mutton scrambling over the top of the local deposit of tins cans, followed by his numerous wives and kids.'

In country of long memories, some at the *Keewong* meeting compare the drought to the bad one in the 1960s. It's 'worse than '66', says one man. 'I haven't had three inches of rain for the year. It's 22 months since I've had water running into the dams. There's no lambing in the Western Division. People haven't even been shearing a third of their wool clips.'

Others, including Rob (who in late 2003 finally leaves *Keewong*), say it's the worst drought since 1900.

They know that even when the rain comes, their troubles won't be over. They'll need money to restock, because many of them have got rid of all their animals.

The two federal ministers – the other is agriculture minister Warren Truss – to whom these families pour out their woes are from the National Party. The Country Party, as it was originally called, was formed about a decade after *On the Wool Track* was published, to give a voice to rural interests and grievances.

The people of the West, according to Bean, had had some 'horrible shocks' from politicians.

Just before the drought broke, the people of Bourke received a visit from their Premier. A deputation waited on him . . . It was hardly necessary to put their case to him because the whole of the world knew by the cables in the papers what the case along the Darling was just then. The grass had long since disappeared; the face of the country was shifting red and grey sand, blowing about wherever the wind carried it. The fences were covered; dead sheep and fallen trunks had become sand-hills . . . the West was literally not different from the Sahara Desert.

Some men's nerves had broken down under it, and they had to flee from it in fear for their sanity. The rest of the world had been watching them fight it as people watch soldiers at the front . . . So there was really no need to put the case to their Premier.

But they did so, for form's sake, and he seemed to listen, looking up when they'd finished.

'What do you do with the country in these parts?' he asked, waving his hand towards the window. 'What – er – what use d'yer make of it?'

They were a little surprised. They had just been telling him for three-quarters of an hour.

But they said: 'Oh, well, we put sheep on it – that is, when there is any grass on it . . .'

'D'jever think of dairyin'?' asked the Premier.

The men went away 'almost sick with disillusionment'.

One of those at *Keewong* is a new breed in the West – the financial counsellor. The men and women of the West have always had banks and pastoral houses. In disastrous times, these sometimes gave help (and still do). But they were also, at the end of the day, the bailiffs.

'It's the toughest it's been,' Brian Dodson tells the meeting. 'The next few years are probably going to be even tougher.' He's had a client whose power and the telephone have been cut off.

Dodson, whose funding comes from the state and federal governments, 'counsels' over a massive area – 23 per cent of NSW in fact.

In his early 50s and born in the Sunraysia district, Dodson is a former banker (some 20 years with the Bank of NSW, now Westpac) and then worked with a welfare organisation, Mallee Family Care. He's trained in family dispute resolution counselling; many years ago he did business studies at Melbourne's Royal Melbourne Institute of Technology (RMIT).

When I talk to him some months after the *Keewong* visit, it's rained – but still only patchily and with not enough follow up.

People are uncertain, he says. 'Even the old guys don't know where they are – whether to restock, and if so, whether with sheep or cattle or go to other alternatives.' And now there's been a fall in wool prices. 'A few months ago people were getting $1000 to $1500 a bale; now it's $750 or $800 a bale.

'If it doesn't rain, or continue to rain, people could spend $100,000 on stocking, and find themselves worse off in a few months' time.'

Yet till they get 'sheep on the ground' the income won't start flowing again and, despite government assistance, 'they'll continue to go backwards'.

The level of debt is alarming. 'I'd say the debt average is $500,000 to $600,000. To service a debt like that you can't afford a drought.' And you need about 10,000 sheep. If the drought has left a property with only a thousand sheep it will take two or three years to rebuild the flock.

He has about 200 clients and, although the pastoral houses and banks were reasonably supportive through the worst of the drought, he reckons that 'there is a pretty fair chance ten of those clients won't be here in 12 months'.

Dodson has great admiration for the women on the Western properties; they have, he says 'enormous durability'.

'They cook breakfast, put on a load of washing, go out and muster, then come back and cook. Most of them work like two men.' Now he's seen in the last decade a trend that disturbs him – what's almost a 'migration' of women from the beleaguered properties into the towns.

In their battle to get some money 'quite a number of families are breaking up. Mum and the kids are coming to town looking for work; Dad is staying on the farm.

'They're physically breaking up, not breaking up emotionally. But it puts strains on and who knows what happens? The guy is working five days a week, coming home and cooking a meal, drinking a bit too much, then it can be a four- or five-hour drive into town for the weekend to see the family.

'It's been happening for the last ten years but it's happening more and more.' In bad times the country women, some of them with professions such as nursing, have to become the family's sole bread-winner.

It's actually not as new as Dodson suggests. Pat Le Lievre, who has property along the Darling downriver from

Bourke, says it was happening from the 1960s onwards. When men married nurses and teachers, the usual comment was, 'Congratulations, mate, you've just drought-proofed your property.'

Drought squeezes the towns. Dodson mentions one, outside the Western Division but apparently typical of many in it, which he says has 18 small businesses and only five still open.

'A lot of these smaller towns are made up of roo shooters, shearers, property hands. With the lack of work they move to larger centres to find work. They won't come to the back country again.'

In these hard times some farmers are depressed enough to contemplate suicide. One of the financial counsellor's tasks is to watch out for danger cases. 'A number of families we monitor on a regular basis.' Calls sometimes come from neighbours. 'We keep as much contact as we can.'

Dodson draws a couple of lessons from the big drought. One is that bad weather forecasting encouraged some farmers to hang on to stock longer than they should in the expectation that rain was imminent. (The forecasters cop it from both directions in the West. In 2004 an angry Bourke grazier, fearing he'd lose lambs he'd mulesed before unexpected rain, wrote to the *Sydney Morning Herald*: 'There is certainly only a 50/50 chance of the weather bureau getting anywhere near forecasting rain until after the event.')

The other lesson Dodson sees is that the tougher breeds of sheep – like the Dorpers and Damaras – often survived better than the Merinos. 'Maybe the days of running traditional Merinos have gone and people should split their flocks between Merino and some foreign stock.'

There's no escape in this country from the heartbreak of drought. The big dries will come again and again, without fail; only the precise timing is unpredictable. And every time they'll catch the graziers in a vice. Even the best providers, the most efficient managers, can't fully insulate themselves against the rainless years.

It was one of these particularly harsh droughts in outback NSW that spawned some of Australia's most striking art.

In 1944 Russell Drysdale went out to the West with a *Sydney Morning Herald* reporter, Keith Newman, and a photographer. The journey was easier and more comfortable than the ones Bean had made; the wartime party was driven in a Buick. The first in the series of articles was headlined, 'Western Inferno. The Country in which there are no Bushfires. There is nothing to burn. An Artist's Journey Into Australia's "Lost World".'

The story has a familiar ring. Newman wrote:

> It is difficult to believe that, after a good season, some 15 years ago parts of the Western Division were so thickly covered that they were the scene of disastrous grass-fires in which thousands of stock roasted to death (and some men, too) . . .
>
> There is no need to watch where you toss your cigarette butts now; you couldn't start a bush fire out here if you tried.

Drysdale's sketches captured the hardness and hopelessness, while the articles gave a lot of attention to the erosion of the land. The drawings as well as the articles caused a storm of protest. *Country Life* raged about 'story after story with "artists' impressions" more hideous than any Archibald Prize picture, more grotesque, more fantastic and more confusing of mind!' It contrasted these with its own 'constructive stories and illustrations'.

In its series, the *Herald* promoted Drysdale as having 'achieved a reputation for his ruthless interpretation of Australia's spacious gauntness and the wear and tear which mankind suffers in its struggle within such an environment . . . The drawings here portray, with subtlety and strength, the fearful and spectral drama of the inferno through which he has passed.'

Reviewing Drysdale's trip 50 years later, Tim Bonyhady wrote that it was 'a turning point for Drysdale'. As well as publicising his work to a wider audience, and landing him in controversy, it led to some of his most important works, including *The Drover's Wife* and the *Walls of China*.

Drysdale with his graphic sketches did for this country what Bean had done with his words. Bonyhady writes that Drysdale 'made what was happening in the outback visible to the majority of people who did not live there'. The sketches of figures suggested the resilience of the people, but the drawings of the country showed the other side of the story – 'skeleton trees, rotting carcasses, derelict windmills and dying soil'.

— 8 —
Women of the West

One of Bean's memorable descriptions of these red plains crossed by black soil river flats is that it is 'a country where bad men are very bad, and good men are magnificent; but where all men are interesting'.

Notably he says 'men'. His story is almost all about men – owners and managers of runs, shearers, station hands, cooks, porters, oddballs.

Although in his day this country was very much a man's preserve, there were of course some women in the West, but in *On the Wool Track* women are depicted by their absence.

Quite a few women were in some towns; we might have expected more women in *The Dreadnought of the Darling* pages because it deals with several of the towns. However, with a few exceptions, they are shadowy figures, apart from their civilising domestic touch. The indications are that Bean was less at ease with women than with men, so perhaps he failed to seek out the detailed stories of women he did encounter.

He tells how the rough but upright men he met idealised the women. 'They have an almost romantic reverence for

any straight woman that lives amongst them in the West.'
  Indeed, a chivalrous

> Western code . . . comes with the force of a sledge-
> hammer on to any man that injures a good woman.
> A woman's life is hard in this far West, and there are
> not many women out there – perhaps not nearly as
> many as there should be. But if devotion, almost
> amounting to worship, shown in little thoughtful
> attentions, in tender consideration in small things
> and large, can help a woman over her difficulties and
> troubles, that attention almost every man in the West
> will lay at her feet.

Bean laments the absence of women on practical grounds.
The 'simple, good men' of the West were not populating the
country: 'as far as producing future citizens for Australia
goes, [the sheep stations] might as well be monasteries.
They want few wives on the outside runs, and no children'.
Station hands were mostly not allowed to marry, he says,
because a family had to be given more in rations but the
property got only the same amount of work. 'In the outside
country women are not encouraged – partly to save them
from hardship, and partly to save the stations from expense
. . . on most of the great runs outside, married men will not
be employed, except in a very small proportion to the
unmarried.' This practice apparently persisted for a long
time, although historian Michael Cannon has expressed
surprise that it was still going when Bean was writing.
  The civic-minded conscious Bean suggested share farming
to increase the number of families. If this was impossible, as

in the far West, 'might it not be wise for owners to recognise the political tendencies of the time, and, even if it means a little sacrifice, to let most of their hands marry? Managers have often found married men easier to deal with than unmarried.'

The legend of the bush has been a predominantly male one but it has also given women a certain heroic part.

As a symbol of the sparseness and frugality of life in the outback, the image of the 'drover's wife' had first come to notice in Lawson's short story published in 1892, in which he tells the horrendous tale of a woman's vigil as she watches for a snake lurking beneath the floorboards of the shanty in which she and her young children await the drover's return. Just as a 'sickly daylight breaks over the bush', with the help of her faithful dog she manages to dispatch the snake after the nightlong ordeal.

While Bean talks of the station hands without wives, selectors often took their wives and families as they set out on their treks to take up land. These women, who included young brides, were brave and ingenious, and often combined physical work with homemaking and constant child-bearing.

Mary Gilmore in her 'Ode to the Pioneer Women' described

> . . . women who at need took up
> And plied the axe, or bent above the clodded
>   spade,
> Who herded sheep; who rode the hills, and
>   brought
> The half-wild cattle home – helpmates of men,

Whose children lay within their arms,
Or at the rider's saddle-pommel hung,
And at whose knees, by night, were said familiar
    prayers.

How much outback women shared men's work down
the century since Bean has varied according to class and the
degree of prosperity or hardship of the times, as well as
personal circumstances (such as widowhood). Many rural
women have always played some part, and often a very
significant one, in the outdoor work around the station,
as well as dealing with a demanding round of 'indoor'
work.

In 1966 the secretary of the Country Women's Association Branch of the Air, who lived in the Barrier Ranges in
the West, replied with this account to questioners who
asked what she did all day.

I get up usually about 7 a.m. and I work non-stop until
8 p.m. at the earliest . . . I very rarely have less than six
to cook for; during school holidays it could be up to
thirteen or more. I often wonder how I coped when the
children were babies and I did everything, including our
big garden. Afterwards, with the baby in the pram, out
to help my husband draft the sheep or lamb mark.

Cooking is a continuous job when you are in the bush.
The cake tins always seem to need replenishing and that
little 'Deli round the corner' is many, many miles away
. . . Next week it will be lamb marking, so off to the
various yards I will go once the tucker box is packed,
whilst the men muster the sheep and help them to lamb

mark. Many women even help with the mustering, not only sheep but cattle, too. Often a friend of mine went with her husband to do fencing, with her babe in the pram and two 'littlies' on foot.

We can see in this account something of a tipping point between past and present. This 1960s woman speaks of the difficulty of obtaining help – a married couple, a gardener – while mostly for the 21st century outback family this sort of help is not an option.

Even if the labour was available they couldn't afford it. And the 21st century woman would usually take shortcuts in the kitchen to spend more time outside.

However substantial their contribution in the past, we can confidently say that never have women played a bigger part than in today's West, whether on the land or in the towns, often to the point of exhaustion.

The stereotype (never really accurate) of strictly divided labour – men doing the outdoor work while women tended the house and perhaps the garden – has collapsed under the practical and especially economic realities, at least as far as the women are concerned. While this division is there in a few families – especially where there are sons or on a company-owned property where the manager's wife isn't much involved in the outdoor work – in most it is not.

The rural entrepreneurs' struggle to do more with a lot less has put women, whether in the 'inside' country or the outback, on a treadmill of work, often to the point of exhausting them. An often-overlooked statistic is that one third of Australia's farmers are women.

Professor Margaret Alston, based in Wagga Wagga where

she's director of the Centre for Rural Social Research at Charles Sturt University, has done extensive research on Australian rural women's lives and the stresses they are under, including women of the far West. She says that farming women in general are taking on a much more crucial role, which ensures their families can remain on the land (at least in the short term). What they do has increased greatly in recent years: this includes extensive on-farm work, the bookkeeping (complicated now by a more demanding tax system), and often paid employment off-farm to bring in vital cash income. As well as all this, they are being left with their traditional tasks of managing the household and caring for the children. In drought, as we saw in the previous chapter, the multiple physical and emotional demands on women are particularly stressful.

Yet these women, many of whom have become involved in farming through marriage, are often publicly 'invisible', Alston maintains; she argues that family farming in Australia remains based on 'patriarchal' principles.

Despite their pivotal role in Australia's rural economy, women still have little real voice in farm organisations or agricultural policy. The National Farmers Federation (NFF) is a salutary example. In 2000 the NFF set a target of having women make up 30 per cent of its council by 2005. At the start of 2004, there were just two women on the council of about 60 elected members.

Efforts that have been made by federal and state governments to significantly lift women's representation in agri-politics in general seems to have failed, although Shelley Spriggs, who heads the federal agriculture department's rural leadership program, says there has been some rise from a very low base.

Women have been put off by the culture of these organisations, which is certainly male and can be brutal. Many of those who do become involved are turning to new single-sex groups like Australian Women in Agriculture, which is the fastest growing farm group in Australia. Another, and perhaps the primary reason why women are not more active in these organisations is that they're just too darn busy keeping up with all the other, more important things.

However, Jenny McLellan, who lives on *Waratah* south of Brewarrina, is one woman who has chosen and managed to add involvement in local government and rural bodies to running her farm. She is third generation in the area, and she has Merinos, Hereford cattle, and dry-land crops. A local councillor for more than 20 years, Jenny is a vice-president (and previously president) of the Western Division group of the Shires Association of NSW, as well as a board member of the Western Catchment Authority, which advises on resource management. She was the first woman on a NSW rural lands protection board.

For a long time Jenny ran *Waratah* and its adjoining property, *Marra Downs*, by herself, after her first husband was killed in 1973 in a freak plane accident in which a pea soup fog suddenly cut visibility when he was mustering.

Bill, her second husband, now helps with her properties, especially with the outside work because Jenny has a bad back. But Bill has his own places 'and we run two separate businesses' – even to having their individual accountants – 'although we work closely together'.

Out in the West in 2003 there was only one woman mayor, Liliane Brady, mayor of Cobar. Slight, red-haired and over 70, Liliane is one of the district's personalities, who came to the mining town from Sydney nearly 40 years ago, wife of the local GP. Originally from Lake Cargelligo, in the Riverina, Liliane wanted her children to have a taste of country life.

Her arrival in the mining town was less than auspicious. She told her husband she'd drive 'and I drove right up the slag heap'. With a cross spouse, screaming child, upset dog, and pet bird that had escaped from its cage flying around in the car, Liliane felt like turning right back to Sydney. 'I thought, bugger this, I'm out of it.'

She stayed of course, and now 'I love Cobar with a passion, and I'm very passionate about the Western Division'. She bought several grazing properties, and threw herself into the local community, getting onto the council, walking off when she didn't agree with some decisions, and later running again and becoming mayor.

We catch up with Liliane at *Mulchara Park*, the station where she and her husband Allan, now retired, live, though not for much longer. Reluctantly, she's just sold up (because of Allan's health) and they're about to move into town, where she plans to build a big home at the back of the old surgery.

It's a wrench to leave the property, where she has run Merinos and done quite well from trapping feral goats. 'I cried for three days,' says the hard-bitten Liliane, as she sits us down for coffee.

The *Mulchara Park* homestead is a simple portable house. Lino on the floor in the living area helps cope with the dust; a big modern wood stove makes the place cosy in cold weather. She will miss the bush view from the kitchen window. 'When I drive over the ramp I always feel I'm home. But you've got to get on with life, haven't you?'

There's the new house to look forward to, 'and you can always throw yourself into local government'.

Liliane was the first female mayor of Cobar, as well as the first woman president of the Western Division shires association, which is the group of 13 councils. She won by one vote, and held the position for three years.

She takes issues head on. One of her preoccupations is law and order, although Cobar itself doesn't have a major problem. When a few young people caused trouble in town, she intensified her campaign. She thinks sentencing is too light, and organised a demonstration at the local court. Extra police had to be sent from Dubbo. Someone told Liliane she'd caused 'merry hell'. She takes it as a compliment.

When she was running for the Western Division presidency, a state MP advised her, 'Don't do it, darls, it's a real man's world.'

'Darls' was well able to cope. 'I had a grandmother who taught me that if you're good enough you'll be good at anything. I did have one mayor who gave me hell. All through the three years he gave me sheer hell. [But] I've got a very good relationship with the men of the Western Division [association] – a lovely, lovely relationship. I don't want to be put there as a token. I will never go on a committee because I am a woman. I think now women have no problems at all.'

Luck, or lack of it, turned out to be Liliane's problem. In 2004 she tied in the Council's vote for mayor – and lost in the subsequent draw.

You don't meet a lot of young women on Western Division properties. One is 30-year-old Megan Mosely, who came to

Etiwanda station in the Cobar district after she married Andrew, whose family have had Western Division country since 1949.

Megan, who shone at agricultural college and in her veterinary nursing course, was runner-up in the 2003 NSW Rural Woman's Award (missing out to a worm farmer), with an entry on 'holistic management' and the challenge of attracting young people to the West. She sees holistic management as providing a way for women to work and be involved in the decision-making process on the land with their husbands and children, without having to work off the farm if they don't want to.

In their quest to better manage and regenerate their country, the Moselys have found it useful to consult Bean's descriptions of the West before the great drought and the impact of rabbits. Andrew had read his grandmother's copy years ago, and been impressed; when the old copy couldn't be found Megan tracked down another through the historical book society.

The Mosely family, including Andrew's parents, live on two and a half properties totalling 70,000 acres; they run a Boer goat stud and also cross Boers with feral goats for the meat market, and a White Dorper sheep stud, as well as cattle and crops.

Megan found that the birth of her two children, 'slowed me up a bit' for outside work. Now that her second daughter is six months and old enough to be left with Andrew's mother Nancy, who lives on the second property, Megan's getting back into station life. She musters, works with the goats and sheep in the yards, prepares animals for shows and 'kids the goats', which involves weighing and tagging the kids from the stud within 24 hours of birth and recording their details.

The only conventional farm group Megan's active in is the Youth Link Committee of the NSW Farmers Association, although she's a member of the wider association. She's not much interested in the traditional farm organisations, finding them a 'bit frustrating – they miss the bigger picture'. She and Andrew are part of Holistic Decision Makers of Australia, a group of environmental farmers – 'they're very open-minded and easy to work with'.

One of the difficulties for the modern, well-educated and savvy young woman who marries into a farming family can be finding herself, as the daughter-in-law, shut out from important decisions. Megan says she's been 'extremely lucky with my parents-in-law, mainly because my mother-in-law had a difficult time – as a young woman she was excluded from financial discussions. In this family, it's everybody around the table.' But she knows of another young woman, a friend, who's kept out of talks about her in-laws' business plan for the family farm.

The Youth Link group is concerned about the drift of young people away from the bush, which is not only a numbers problem but draws away energy, money and services.

'There are young people in Cobar because of the mines but they are thin on the ground on farms,' Megan says. This has all sorts of implications. For instance, there is only one other family that can bring children to a play group with Megan's children – and the mother, who has two children, is 40.

'The average age of farmers is 58 – what's going to happen in five or ten years' time? There will be millions of acres of the Western Division and who's going to manage it? Large companies, which will put managers in? Andrew and I often talk about it and wonder about the future of the Western Division land. My belief is that the key is holistic management to revitalise the land so young people can make a living out of it.'

With rural women's work getting harder by the year, and city folk no longer feeling the closeness to the land that previous generations did (even if they'd never lived there) there's less incentive for young women to marry into farm families.

'It's a fair challenge to live out here. The bright lights of the city are pretty appealing for a lot of women. It's horses for courses. I couldn't stand to live in the city, but I have friends who nearly die when they step out of the car,' Megan says.

'You often hear of the young bachelor who can't find himself a lady to marry. He's often working with Mum and Dad on the farm. Young rural women are scarce.'

This, no doubt, is something that would have worried Bean.

— 9 —

Falling off the Sheep's Back

Bean's series on the wool industry ran in the *Sydney Morning Herald* under the title 'The Wool Land'. It was true, he wrote, that this red country did not contain anything like half the wool-growing in Australia. But out here, sheep and wool defined the life of the people.

The romance between Australia and wool had been growing for four or five decades before the flock owners moved out to the Darling. From quite early in the 19th-century wool growing had been the driving force in the takeover of the land, and a great chain of wool activity led from the settlement frontier, with riverboats and wagons moving through the wool hamlets to the port cities and then clipper ships racing across the oceans carrying the wool to England, where the textile mills had an insatiable appetite for the lustrous fibre.

This actively drove an unending quest for new pastures and Australia's national sheep muster grew rapidly to 98 million in 1890, but was dramatically knocked by the great drought that started in 1895, falling to 54 million in 1902. By 1908 it was back to 87 million, with about half the flock in NSW. Australia was by far the largest sheep-raising country in the world. For every one Australian there were about 20 sheep – and 28 for every person in NSW – and the total value of the wool clip was about 23 million pounds. Almost all the clip was exported, and the United Kingdom was by far the biggest buyer.

Now at the beginning of the 21st century it's come to this: less than 100 years after Bean surveyed the nation's premier income earner, wool has been reduced to a relatively modest contributor to national export income and it is only a mild exaggeration to say that in the West, the sheep resembles an endangered species. The national flock reached a peak of 180 million in 1970. It has dropped by 40 per cent since 1990, when there were 170 million sheep and lambs; by mid-2003 the estimate was 91 million. Wool production had dropped by more than half, and it represented less than 10 per cent of the nation's agricultural output.

Despite this, Australia retains its pre-eminence internationally. We're the world's largest wool nation, accounting for nearly three-tenths of world output.

When Bean went through, sheep numbers in the West had partially bounced back from the dreadful drought. In the 1895–1903 drought, they'd dipped just below four million. By the time Bean got there, numbers had climbed above six million, but still varied substantially from year to year. Another low of about four million, caused by drought, occurred in 1945.

After another drastic drought marked the early 21st century, Geoff Wise, the Western Lands Commissioner, reported in July 2003 that there were only about two million sheep in the area. This is a remarkable, and disturbing, figure. The number of sheep was half of what it had been in the drought of a century before.

However, the 2003 small number also has one very positive side to it. Wise said it represented not just the severity of the drought but 'responsible management' by landowners in response to it. 'Landowners have used modern transport and marketing facilities to respond quickly and prevent long-term damage to their property,' he said.

Wise had some other interesting figures and facts about the West's sheep. From 1885 to 1887, average sheep numbers in the area were more than 13 million. But the 20th century did not see them rise again to 10 million – not even the best of seasons or the better distribution of watering places could coax them back anywhere near to the old levels.

Indeed the average annual sheep number in the West throughout that century was six million, and the last peak was less than eight million in 1990, when the 'reserve price' for selling the national clip was operating. Since then, numbers have progressively declined.

Peter Austin is a long-time journalist who writes for *The Land* and other publications. He was briefly, in the mid-'60s, a stock agent in Brewarrina. In those days, he says, when the Western land was 'as settled as it's ever been', people believed a flock of 3000 to 4000 sheep would give them a viable enterprise. But by 1969–70, the worry was mounting. The *Western Herald* noted that Bourke had been known as the largest wool-producing centre in the world, but the wool market made it 'increasingly difficult' for graziers to cover escalating costs.

Perhaps 'sidelines' such as cattle and irrigated crops could

Falling off the Sheep's Back

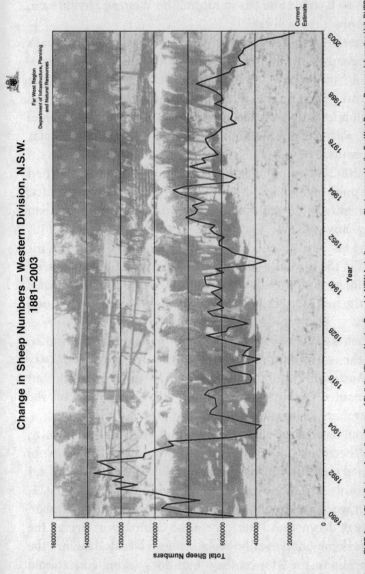

Change in Sheep Numbers – Western Division, N.S.W.
1881–2003

Far West Region
Department of Infrastructure, Planning
and Natural Resources

Source: RLPB Annual Stock Returns, Australian Bureau of Statistics (Sheep Number Records), NSW Agriculture, The Department of Infrastructure, Planning and Natural Resources.
2003 Figures derived from Departmental field staff observations and RLPB feedback.

Chart prepared by the Far West Region, Resource Information Unit, DUBBC
6th June 2003
Disclaimer: All figures based on estimates provided by various sources.

assist to balance budgets in future, the *Western Herald* said, but only 'time will tell'.

What's happened in the West is, pretty much, what's happened elsewhere. But despite wool's drastic fall in economic importance, the romance of it is still strong in Australia's national psyche. Our commercial image abroad is still bound up with sheep and wool, which share the limelight with the unique natural wildlife – kangaroos, koalas and emus.

In 2002 a book of magnificent pictures and evocative text was published called *Wool: The Australian Story*. In fact, we might say the real story is that wool isn't 'the Australian story' anymore.

The modern 'wool track' has become a hard road for most in the industry, and this has taken its toll. The vagaries of climate and price of wool can still bring ecstasy or agony, but the industry is tough going for those in it, even in good times.

'Such as it is, Australia has been made by wool. And so has the Australian,' Bean wrote. 'If ever the wool industry of Australia were to be not merely supplemented, but supplanted, by other industries, the old types of the Australian, such as they are, would go with it.'

Wool has been well and truly 'supplanted' and so, mostly, have been the 'old types'. As recently as the 1960s, wool formed one-third of Australian exports. It has shrunk to 2.4 per cent. The big change was between 1951 and 1971, when wool went from 64 per cent of the value of Australian exports down to 13 per cent. One comparison brings the point home dramatically. Wool brings fewer dollars into the Australia of the 21st century than does selling educational services abroad. In 2002, the figures were $3.6 billion for wool and $4.2 billion for education.

But significant as it is and however much it grows, the industry exporting educational services can never aspire to the glamour of even a struggling, diminished wool industry.

Wool's troubles are neither recent nor passing. They have been exacerbated by drought but will exist in good seasons. The industry has been in a long-term decline, battling fierce competition from synthetics, and other problems.

A 2002 report by the Centre for International Economics, a private research agency, points to one less-talked-about reason for the squeeze.

Demand for all textiles, wool and non-wool, has weakened as consumers spend a smaller proportion of their income on these items and more on other goods and services.

In Australia, for example, in 1984 households spent more than 14 per cent of their total spending on clothing, footwear, furnishings and equipment. By 1999 this was only 10.6 per cent.

Most studies have concluded that Australia's dependence on wool as a key driver of its economy remained until the 1950s – or even the 1960s.

Controversially, this is challenged radically by research published in 2002 by Paul Cashin of the International Monetary Fund and C. John McDermott of the National Bank of New Zealand. They studied data from 1862 and 1995 on how the wool export cycle synchronised with the business cycle to find when the Australian economy 'fell off the sheep's back'.

Their answer is, after the First World War. The idea that Australia's dependence on wool exports continued into the

1950s is misplaced, they argue. The wool boom from the Korean War – the golden days when wool fetched 'a pound a pound' was 'a temporary aberration'. 'Fundamental changes in the Australian economy had overturned its dependence on wool at least three decades earlier.'

Many graziers who used to produce only wool have had to diversify into other things; some have given up wool-growing entirely. Faced with tough times, those who remain are responding in two ways. They are moving towards finer wool, because that's more valuable. And they're turning to meat sheep.

Charles Massy knows as much about wool as probably any person in Australia. His *The Australian Merino*, published in 1990, runs to more than 1000 pages. It is an astonishing piece of work – and he is busy on a sequel.

In *The Australian Merino*, Massy captured the importance of the industry not just for its dollars but culturally.

> The Merino sheep and the wool industry are synonymous with Australia. For most of our European history the Merino was the backbone of a developing economy and society, and for a hundred years from 1860 Australia really did 'ride on the sheep's back' . . .
>
> From the Merino also, and its associated occupations such as droving and shearing, came much of our cultural heritage – in art, literature, poetry and music – and our essential images of Australianness.

Massy himself is a wool producer, living at his property *Severn Park* near Cooma. His main work, however, is as a consultant to more than 100 breeders. 'It's a fulcrum moment in the Australian industry,' Massy says. 'If it gets any worse, the industry falls below critical mass.'

'Critical mass' is a key phrase in the debate about the future of the industry, which has found itself suffering from falling demand and falling supply. Growers got some welcome high prices in 2003, but that only masked the problems.

If Australian wool loses its critical mass as an industry, it doesn't have the clout it needs in the international fibre market; buyers become even more inclined to turn to other fibres, and it risks being too small to support the research and development vital for a competitive future.

Some things haven't changed since Bean wrote. Most Australian wool is still exported, and still sold by auction, and remarkably little is processed locally. 'Nearly all the Sydney wool goes to foreigners', Bean reported. 'Last year it went mostly to France. France took 264,000 bales, England 245,000, and Germany 225,000, Belgium 91,000, America 27,000, and Japan 8000.'

If we take the value of Australia-wide sales in 2002, that list is very different, with a big shift from Europe to Asia. Only one European destination was among the top five. China was by far the largest market for Australian wool, followed by Italy, South Korea, Taiwan and India.

The CIE study into the prospects for further wool-processing in Australia is deeply pessimistic. With the wool-processing industry suffering internationally from overcapacity, it says the Australian processing industry could only grow at the expense of somewhere else.

For this to happen, Australia would need to be able to process more cheaply than elsewhere or with better quality.

'There is no evidence to suggest that Australia is able to achieve either of these outcomes,' is the gloomy conclusion.

The Land newspaper in 2003 was full of stories about the uncertainty surrounding wool. No wonder even small straws of hope are seized upon. 'Suits back in business: strong signs for wool industry,' the headline declared. The story reported that 'dress down' Fridays (and other days too) were going out of fashion. Also in *The Land* we learn that wool is hitting back at synthetic 'polar-fleece', with non-woven outdoor garments that had 'the look, feel and appeal' of the coveted synthetic stuff but were actually made from 'good old natural wool'.

— 10 —
The New Merino

The Brown family, one of the largest wool producers in western NSW, has built a shearing shed that looks just like a convention centre for sheep.

'Have you seen the *Reola* shed yet?' we were often asked as we travelled in the West. No, we said, as it became clear we must. So when we reach the old opal town of White Cliffs, we find a local with a four-wheel drive and set off to see the super-shed of the West.

Some people speculate this great shed cost a million dollars, or even more. Graham Brown declines to put a figure on it.

Whatever its price, the shed is so impressive that tourists who travel up the 110 kilometres of dirt road north from White Cliffs, or fly in, are willing to pay $10 each for a guided tour of the remarkable complex. Between Easter and the end of October, around 1000 arrive.

They might be told that the Browns' daughter Sally had her wedding reception there. Friends came in light aircraft for the occasion. A week later (with all the catering gear still in place) a select band of about 50 sheep from studs in

Victoria, South Australia and the Riverina moved into the shed's luxurious quarters while their owners talked about them at a two-day workshop. These sheep were the elite of the New Merinos. We will return to them.

Sixty metres long and 42 metres wide, *Reola*'s shed has four levels. The sheep walk up to the top, into the pens from which the shearers drag them onto the 'board'. The fleece is handled on the next level down. It is then sent to the fourth, and lowest, level (one-and-a-half metres below ground) for pressing. Finally, back the bales come, to ground level, for storing, until they are trucked away.

Unlike the conventional, older-style shed, where shearers and shed hands work in a common space, the shearers here are on an elevated, horseshoe-shaped platform. Think of them and their sheep as performers on a stage about a metre high. The wool is gathered up by a team operating where the audience would sit. The theory is that shearers and rouseabouts don't get in each other's way.

At another property we visited – *Abbotsford* near Ivanhoe – which has a similar raised 'board' in a six-stand shed designed after a time and motion study, the owner said the configuration means he needs one or two fewer rouseabouts. This is a cost-saving of about 40 cents a sheep. The only complaint we heard about the elevated board is that some women rouseabouts aren't tall enough to reach up comfortably.

The *Reola* shed can hold up to 4000 sheep under cover at one time. During the July shearing, some 8000–9000 will be on the move each day, coming to the shed or returning shorn. About 2700 will be shorn daily.

Despite its size, the *Reola* shed has stands for only 16

shearers. In contrast, there were 58 stands at one of the old *Momba* sheds.

The opening of the *Reola* shed, in July 1990, was a red-letter occasion. As with all big projects, there was a last minute flurry to get everything finished. The builders worked through the night on the final touches. Some rouseabouts who had arrived early for the shearing gave them a hand.

The shearing contractor was to have the honour of christening the shed by taking the wool off the first sheep. So he was mightily annoyed to discover one already shorn – by a rouseabout at around 3.30 am.

The Browns (Graham Brown went to Bean's old school of All Saints' in Bathurst) have 430,000 acres in six properties in the district, which are run centrally. Seven people live permanently on this area. In the 1950s it would have been about 50.

Two of Graham and Deirdre Brown's four children work with them. They both returned after doing degrees; a third, recently out of school, also wants to 'come home'.

This is young people's country out here, Graham says. He finds the new generation very committed – and very aware of the need for conservation of the land. But a lot of the younger people have left, because of the economics. Smaller properties can't support several members of a family.

Graham's father drew a block in the late 1940s, part of what had been *Salisbury Downs*, a Kidman property. 'Cattle King' Kidman had opposed the carving up of the outback stations into smaller blocks, predicting they'd end up being put together again. That's exactly what's happened, and is still happening. Before the drought the Browns ran

45,000 to 50,000 sheep. 'You can't live on 5000 sheep [in this area]. For a family, you're looking at 15,000 to 20,000.'

In Graham's father's time, the *Reola* land was 'just sand'. After a dust storm you could walk over a fence, the woolly sheep would lie down around the water bores, their backs against the wind: sand would pile up behind them, discolouring and weighing down their fleeces.

Now woody weed is over much of the country. It reduces the land's sheep-carrying capacity, but it also makes for cleaner wool. This is another positive point we hear about woody weed, which has a bad name among many in the West. 'Before 1950, because of the sand, 35 to 40 per cent of the [fleece's] weight was wool – now it's 70 per cent,' Graham says.

There's only one reason why the country regenerated, he says: myxomatosis killed the rabbits. 'We haven't had a lot of rabbits since the 1950s. It's a novelty to see a rabbit – although the odd one is popping up.'

The Browns are among a minority of Australian wool growers who are converts to a new type of Merino. They're called by their unlikely, although appropriate, trademarked name of 'soft rolling skin' (SRS) sheep.

The SRS sheep are large, plain-bodied animals, with white, soft, fine wool. They also produce good meat – and heated, sometimes bitter, debate among the sheep fraternity. The Browns have been changing over to these sheep since the mid-1990s. There is an unusual story behind this. Daughter Chrissie, doing a wool and pastoral science course, became very interested in SRS sheep. Graham says, 'She had to do a thesis, and she wanted to do it on something of benefit to us. I said, "Our main income comes from the skin of sheep, the wool factory." She did it on this.

'We helped Chrissie in a lot of her experiments. She took 260 skin samples to count the wool follicles, and the skin thickness. That was a very big turning point for us.'

In the early days Merino studs in better-rainfall areas provided the breeding stock from which the back country flocks were built, and because of the vast acreages available in the West, there was a greater willingness to innovate.

Inevitably this led to a serious mismatch when a leading breeder, Samuel McCaughey, became convinced that the Vermont strain of Merino he had imported from the United States was ideal for his vast domains beside the Darling. The Vermont was a highly wrinkly sheep, and McCaughey's critics vociferously condemned them as unsuitable. They said the claimed benefits of the wrinkled skin – the production of more wool – were illusory, and the breed had a poor constitution that couldn't adapt to harsh conditions. European buyers became critical of the Vermont-type wool. The critics won: McCaughey finally admitted he had been wrong and from 1904 he made a complete change to the plain-bodied Merino, setting aside 20 years of misguided attention to the Vermont 'wrinklies', which had done great damage. It was to take years for the Vermont influence to be suppressed in favour of the prevailing Peppin blood.

But the SRS advocates say the retreat from the wrinkled Merino didn't go nearly far enough.

The main man behind the development of these SRS sheep is Jim Watts, a veterinarian who began his work on the sheep when he was with the CSIRO in the 1970s and 1980s.

He and a team produced a 'biological blueprint' for a sheep with better wool. Watts, based in NSW's Southern Highlands, is now a consultant to Merino studs around the country, and an evangelist for the New Merino.

In simple terms, SRS selective breeding produces animals with wool that is both denser and longer than standard Merinos' fleeces. On Watts' figures, an ordinary Merino ewe producing 18 micron (fine) wool would clip between 4 and 4.5 kilos a year, earning about $30 gross for her owner. Her SRS cousin cuts 6.5 kilos of 15.5 (finer) micron wool, producing about $120 gross return.

'This is a quadrupling of income in what is a failing industry,' Watts says.

You'd think everyone would be onto it. But they're not. Of some 35,000 Australian wool growers, only some two per cent are producing this lucrative wool. Although they have been gaining popularity, SRS sheep are rejected by many of the traditional Merino studs.

Watts is frustrated. The stud masters have been used to looking for thick 'staples' (units of fleece as thick as a person's finger) and a fine 'crimp' in their breeding sheep.

Now Watts is telling them that to get the densest longest wool, the staples have to be replaced by very thin fibre bundles (about as thin as a matchstick and twice as long as wool is normally grown) and the 'crimp' should be deep and bold rather than fine. He admits his case is made tougher by the appearance of the New Merino, whose long wool falls under the effect of gravity, giving the sheep a shaggy, floppy look. Watts describes it as looking like a thatched roof. 'It's a little bit off-putting. But the bottom line works for us. The return per head can double and double again. That's helping us to gain acceptance among the commercial wool growers – not among the stud breeders.

'It's Catch 22,' Watts says. The wool is in strong demand from processors, because of its soft, long, silky quality. 'Wool buyers and processors are saying "we can't buy enough to meet our orders", but it's very difficult to influence the major breeders. We are only a small team of private individuals who've come across something vital for the health of the industry. How do you get the industry to change its culture?'

The critics of the SRS sheep are sometimes shy of going on the record. One Western grazier, who was sticking with the older-style Merinos, told me that 'traditionally sheep producing lower micron wool are smaller and cut less. They always do and always will,' and 'to change a flock is a radical call. It's almost a new breed of sheep – it's a ten-year program' with high costs.

Nevertheless, 'I'm still keeping my options open' and watching with 'the greatest interest', because the innovators might be proved right.

Eventually, the market will be the arbiter of the fate of the New Merino. In the meantime, the Browns don't need further convincing. Their approach is to reduce their number of sheep while getting more wool from them individually. 'Our aim is to halve our stock and produce more income-wise,' says Graham.

The Browns have paid between $10,000 and $22,000 for their SRS rams. A favourite when we were at *Reola* was 'Sweet 16': he cost $16,000 and had 16 micron (fine) wool.

Graham described him as 'a most likeable fellow'. We didn't meet Sweet 16 – he was resting under a tree out of the

January heat – but we saw his fleece, bundled up in a green bag and kept for show and we were given a small portion of it. The fleece weighed perhaps 10 or 12 kilos. Sadly, Sweet 16 didn't survive the drought, which hit *Reola* badly.

In 2001 *Reola* had half its average 10-inch rainfall, the following year a little over a quarter, and in 2003, about three-quarters. The Browns spent large sums on feeding to keep the core flock; in the end only a few thousand were left, the others sold or dead. The area was still listed as being in drought at the start of 2004, although *Reola* had some areas of feed. With the prices high for replacement stock, the Browns plan to breed up again from their own much-diminished but still quality flock.

Another enthusiast for SRS sheep is Bob McFarland. We called in at the McFarlands' *Oxley* on the Lachlan, a station of 25,000 acres just outside the Western Division. *Oxley* has been in the McFarland family since the early 1900s, and it now runs about 7500–8000 sheep.

Bob and Errolly McFarland are deeply committed to 'holistic' farming, including resting grazing land, planting saltbush to regenerate the land, and breeding 'easy care' animals. As he drives us round *Oxley*, Bob gives us a big sales pitch for the lowly saltbush.

He has also pioneered Charlie Carp fertiliser, which turned a menace in the river system into an environmental and commercial benefit. The carp undermine the banks and trees, eat the vegetation, and take oxygen out of the water. McFarland calls them 'the rabbits of the rivers'.

The McFarlands have found the SRS sheep not only easier for the shearers, but less susceptible to fly strike, a useful saving.

Keri-Keri, near Moulamein, also a little outside the Western lands, is the source of many SRS rams into the Western area.

The SRS sheep continued a direction in which *Keri-Keri*'s Dowling family had been going for decades. In the mid-1920s Ray Dowling bought huge, plain-bodied rams from South Australia – the sort of sheep that could cope with marginal country.

But additionally, *Keri-Keri* boasts of being the home of the 'Australian Milking Merino'. The story goes like this. In 1990, when he was involved in an artificial insemination program at the stud, Watts noticed some of the ewes had four milking teats, instead of the usual two.

These sheep were selected out; gradually, a flock of more than 1000 'Milking Merinos' has been built up. The result is more lambs which grow bigger, faster. Combine the SRS and 'Milking Merino' stories and Watts believes that 'we're in the process of breeding sheep that will do away with the "first cross" ewe'. She – with Merino and Border Leicester parents – is the traditional mother of the fat lamb.

The 'cull' – that is, reject – ewes from the *Keri-Keri* flock sell well to producers of prime lamb because they have a double advantage over the first crosses. Their lambs, between birth and market age (about six months) grow to a butchershop weight of about 27 kilos, compared to about 22 kilos for the offspring of the first cross mother. And the ewe herself yields a fleece worth about $40 compared with $10–$15 for the wool from the first cross ewe.

There is another intriguing aspect to the SRS sheep. A sheep growing a fleece of 200 millimetres annually – twice the standard length – needs to be shorn twice a year. Partly, this is obviously for the convenience of the sheep. Also, the machines handling fine wool in our export markets are used to coping with much shorter wool. Double shearing has upsides and the obvious downside of the higher cost.

'I thought the double shearing would have problems,' Watts says. But most SRS wool growers who go that route have seen the advantages. Not only are the number of bales per year significantly increased, but the wool contains less dust and plant matter and lambing is easier.

Growers have to bring their sheep in for 'crutching' anyway which, although it doesn't cost in shearing as a full shear, also doesn't pay much in returns from the small amount of dirty wool. And there is all the same work of mustering sheep as for the general shearing. It's a matter of 'when you bring your sheep in, make it count', Watts says.

He sums up his New Merino story: 'It's not us who are clever – it's the Merinos.'

— 11 —
The Old Trade in a New World

The essence of the shearer's trade hasn't changed in a century, although its status and prospects have taken a dive.

Shearing might be 'well-paid work' and the conditions 'good enough', Bean wrote, 'but no one attempts to deny that it is real hard work – eight hours of sweating, aching, vibrating work, carried through honestly at top pressure'.

A recent academic study with a dozen authors from three institutions suggests, in modern language, precisely the same about the nature of the occupation, which is so identified with the Australian legend. 'Sheepshearing has a strong identity in Australia', the researchers note, before homing in on the hard realities.

> It is a task that represents almost everything that is associated with an injury risk – hot, live, heavy unwilling animals are caught, restrained and dragged to a variety of work station settings in extremes of environmental conditions. The fleece is removed cleanly, in a stooped position before the animal is ejected from the shed.

The shearer is one of the characters at the centre of *On the Wool Track*, and Bean romanticises him, seeing him as a superior type to station hands. Indeed then – as now – many shearers were 'employers themselves – farmers or farmers' sons shearing in their slack season'.

The shearer, 'in spite of all that is sometimes said of him', was 'a surprisingly high class of workman'. Shearers usually spent their money deliberately (unlike the station hands); they had 'libraries in the huts, and a committee of their own generally arranges for all sorts of newspapers'.

'I heard conversations on every topic better worth listening to than you would hear in the lobby of Parliament', Bean enthused. 'The conversation in the hut after tea . . . covers slow sheds and fast sheds, ringers and records, racing, farming; but more especially politics. Some M.P.'s have much less political philosophy in them than the Australian shearer . . .'

In his first edition of the *On the Wool Track* Bean reported that the shearers had sent one of themselves to Parliament, 'to be the ablest man there'.

At the time of writing, the man to whom he referred had far from reached his peak. In a later edition he made it clear he was talking about Billy Hughes, 'a great Prime Minister and the *enfant terrible* of the Versailles Conference'.

As an aside, it might be mentioned that there is an alternative take on Hughes' country sojourn. In a profile of perhaps the most colourful of Australia's PMs, historian Geoffrey Bolton has written that Hughes was prone to romanticise his 18 months spent in outback Queensland and NSW, while the real story was rather different. 'A scrawny new chum without bush skills, he lived rough and earned little, aggravating his deafness and dyspepsia, and – so he admitted in old age – fearful of homosexual rape.'

Bean even saw virtue in the racism that shearers of his day shared with most of their countrymen.

> Shearers are more consistent with their political prin-
> ciples than is often admitted. They will not have a
> Chinaman or an Indian or an American negro amongst
> them; but they will work with a Maori or an Australian
> black-fellow. That is simply because they do not think
> the former should be allowed here; but they recognise a
> duty to the latter.

Shearing has always been a tough existence, and no doubt more attractive in its great legend than in the nitty gritty of real life. Throughout our history, the shearer has been an important character in Australian folklore, and in literature, film, and song. Half a century after Bean's characterisation of these aristocrats of the outback wanderers, Jack Thompson starred as the gun shearer in *Sunday Too Far Away*, a tale of mateship and a union struggle on an outback station. Recently, shearing has been given a fresh kind of celebrity status, with the opening of *Shear Outback*, the Shearers' Hall of Fame exhibition at Hay and even a calendar of 'pin-up' shearers.

Behind all this is the less encouraging reality: shearing is a declining occupation in the 21st century, without a lot of future. The job outlook is poor and many shearers are depressed about their lot.

Also, in an occupation where the union was once so strong, unionisation has disintegrated in a big way. A survey released in 2002 by the Australian Workers' Union of nearly 200 shearers and shed hands (all union members) found the nation's shearers are ageing, with one-third over 46, and only 6 per cent under 25. Just over half had been working in what the union calls 'the profession' for more than 20 years. Most full-time shearers averaged nine months of work annually; they went to 24 properties and worked for 16 employers. Most shearers earned less than $35,000 a year, and shedhands earned around $18,000. And while the modern shearer has to contend with fewer wrinkles in his sheep, the size of the animals has grown!

Long-time shearers used a very practical measure to argue they were financially worse off since the 'wide comb' dispute of the 1980s, which had major implications, including the breaking of unionisation. Once, shearing a sheep could buy a pot of beer. At the time of the AWU survey (Christmas 2001) the shearing rate was $1.78 and a pot cost $2.50.

Shearers also believed they were treated respectfully by their employers, but that they were poorly regarded by the community.

In her comprehensive book on shearers, published in the early 1980s, Patsy Adam-Smith wrote that the Australian shearer developed a unique skill 'finer to this day than anywhere else in the world'. Despite this, in the new century a majority of shearers, it appears, would prefer to be doing something else – and certainly would not, by choice, put their sons in the sheds. About seven out of ten would take up another job on similar pay if the opportunity arose; the same proportion said they wouldn't encourage friends, family or children to become shearers. They think the work too demanding, and the industry declining.

David Stuart is an expert in exercise science from the University of South Australia's School of Health Sciences. He and colleagues have studied shearers and their working conditions since the 1970s. They've come to some startling conclusions about those who practise what they describe as 'one of the most physically, and perhaps mentally, demanding occupations that humans currently pursue'.

Most shearers don't keep themselves nearly fit enough, the researchers found, and 'many of their daily work habits appeared to be based on myth rather than on sound ergonomic practice'.

One wonders what Bean and the shearers he met might make of 'sound ergonomic practice', but the researchers had some practical suggestions. These included changed designs for the floors of catching pens and the chutes for releasing the shorn sheep. They also studied, and had proposals for, the geometry of what they called the best 'drag paths' – the route for the shearer dragging the sheep from pen to board.

In Bean's time, shearers were heavily unionised. Some of them would have been veterans of the great, sometimes violent, industrial struggles of the 1890s and before, as the shearers battled to establish their union and win better conditions. In Bourke, Bean heard from Captain Pickhills, retired former master of the riverboat *Jandra*, the dramatic story of the shearers' burning and sinking of the *Rodney*, which was bringing non-union shearers to *Tolarno* station. Although three men were arrested, solidarity was tight, the men were given alibis and no one was convicted.

Now, only a minority of shearers are members of the Australian Workers' Union or the Shearers and Rural

Workers' Union, which broke away from the AWU in an internal power battle a decade after the bitter 'wide comb' dispute, the shearers' last great industrial struggle, and the one that dealt the death blow to unionism in the industry. While this dispute was nominally about the wide comb, it was actually, as one unionist puts it, 'about the clash of regulated and deregulated pastoral cultures'.

Paul Houlihan, who as National Farmers Federation industrial director was in the thick of that dispute, has described the controversial comb that caused all the trouble as 'basically the same implement as we see at a hairdresser'. The comb at the end of the shearer's handpiece separates the wool; an attached cutter severs it.

The wide comb came in with the influx of New Zealand shearers, and it contravened an old pastoral award laying down that the comb should not be more than two and a half inches wide.

The shearers feared the wider comb because they thought it would mean more Kiwi shearers, and increase the number of sheep that each shearer was expected to do a day. According to one shearer we met, the eventual triumph of the wide comb lifted the whole standard expected (although shearers are paid per sheep). Now, he said, shearers need to be able to do 150–160 sheep a day to get a job, where previously it was 80.

A high-profile protagonist in the wide comb battle was Robert White, a former member of the AWU. White, a contractor in Mandurama, in the NSW central west, was not just a campaigner for the wide comb but also declared provocatively that he wouldn't rejoin the union 'until the organisers get out of the pubs and into the sheds'. At one point the employers organised a demonstration shear with the wide comb at Sydney Showgrounds. The AWU was furious when the TV cameras turned up. When the union argued the comb was not suitable for Merinos, the National Farmers Federation went from shed to shed to show it was.

Duncan Fraser, who has a property near Hay and is active in farm politics, remembers one of his shearers – who were all unionised at the time – going to a 'scab' shed where they were using the wide comb. 'He went along out of curiosity, and one of the shearers said "why don't you have a go?", because he was bagging the shearers using them. So he did, and actually he was quite amazed it didn't lead to a lot more cuts . . . it was just as easy to push a wide comb through the fleece as a narrow comb.' At a meeting later organised by farmers, this man got up and said, 'I was anti wide gear and now I reckon that shearers should make up their own minds about it.' He was blackbanned by the union, but later other shearers came to the same conclusion.

In late 1982 the Industrial Relations Commission gave the okay for the wide comb, while protecting shearers who didn't want to use it. After the AWU lost an appeal against this decision, it launched a prolonged national strike, the last great (and nasty) battle between union and employers over shearers.

After it was over, the wide comb was in and within 12 months the AWU had lost 60 per cent of its pastoral membership. Resisting something that made for greater productivity was, as one of today's union leaders puts it, 'cruising for a bruising'. The wide comb issue was also a catalyst for wider discontents with the union; it came as unionism generally was on the wane.

Not one of the nine-person shearing team we meet at

Polpah station, just north of White Cliffs, is a union member. Clinton Bell, a shearer by trade but having a change of work on this trip by being the team's cook, says none of his shearing friends is in the union. 'The new generation of shearers [is] completely illiterate about what the union stood for.' They think in terms of the union's (futile) fight against wide combs; 'they don't know what they did for conditions'.

Clinton, though not a union man himself, reckons the pendulum has swung too far. 'Young fellows are not getting into the industry, and the Kiwis are not here. It's probably a good time to join the union and get things back on track. But it's not going to happen.'

Clinton has an interesting story. Dubbed the 'global shearer', he's worked through the American Mid-West, as well as doing several seasons in Britain. And he is one of the shearers used by Prince Charles.

The sheep in Prince Charles's flock are a far cry from the Merinos here at *Polpah*. They are a flock of about 600 Outer Hebrideans (horned, with black wool) and Mules (a meat producing breed). Nor does the Prince have a conventional shed. The job is done in a general barn or a portable trailer. It is finished in a day.

Clinton's shearer father learnt his trade with the blades, and, unlike most of today's shearers, shore until he was 65.

Both Clinton's shearing start and his ambitions are different. Clinton's in his 40s and wants to get into another occupation: he's studying to become a teacher of English as a second language. (When I check back just before this book goes to press, Clinton has finished the course and is soon off to Thailand to teach.)

Clinton and his mate Tony Helps, usually a contractor but

when we met him one of the shearers in the team at *Polpah*, trained at a shearing school. The course ran 12 weeks and took in three properties. Tony remembers, 'You'd dream shearing at night – then you'd wake up and have to do it.' The tyro shearers would find tears smarting their eyes as they drove to work, in anticipation of the pain to come. Mod-cons can't eliminate the strain of this physically hard job, but they can ease the backbreak a little. Most modern shearers wear a harness. Tony couldn't shear without it; 'two years ago I did my back in – I couldn't shear for 12 months.'

The wool industry is perennially searching for cheaper, more efficient methods of separating the sheep from its wool. Chemical shearing sees the sheep injected, the wool stops growing and is then shed. Recently the ABC's 'Lateline' reported on the use of 'Bioclip': animals are injected with a protein that 'breaks' their wool within days. 'Something resembling a boob tube is stretched over their torso. And in about a month's time, when they have protective stubble of new growth under their woolly jumper, the fleece will simply be peeled off.'

Recently there have been trials with a system that would turn shearing from an individual encounter between one man and the sheep into a conveyor belt operation. Shearers would become wool 'harvesters' and the sheep would be 'de-fleeced'.

But Australian Wool Innovation, the industry body that sponsors research, pulled out of the project in late 2003. There were other problems but one reason was that it thought the system would not be economic.

For the forseeable future, the shearer remains as central as he's ever been in relieving the sheep of its fleece.

3

Back on the Track

3

Back on the Track

— 12 —
The Start of Bean's Wool Track

Although Bean concentrated most of his travels for *On the Wool Track* in the far West of NSW, he did write about two areas closer in: the Snowy Mountains and properties outside Gunnedah in the north west. The former he used to illustrate the legendary status of Australian mountain horse riders, the latter to highlight the 'genius of the Australian'.

We set out from Wagga Wagga to Gunnedah and the country of the great wide northern rivers in search of two stations. It was here, near the Namoi River, in the good rainfall country, that Bean began his research for *On the Wool Track*. For me this trip to Gunnedah, which starts routinely enough, will turn into a much more personal journey into my own family's past.

Along the way we drive through the neat towns of Forbes and Parkes. Forbes was the site of Australia's first sheep dog trials, in 1872. Parkes has a more modern claim to fame, the radio telescope, which opened in 1961 and was used for monitoring during the Apollo space voyages. The town these days is making one of its tourist selling points its fame from the film *The Dish*, starring Sam Neill, which told the story of Australia's role in the moon-landing drama.

Gunnedah, which sits on the banks of the Namoi, has the natural advantages of rich soil and large seams of coal. Unlike the land further out, this is cropping country and within a few years of the first land sales in the 1850s wheat had become a staple crop. Today, with a population around 8000, it is the centre of a thriving rural district producing wheat and wool, cattle and canola as well as the more controversial cotton crop. The arrival of the railway in 1879 brought the town into the orbit of Sydney, and it still has one of the largest livestock markets in the state.

The particular interest for Bean in the Gunnedah district was *Kurrumbede*, a property that had recently been purchased by Charles Mackellar, Bean's 'revered friend'. Apart from being a leading Sydney doctor, Mackellar was a public figure and, for just a few weeks, a Protectionist senator in the fledgling federal parliament.

Mackellar installed his sons Eric and Malcolm on the new property and the brothers may have been models for various flattering references in Bean's writings to the young bosses of the outback.

The main interest of *Kurrumbede* today is its one-time connection with poet Dorothea Mackellar. According to Dorothea's own account, her 'My Country' poem (originally called 'Core of my Heart') was inspired by the drought-breaking rain at another of her parents' properties, *Torryburn*, out of Maitland.

This has not deterred Gunnedah from promoting its ties and anyway, there are competing claims. The *Reader's Digest Illustrated Guide to Australian Places* insists that it was the drought breaking around Gunnedah that was the inspiration.

The town has made itself a shrine to Mackellar, with a room of memorabilia at the tourist centre and a statue in Anzac Park where she sits, side saddle, on her horse, gazing towards *Kurrumbede*. A memorial society runs a poetry competition for school students, attracting more than 10,000 entries from around the country and even overseas.

The Waugh family has lived at *Kurrumbede*, a short run out of Gunnedah, for more than half a century. No wonder they feel a certain frustration when people still think of the station as the 'Mackellars' place'.

The Waughs are hospitable. Come out to dinner, they say, when we explain what we're doing. But please, no pictures of the modern *Kurrumbede*. They like to keep their privacy.

We're disappointed. But perhaps we don't need a photograph. Bean, who saw in the Mackellars' house a great example of Australian outback ingenuity, has left one of his wonderfully precise word pictures.

Between Gunnedah and Boggabri, overlooking the Namoi River, is a handsome modern homestead built of what seems to be rough-hewn stone. Actually, the blocks are not stone, but clever imitations in concrete. Every block was moulded and squared and dried on the station itself. The walls were built by station labour. The floor joists and roof beams, the wainscots and window frames, every atom of woodwork was fitted, joined, mortised by the station carpenter; some of it cut by the station blacksmith at the station sawmill. The plans were designed by the station owner.

Bean uses this to illustrate what he regards as one of the great strengths of the Australian – and one that he made much of in his war histories – the ability to turn his hand to anything. 'The Australian, too, has his shortcomings, a full round share of them, and one would be blind to deny it. One would be equally blind not to see that he possesses one virtue in a degree in which, as far as one has experience of them, no other people possesses it. He can do anything. He is aware of it.'

Today the house stands larger and even more 'handsome'. Its drive sweeps through immaculately maintained lawns and gardens filled with white and blue agapanthus, geraniums, plumbago, red hot pokers, oleanders and roses. The gardening is all done by Lennox Waugh and his wife, Ann Maree.

The homestead was renovated and extended many years ago in the original style after Lennox's father found the brick mould in Gunnedah and used it for the additions. The modern 6000-acre property carries shorthorn cattle, which are being fed in the drought. There are no sheep, unlike earlier times. Dorothea described in her diary (1911) watching drafting and shearing, and riding out to move sheep on a '[h]ot thundery day, pinky iridescence in the clouds, blue haze and mirages everywhere . . .'

In Gunnedah, one of the popular restaurants is called Fiorella's. Sit at one of Fiorella's tables, and you are touching the wood from the woolshed that stood until recently on nearby *Gunnible* station. Bean went the relatively short distance from *Kurrumbede* to *Gunnible* to watch the shearing.

The Hoddle family, who own both *Gunnible* and the restaurant, pulled down the old shed because it was becoming dangerous. Fiona Hoddle is still sad about letting a piece of history go. But it would have cost $500,000 to restore. And recycling it to the restaurant is a way of preserving its past.

When we go out to *Gunnible*, which is very close to town and has a sprawling old house and a shady garden, we walk over some of the shed's wood, still lying on the ground near the shearers' quarters, built of stone. Only the better timber went into constructing the bar, beams and tables at the restaurant.

On the summer day we visit, the Hoddles are away, but we run into Matthew McCorkle, who with his wife Anna have been renting the cottage on the property.

The McCorkles have both been working at Gunnedah – Matthew on a property nearby and Anna at a local school. They are, however, people of the Darling, and they're just packing up to move to Bourke.

Big Matthew, who takes us round the site of the wool shed and the old shearers' quarters, is half American, with a lilting accent. He was brought up mostly in Atlanta and Birmingham. On his mother's side, he is one of the Murray family who have extensive holdings along the Darling, including what's left of grand old *Dunlop* and other properties which used to be part of it or lie close to it.

Anna is a Mitchell; her family also comes from around the Darling townlet of Louth, and goes back a long way. Despite the families living for generations in such a small community, theirs is the first marriage between the Mitchells and the Murrays. The 2001 wedding, with the bridal vehicle decked with Australian and American flags, was in the little Louth church.

The pull of the Darling is strong, and now they've both lined up jobs – Anna teaching, Matthew with the Bourke council – to get back as close to the river as is practicable.

We have a little time to while away in Gunnedah. Margaret says that while we're there we must call in on Joan North, a friend of a friend of hers.

Joan's father Joe Innes sold a property, *Sandside*, between Jerilderie and Narrandera in the Riverina, to Margaret's and my grandfather William Younger in the 1920s. *Sandside*, which is on the broad and gum-shaded Yanko Creek, is still in the family, and now owned by Margaret's brother, Don Younger.

Joan has lived her life on the land, and only recently moved into a retirement complex in the town. We drive round to it on spec, and find her just arriving home. Like the homes of many retired country people who've moved to country towns, Joan's unit has some elegant, distinctly 'station' pieces of furniture. She's delighted to dredge up some old memories and we settle down over cups of coffee.

Joan was only a small child when her family moved from *Sandside* up north in the state. I expect her recollection of the property and people to be dim. We are talking three-quarters of a century ago, and the two families didn't spend a lot of time together, although some of my relatives did call in at her father's property during stock-buying trips.

Amazingly, however, Joan recalls everything in extraordinarily sharp detail. She remembers the intense liveliness of my mother Midge, then in her late teens. When Midge was at *Sandside*, what she wanted was what happened, Joan says. And she speaks as if it were yesterday of my uncle Ron, who was very young at the time, advising her to enter the competitions for children that the newspapers ran. By good fortune, I've brought with me a couple of copies of Ron's book *The Romance of the Stockman*, and give one to her.

She talks about *Sandside*, and the horses they had there. My mother's conversations of years ago come flooding back to me. Joe Innes had left some of the old horses on the property, for which my grandfather cursed him when they were unable to get up and there was the terrible business of having to destroy them.

Joan is sure she has some pictures of *Sandside*. She doesn't think she'll be able to find them immediately, however, in the muddle of having just moved.

We arrange to meet the next day at a cafe in town and by the time she arrives, Joan's not only read half of Ron's book – she's turned up the old photo albums. We pore over the little black and white pictures labelled *Sandside*.

Here is one of a group, neatly lined up, staring straight at the camera, the Youngers and the Inneses, on the *Sandside* lawn just before the property was handed over in 1925. It is the first time I'd seen a picture of my mother at that age, or of our family of that time together.

We go on our way, and Joan promises to send copies of the photos. They arrrive a little while after. I promise myself to contact her again, for another talk in search of more detail about those old family days. I leave it too late. Less than a year later, I hear that Joan, so vital and active, in spite of her age, has died, struck down quite suddenly. The little picture, now in a gold frame in my bedroom, seems even more precious, a chance reunion with the past.

Although my grandparents were bush dwellers only in part, having grown up in or near Melbourne and always sharing their time between city and country, my grandfather came from a long line of Scottish handlers of livestock, and he followed in the tradition.

He bought *Sandside* because he considered it ideal for cattle fattening, and after the sheep were cleared from it he would bring successive trainloads of bullocks from northern NSW to fatten on the rich flats of the Yanko, to ready them for Melbourne's Newmarket Saleyards, where they regularly topped the market.

My grandfather would never have considered moving to the West, but his grandson Bill (Margaret's other brother) had early good years when he took up his Ivanhoe holding in the 1950s and he has never lost faith in the remote country.

— 13 —
The Town with Iron Windows

In 1909 Bean could travel to Bourke by train; today the rail service no longer operates.

Margaret and I drive along a modern Mitchell Highway from Nyngan, crossing into the Western Division along the way.

When the young Sydney journalist arrived with his notebook to set out down the Darling to *Dunlop*, the town, which he called the Old Port, was already past a prime that had been full of hopeful promise.

Bourke, by then heading for its half-century, had lost a good deal of its former spark. Its population had peaked in the 1880s and early 1890s. Then it had been battered by drought and the financial crash, although in 1901 it still had 20 hotels. The population was down to about 1600 when Bean was there, less than half of the 1890 level.

Once Bourke 'lay at the chief shipping port of Central Australia, the last town for 460 miles, as the crow flies (or 1200 as the river runs), to which any railway comes', he wrote.

'It is hard to believe now that, only thirty years since, they thoroughly believed that Bourke was going to be "the Chicago of the West",' Bean wrote.

He found 'a sleepy country town – a town of thistles, and goats, and backyards, and scraps of old iron, and other signs of prosperity long gone bad – a town which most people have forgotten to be a port at all . . .'

The river trade had suffered some of the knocks of hard times, although it was still a functioning riverboat town.

Today there is no 'port'. The riverboats with their huge and valuable cargoes are a lovely dreamy tale. Bean lamented that a mail train, which had run daily, was down to two days a week, which is a lot better than today's no train.

There is still a steep wooden wharf. But it is not the one Bean peered down, nor has it ever been used for commercial boats and passengers and cargo. It is a fake wharf, recreated in memory of a busy past and in the hope of building a future on the tourist trade.

It is on a hot Sunday afternoon in December 2001 that Margaret and I first arrive in Bourke. We go straight to the Darling, which lies quiet and deserted. Looking at the sluggish water, it takes a feat of imagination to picture this as the bustling inland port of the late 19th and early 20th centuries, crowded with boats and barges and bales of the golden fleece that sustained the country, and the 'Sydney passenger', as Bean referred to himself, a little flustered, rushing to climb aboard his trusty little vessel for the trip downriver to *Dunlop*.

There's hardly anyone to be seen. The great river is green-coloured, low and slow between its high banks.

After watching the water for a while, we go to check out nearby Oxley Street, Bourke's main commercial drag, which is also deadly quiet. Here's a shock. The shop fronts are all covered by iron roller blinds, painted in browns and greens. Bourke looks as though it is wearing armour.

As it is. The war against vandalism is a running, only partly successful, campaign in a town that struggles with its reputation, and to acquire a better one. At the crossroads of this street, the blue overhead structure appears at first glance just a bit of civic decoration.

Then, at the centre of it, you notice the camera. It beams back into the police station. Other cameras are set at strategic points along the road, which contains Fitzgerald Post Office Hotel.

When we're there on our first trip, many Aborigines are drinking at this pub. It closes around 6 pm, to stop fights, and a bus is provided for patrons. Even so the licensee, who we meet outside where a clean up is underway, tells us it is 'still a battle every day'.

When we return to Bourke 15 months later, the Fitzgerald Post Office Hotel is about to undergo a major identity change and become a Tai Chi centre. We'll get to that story a little later.

Bourke is a town with a complex character. A tough town. A friendly town. Often failing. Always striving.

The police station has a startling poster. It tells parents: 'There's a limit on physical punishment. Don't hit or use force above your child's shoulders. Don't hit or use force below your child's shoulders that could harm them more than briefly'. At a supermarket, one of Bourke's three, a sign warns that children under 16 aren't allowed in unless accompanied by an adult or a staff member.

In Bourke, house break-ins are routine and many people

keep large dogs. We find they're often more benign than their bark suggests, but this mightn't be everyone's experience.

There are 36–40 policemen for something over 3000 people. The young Aborigines are 'refugees' in the town, one man tells us on our initial visit. The night before, he'd seen 15 to 20 young kids sitting on the corner near his centre-of-town house. He presumed they were afraid to go home.

That summer the street kids were out each night, throwing bottles and making a noise. The local community eventually held a meeting in the park about the violence. The next summer the gang of street kids aren't to be seen. But the kids still roam, especially in the lanes which houses back onto. We're told they whistle to each other, sometimes when they're casing out houses. A 'cockatoo' will stand at the corner of a street, messaging a mate by the nature of his whistle. One local says you can set your watch by the whistling, which starts around 12.30 or 1 am. Margaret, the lighter sleeper, reports hearing whistles in the early hours.

A prominent local tells us Bourke is 'a tale of two cities. Bourke is the best of towns, Bourke is the worst of towns'. On the one hand, he says, townspeople help each other; on the other, there's 'the abandoned generation'.

'Any day you go down the town you'll find children who are on the streets, not at school. I don't see it as an Aboriginal problem. We have white no-hopers too. There are so many good Aborigines. It's not an Aboriginal problem per se – it's [a problem of] undisciplined children.'

More than three in ten of the town's population are indigenous, and one-quarter of the wider Bourke local government area – compared with an average for the state of NSW of less than 2 per cent. About half the indigenous population is aged between babyhood and 19.

The Catholic Church had 11 priests, brothers and nuns in Bourke in 2001, a large religious community for a town of 3300.

Five are Mother Teresa (Missionary of Charity) nuns. Members of the order were first sent to Bourke in 1969. The little smiling nuns from India do most of their work in the Aboriginal community.

They drive a minibus and get about in the heavy regalia that most orders in Australia have long abandoned, its bright whiteness giving the impression but not the reality of coolness. Their dress might be old-fashioned, but the nuns are not. When a parishioner asks, after a mass for the beatification of Mother Teresa, whether the nuns will be able to find out what is happening at the Vatican, one of them says that pay TV has arrived just in time and they're going off to a neighbour to watch the Rome ceremony. We're told that when they leave Bourke, perhaps with little notice, they are only allowed to take a couple of photos and one possession. One got round the stricture by making her 'possession' a photo album.

The nuns and the other church people point to drink and drugs as the main problems, which often lead to child neglect or abuse.

One member of the Catholic religious community finds the Aboriginal people 'taken up with the fact that they feel they are very much second-class citizens. It's a racist town in many ways. The indigenous people aren't accepted as they ought to be. Not that I blame the white people. There's a history behind it. Some of them have had bad experiences in their relationships with indigenous people.'

This is a franker view than most townspeople will give you.

Louise Brown is an Aboriginal woman who counsels problem gamblers, has mentored school children and works at the youth centre. She's a no-nonsense woman who's been in the town 22 years; when she was young she lived on a reserve and left school at year 9.

Her approach seems one of tough love. She says the court system is failing because 'criminals' get let off. 'The [young criminals] are attacking the elders of the community,' she tells us. But that's only one side: she loves Bourke and its people – the place is 'laid back, and you don't have to rush'. When we meet her, Louise is hoping to go away to Wagga Wagga to study, taking her schoolgirl daughter who is, however, reluctant to leave. 'I tell her, "You need to go to university and get a piece of paper".' For her part, Louise says she would use whatever training she got (she started psychology but found it too hard by distance education) to help indigenous people, rather than to go into the 'mainstream'.

Bourke's Aborigines have the health problems sadly common to Aboriginal communities, but they have also, over the years, attracted doctors who are anxious to help them.

Jeremy Cumpston is best known to urban Australians as an actor, but he's also a doctor who spent seven months in Bourke in 2002. He particularly wanted to work with the Aborigines, and when you know his background, you understand why. Jeremy's family is from the West: his great-grandfather was an Afghan camel trader who married an Aboriginal woman.

The average Bourke Aboriginal's life expectancy, according to Jeremy, is 20 years under the national average, and the Aborigines lack a sense of their history or economic base. 'If you haven't got hope for the future you often tend to use alcohol to circumvent the pain.' But plenty of people in the white community drink a lot more than the Aborigines, Jeremy says. 'People drink out there. It's the last bastion of the Wild West. They're tough people – and they've a lot on their plate.'

Despite everything, when we are first there Bourke has about it an optimism and a feeling of greater prosperity than some other places in the West. It's a town determined to present its best face, one reason why there is a certain defensiveness. The local tour guide volunteers, without being asked, to the small group he's showing round, 'We do have social issues, but so do they anywhere in Australia.' He makes the point not once but several times. So do others.

While it is hard to chart precisely what's happening to attitudes, Bourke in the last few years has certainly spruced up its appearance.

The streets are kept exceptionally clean. A man is slapping paint over graffiti on the walls of the Fitzgerald Post Office Hotel, which dates back to the building boom of the 1880s. We are told (this is before the hotel changes hands and character) the touch-up is done monthly. Gardens are lushly green in the summer heat. Even the 'armour' is neat. The council had the old grilles on Oxley Street's shops – which didn't match and gave the streetscape the appearance of a jail – replaced by the rollers.

A traveller we run into outside the (closed for Sunday) tourist information bureau, who's driving through to Dimboola in Victoria, tells us that when he was here 26 years before, Bourke was a good town. On another visit, several years ago, it had been 'terrible', but it has improved again. A local says, 'People are doing more to get things better now there is more investment.'

There are relatively few Bourke shops but they are well-stocked in the weekend before Christmas 2001. Shoppers rush the toy sale set up outside the newsagency. Even in comparatively good times, however, it's a struggle.

Tradespeople don't want to come to what is still a remote spot. We meet a recently arrived motor mechanic at breakfast in the Port Of Bourke Hotel where we stay the first time. He's planning to stay a couple of years and retire young, confiding, 'You get paid twice as much here.' And houses are cheap – provided you want to buy rather than rent.

He's just made an offer of $25,000 on a house which he thinks he could let for $140 a week.

When we're back in Bourke in early 2003, spirits are gloomier. The drought has really knocked the town around.

Bill Crothers arrived in Bourke in 1952 as a young chemist. He's recently passed on his pharmacy – a big shop that sells glass and china as well – to son Peter, who lives in Canberra. But Bill still spends a lot of time at the shop, playing with the computer in the back room.

'The shops are doing badly. We used to sell a lot of giftware – we don't sell as much now. The prescription side keeps going on – there are more people with prescriptions for depression.

'The bloke next door is in hardware. He was getting eight pallets of goods a week – now it's only one and a half. The grocery places are feeling it.

'It's dreadfully hard to sell country pharmacies – no one wants to come out here.' When the pharmacist left Brewarrina, some 95 kilometres away, the prescriptions had to be ferried each day to Bourke for making up. The esky would arrive in the middle of the morning. The Bourke pharmacy was notified about any emergency ones, so they were done quickly.

Hard times notwithstanding, one Bourke businesswoman has her eyes on expansion. Yi Bing Wang (Bing to all) is one of the most remarkable women we meet in the West. We hear of her because everyone's talking about how she's just paid $50,000 for the Post Office Hotel.

A ball of energy, with her black hair cut in a short bob, Bing's story is an unlikely one. Yet as a Chinese in the Western Division, she is following a tradition of many of the early Chinese, who'd come to Australia in the gold rushes and spread out through the country areas, as hawkers, market gardeners, and general workers. Most of the big properties had a Chinese garden, supplying vegetables and fruit to the sizeable communities on the station.

Bing says she left China in 1989, first to study English in New Zealand, then to settle in Melbourne, where her sister has a Chinese medical centre. Bing worked with her for a while.

A few years ago she saw an advertisement for a cafe in Bourke. Bing, husband Keith and son Gary (now in his mid-teens) moved north. As well as having the Elysian Cafe – where, when she's not working, you'll occasionally find her up the back watching a video of a Chinese love story – Bing teaches the locals Tai Chi.

Tai Chi might sound a bit of an oddity in a place like Bourke – or at least that's how it seemed to us when we first heard of Bing's classes in a little park at the back of the cafe.

But it's become quite a hit with the locals. Margaret and

I pay our $6.50 each and go to an Easter Saturday session.

Bing says she'd been planning to have a rest over the holiday weekend, but the pupils wanted their classes. At least that's what they told her. Only one other woman, Brenda Porrelli, who's come the short distance from North Bourke, cavorts around the tiny park with us. Margaret and I can't quite get a grip on the basics, but Brenda is working on more advanced movements with a shiny silver sword.

Now Bing has a new project. She plans to move the cafe to the Post Office Hotel, just across the road. She'll have accommodation for travellers, and run a Tai Chi centre, also offering acupuncture and massage.

Tai Chi, says Bing, could be one answer to some of Bourke's problems. 'There's too much drink and gambling.' Tai Chi could reduce the drunkenness: 'It's good for mind and body.'

She is on the look-out for a Tai Chi instructor, and wants to expand into Brewarrina, Dubbo and Cobar. 'I have 27 people interested in Brewarrina.'

Bourke, says Bing, is 'OK. We have problems, especially for the kids. They have no education, so no respect. People drink, when they're drunk they do terrible things, smash things up. This shop has been broken into three or four times – they come in to steal drinks. By the time we get to know them, it's a little better.

'On the other hand, we have very good regular customers. We make good price, we're friendly to them. Local people come to our shop, mostly black people. They like it because of the low price. We don't earn that much profit.'

Wool is still important to the Bourke area, but by 2001 the irrigation-based cotton industry, supplemented by fruit, had outstripped it in generating wealth. In the drought that opened the new century, there was no cotton planted for two years (2002 and 2003), because the water didn't come down the river. The town drooped.

Like a number of other outback places – Longreach with its Stockman's Hall of Fame, Hay with its shearing hall – Bourke wants to trade on its past to help secure its future.

History has become business. Tourism is growing. A hotelier tells us, 'The Back-of-Bourke catch-phrase is known throughout the world. Seven to ten years ago Bourke was a bit in the doldrums. They've marketed the area successfully as the accessible outback.'

The unassuming Bean would be surprised to see his face and words on the brochure for the Back O'Bourke Exhibition Centre, a work-in-progress. The photo is of a serious, quite elderly man. But quoted is the young man on the wool track: 'Out here you have reached the core of Australia – the real red Australia of the ages . . .'

Paul Roe is one of the activists in getting the centre started. A teacher and a founder of the evangelical Cornerstone movement, who set up a Bible college just outside Bourke in the 1970s, he is a Bean enthusiast.

When I first rang Paul to say we were retracing Bean's tracks he was delighted. Paul takes people on poetry and history treks, along the road to Hungerford that Lawson walked in the 1890s.

A cluster of stones and plaques on one road in Bourke commemorates iconic names of the bush writers: Henry Lawson, Will Ogilvie and Breaker Morant. All spent time in the area. A plaque has been made for Bean as well, and a stone mount awaits it besides these other writers.

Roe says Bean the war historian 'had met the Anzacs in Bourke before the war. I was really impressed with *On the Wool Track*. Its lyrical passages touched the essence of the bush. I was drawn to the fact that he told the story through people – we're adopting the same approach with the Back O'Bourke centre.'

In 2002, Year of the Outback, the Back O'Bourke Exhibition Centre opened. When we talk to people just before the opening, they are full of enthusiasm. A year later, the centre and its backers have an enormous struggle on their hands. Its construction has stalled for want of funds. Here's another blow on top of the drought that has hit the cotton and sheep industries.

The centre's modest first stage is operating for tourists, but the rest of the area is part-finished buildings and hazardous rough ground. No more government funds are available – the locals are trying, so far without great success, to raise business money in Sydney.

Bourke's historical buildings don't quite match those of Wilcannia, down the river, but they are usefully rich assets in the effort to develop the tourist industry.

Bean would have seen the Carriers Arms Hotel, from the 1870s, where Henry Lawson drank. Close to the river bank in his day was the Telegraph Hotel, now carefully restored as the Riverside Motel, where we stayed on one visit.

The grand London Bank building, constructed in 1888, was in its heyday in the early 1900s. After ceasing to be a bank in the 1940s, it fell on hard times. It was used to house abattoir workers, and later as a boarding house, before being abandoned and vandalised.

The council bought it, but initial attempts to do it up

didn't amount to much. It's being restored by Chris Ware and Kristie Smiles and two other partners. The Ware-Smiles, who have come from the NSW town of Mudgee, receive no government help, but are promised the title to the building as soon as they finish the work to heritage specifications. At last the old bank building could have a new life although it will never see another teller. Even the tradesmen are enthusiasts for this massive task: a bricklayer from Mudgee is an expert on rendering historical buildings.

Alongside the London Bank building are accommodation units which the Smiles have upgraded and run as a motel. They call their business Gidgee Guest House, after the strong-smelling acacia that is a feature of the area, about which Bean wrote: 'Some even say that when rain is falling across the Darling and the wind happens to blow from the north-west they can smell the Gidgea [Bean's spelling] in Nyngan, 130 miles away.'

Even the cemetery is playing its part in trying to attract the tourists to Bourke. The most famous grave that visitors come to see is a very modern one, and that of a man who was not a local but became a local hero. Fred Hollows, the famous eye specialist who died in 1992, chose Bourke as his burial place. As you drive into Bourke along the Mitchell Highway, an avenue of trees called The Vision Way remembers Hollows' contribution. His grave in the cemetery, with a ring of rocks around a central spot, represents the eye, the focus of work that helped people in many countries including, and especially, Aborigines around the Bourke district.

Hollows recounts in his autobiography his experience in Bourke, to which he went in the early 1970s after a psychiatrist he met at a party asked him to take a medical team there. He found a lot of trachoma among the area's Aborigines. He also found Bourke 'still quite a racist town' and prided himself on helping 'bring down a few barriers'.

Team members were issued with honorary memberships of the Bowling Club, the Gold Club and the 'exclusive' Oxley Club. For Hollows, 'Walking into the Oxley with [Sydney Aboriginal woman] Shirley Smith, getting the barman to back off and serve us, and sitting with the Shire President and the Town Clerk and the local priest, was an event to remember.'

The richness of Bourke's past comes through in a little book, *100 Lives of Bourke,* telling the stories of people who lie in the cemetery. As the authors say, the graves provide a glimpse into 'the world of riverboats, cameleers, drovers and pioneer settlers'. Muslims and Chinese are buried here, in a town that was 'multicultural' before the concept, let alone the word, became fashionable. And anyone who wanders around the graves is reminded how epidemics of diseases like typhoid and diphtheria were once commonplace.

The three authors are now part of the small army of custodians of Bourke's past. Barbara Hickson, as a heritage adviser, visited Bourke regularly for eight years to explore and document the old buildings. Heather Nicholls, a town planner and historian, came to Bourke history through her interest in Cobb and Co. And Ann McLachlan manages the Bourke Library and has a passionate interest in the town's past, which is also its future.

— 14 —

A New Industry and a New 'Church'

On one of our later visits to the far West, dawn is breaking on Easter Sunday in the cotton country round Bourke. Except this year the cotton fields, where harvesting should be in full swing, lie fallow. With drought's iron grip strangling the land and the river, there's no water for this ever-so-thirsty crop.

We are among some 200 people huddling round bonfires before the simple service starts. They've come 20 kilometres from Bourke, and from nearby farms. A spare, elderly man sits towards the back of the congregation, singing the hymns in a firm clear voice as the sun comes up in a red blaze. Walking aids are propped nearby. Later, with the other worshippers, he enjoys the pancakes ('hotcakes', he calls them) that follow the service, although with his bung legs he has to balance precariously to eat standing up.

This is Jack Buster, former US marine and big man of Bourke, who lives with his extended clan of four generations at *Darling Farms*, across the river from the main town, where they grow cotton and fruit.

Officiating at the Easter service on this chilly morning is

Paul Roe, a founder of the evangelical Cornerstone organisation which, like the Buster family and in lockstep with that clan, has become a significant presence in Bourke life.

Cotton and religion have joined forces in an experiment in the outback. The relationship between a major local business and a Christian movement, and the importance for the town of that joint force, make modern Bourke quite an unusual place.

Jack's brother-in-law Frank Hadley and fellow American Paul Kahl were cotton pioneers at Wee Waa, on the Namoi in the early 1960s. They were Californians from around Merced. Jack Buster and wife Harriett (also from Merced) were encouraged to follow, and they too settled initially at Wee Waa.

This part of the Namoi became a little bit of America. John Yeomans, in *The Scarce Australians*, who visited in the '60s, was mightily impressed. The Hadleys' new house, he wrote, while externally like any other farmhouse, was filled with not only 'large and glossy Australian-manufactured household appliances but also with rarer comforts imported from the United States'. Colonial furniture, a piano and an electronic organ had all been shipped from the US; Mrs Hadley, 'a smart young American matron' played 'Them Thar Eyes' on the organ.

The Americans also shipped in religion. They revived the local Protestant (Presbyterian) church, which became a centre of intense activity. This gives some context to what happened later in Bourke.

Jack formed a partnership with fellow American Owen Boone and soon they were driving to Bourke to look at properties. The Buster family tells the story of how the ex-marine and the former military policeman had to bunk down in a double bed because that was the only accommodation they could find in town.

They lit on the pioneer station *Fort Bourke*, and in 1966 the Busters and Boones settled in, dividing the land. The Busters called their property *Darling Farms*; Boone kept the old name. Later the Busters bought *Fort Bourke* from the Boones.

Although comparative newcomers to Bourke, the Buster family are among its most prominent people, wielding influence because they provide such an economic dynamic for the town. Jack is larger than life, with a distinctive language of expletives that he insists comes from his youth rather than his three years in the US marines in the early 1950s. Favourites include 'horse-feathers', 'Judas Priest' and 'Dad Gummit'. His crippling injury was a result of a truck carrying bee hives colliding with his ute. It left him physically impaired but failed to dent an indomitable spirit. 'I'm as slow as a seven-year itch,' he says laconically, when you ask how he is.

Jack loves planes and one of the more colourful stories told about him is how he fought back when his flying licence was taken away because of a leaky heart valve and his other health problems.

When he drove to the doctor in quest of its reinstatement, the medico promptly declared he wasn't fit to be in charge of a car because his pulse rate was so slow. There went the car licence. So the next day Jack booked into a hospital, had a pacemaker installed, and got back both licences. Since then he's lost the pilot's licence again. But he still takes up a light air machine that he built from a kit.

Buster, who's now in his 70s, has handed over the running

of *Darling Farms* to his family. The *Darling Farms* folk are very generous to community causes, and hospitable. For all this, they have a certain air of mystery about them.

A few years ago Buster bought the Bourke newspaper, the *Western Herald*. Pick up a copy and you see just another little country paper. But the *Herald* is rather special, and not just because it is one of the few in rural NSW still in independent ownership. Its distinction comes from a famous contributor, Henry Lawson, who wrote for it during his stay in these parts in the 1890s.

The potential of the land around Bourke for agriculture was seen early. In the late 19th century, an artesian bore of more than 1000 feet produced over 600,000 gallons a day, and irrigated crops, orchards, and vine growing. The Pera Bore oranges became world famous. In 1906 the *Bourke Banner* reported that the Department of Agriculture had sent to the Agent-General in London for display Pera Bore oranges. Word had been received back that the fruit 'arrived in magnificent condition and were greatly admired'. However, the bore water polluted the soil and the venture faded. Cotton was tried around that time, and the manager of the government experimental station was highly optimistic about its potential, declaring himself convinced that cotton of good marketable value could be produced and 'if we can dispose of it locally, the cotton industry in the West ought not to be long in establishing itself'.

In fact, it was still a lifetime away, and even then it began slowly. But by the 1980s, when river water started to be stored on the farms, it was flourishing.

The amount of export income cotton produces for Australia nationally – almost $2 billion in 2000–01, before the drought – comes as a surprise, especially when put against the nearly $4 billion export income from wool that financial year. Although it produces only a small amount of the world's cotton, Australia has been the third largest exporter of the fibre behind the United States and Uzbekistan.

The Bourke cotton growers strongly defend their industry against the numerous critics who say irrigators, especially cotton growers, here and further up the river are sucking too much water out of the Darling, adding to South Australia's serious salination problem.

Cotton Australia, the peak industry body for Australia's 1200 growers, argues that with new methods such as 'drip' and 'trickle' irrigation water use is less, and the water is recycled.

With the overwhelming majority of Australia's cotton growing happening in the catchment of the Darling and its tributaries, the sceptics are not convinced and say that country like Bourke should not be used for such a water-intensive crop. Local Bourke producers tell us former federal environment minister Robert Hill, a South Australian, declined several invitations to visit. They are chuffed when his successor, David Kemp (a Victorian), arrives within a month of taking up the job.

In its second incarnation in the area, since the 1980s fruit has developed into a big industry, with table grapes and citrus the specialties. In 2001, the Bourke district had about half a million sheep and 18,600 cattle, and grew 34,550 acres of cotton. Five hundred acres were planted with citrus; 420 acres with table grapes.

According to a January 2001 consultants' study for the local cotton industry – prepared as ammunition in the argument about water – cotton and fruit brought $65 million a year (most of it from the cotton) to the economy of the Bourke shire, and provided 715 (fulltime-equivalent) jobs. Clyde Agriculture produces more than half the cotton, and Busters about one-third. There are various smaller producers.

In normal times the Busters have between 7000 and 11,000 acres of cotton. It is planted in the spring and harvested in the autumn. They have some 120,000 citrus trees, almost all navel oranges, and 70 acres of vines. But in 2002 and 2003 the Busters planted no cotton and the hardship of the drought just made the locals angrier about the inexorable move to restrict water for irrigation.

The cotton-farming Busters have had a symbiotic relationship with the Cornerstone community since it was established in the area in the late 1970s. Cornerstone takes in recruits for training, its two-year course melding work and religious study. *Darling Farms* contracts Cornerstone to supply some of the cotton enterprise's labour force. The students spend a morning chipping cotton and an afternoon studying, or vice versa.

Cornerstone would prefer not to be called a church. It had a debate about this some years ago, when the Anglicans became twitchy. They wanted to know whether Cornerstone was in the baptism and burial business.

'We explained we were more like a mission order – more a religious order like the Franciscans or the Dominicans,' says Paul Roe who is Cornerstone's assistant national director. Director and co-founder Laurie McIntosh, a one-time engineer, runs their central office in the town of Dubbo.

Studying for an honours degree in history at the University of NSW in the early '70s, Paul was active in an informal group who lightheartedly called themselves, in the revolutionary spirit of those days, the 'Jesus Christ World Liberation Front'.

Laurie, now in his 60s, had come from an atheist family; he was a relatively late convert to faith. He became a mentor to the younger Paul.

Paul and Laurie, who had gone to Bourke to help his family set up a dairy, were involved in religious work in Sydney, where Paul took up school teaching. Laurie suggested starting some permanent mission work in Bourke, centred on farming. 'We talked about a teaching community that was life-related and vocational,' Paul recalls.

Meanwhile Jack Buster and Owen Boone had already started a Baptist fellowship in Bourke. But they didn't have a pastor; when Laurie arrived, they asked him to do the job part-time. It was a matter of opportunity all round: Laurie told Paul he'd talk to Buster and Boone to try to get a block of land that they could share-farm.

Paul and his wife Robyn set off to Canada for Bible studies; while he was there, Laurie secured an arrangement. The Roes moved to Bourke to run the Bible school which began teaching in 1978.

They started with eight students – two girls and four boys and a married couple with two children. The girls lived with the Boone family; the rest were in caravans, as were the Roes. In later years students were recruited by the Cornerstone 'teams' that have spread far and wide, as well as by advertising. But the early ones came mostly through the Roes' personal contacts.

When the Roes moved into a house, it was the old

shearers' quarters. Another house literally grew around the bathroom that had serviced the caravans.

'In the first year it was a rude shock after Sydney,' the softly spoken Robyn remembers. 'It was a drought – my welcome to Bourke was in the dry times. We had to chop our wood to heat the water. It was called a "bush donkey" – there are drums over a fire, you heat the drums. It's very effective' – so long as you have an adequate supply of wood at the ready.

Did they ever think of giving it away?

'Numerous times.'

So what kept them going?

'A belief that that's what God had called us to do. And seeing lives change. It was the people experience – that was hard at times too! The love of the country came in time.'

Paul explains the Cornerstone approach: 'We focus on the character issue. It's our responsibility to live what we teach – [the religion] is caught, not taught.'

And speaking of catching, the Cornerstone people keep an eye out for opportunities to spread the message. Robyn and Paul, separately, make polite inquiries of Margaret and me about our religious 'journeys'. Margaret clothes herself in her family's Presbyterianism. I feel confessing to godlessness here is like proclaiming yourself a Liberal at a Labor Party barbecue.

The handbook for Cornerstone's diploma in Christian studies says that typically, each student will work 20 to 25 hours a week. Students' work pays for most of their course fees and board.

Alan Parker, formerly from Blacktown in Sydney, is teaching Old Testament theology when we meet him. An engineer until he was 35, he then trained as an Anglican minister.

'I worked then as an engineer to earn money, and assisted in parishes. My youngest brother decided to sit on the Darling and find out what God wanted him to do. He got found by the Cornerstone people. Later he told me, "I've found the best Bible college in Australia." I said "where?" He said Bourke. I said, "pull the other leg". So we came out on holidays and we were very impressed. That was the early '90s.'

Cornerstone has grown strongly. It presently has more than 100 staff, about 130 students, nine 'mission' teams in the field, and teaching centres in Broken Hill, Dubbo, and Canowindra as well as Pera Bore. Its handbook reports that since 1979, more than 100 teams have been commissioned for at least a year of 'focused mission' in more than 50 places in the eastern and southern states.

Its greatest strength is in NSW but it is also operating in Victoria, where it is considering establishing a training centre, and South Australia. However it has had to pull out of Queensland because of what Paul described as 'logistical' problems.

One of the big surprises has been the interest from overseas. The school has had students from Papua New Guinea, Indonesia, Sri Lanka, Poland, Germany, Holland, Britain and America. A Cornerstone centre has been set up in Ghana by a former student (a Ghanaian) and one is just beginning in West Papua.

Cornerstone doesn't believe God and mammon mustn't mix. Quite the opposite. It runs numerous businesses. They include several pizza shops, a turf farm, a laundromat, a carpet-cleaning business, and a house-moving and relocating business. A labour contracting scheme supplies farm-help for jobs such as trimming vines and harvesting pumpkins and melons.

It hasn't all been smooth sailing. The turf business became controversial because it enjoyed a tax break and its secular competitor didn't. There were red faces at Cornerstone over its involvement with a certain Mr Foo, a high profile illegal immigrant, although they had parted ways when the fuss blew up.

At Bourke Cornerstone also runs a Christian school, with about 100 pupils, to which some townspeople send their children for educational rather than religious reasons. Bourke's social problems make the school a drawcard.

Although the Busters and Cornerstone are separate, they're interlinked well beyond the ties of contract and convenience. Two of Jack Buster's five children went through the Cornerstone course, and the family are enthusiasts.

The drought hit Cornerstone, because of its dependence on the cotton industry. 'Christmas [of 2002] was awful – very, very depressing,' Paul tells us. Because there was no cotton crop that season, Cornerstone has had to downsize its Bourke operations.

When we go out to see the Roes at Easter 2003, Cornerstone's second Bourke settlement, at Gidgee Lakes, has only two families, and three houses are empty. Pera Bore is still taking theology students but the Gidgee branch is closed for business, waiting for the heavens to open. The drought has made no exception for devotees.

A few months later, things are still quite grim. One day, Russell Mansell's wife Suzanne drops in on Robyn, and the two women say a prayer for the rain still needed for the cotton and the fruit, and for the religion too.

— 15 —
The *Jandra*
Sails Again

A half-century before Bean's visit, the paddle-steamer, *Gemini*, made the first long, tortuous trip up the river to the spot where the town of Bourke would be soon laid out. When he was in town, Bean interviewed an old retired riverboat captain, Captain Pickhills, who had been a *Gemini* crew member on a rather spectacular rescue mission in the early 1860s for the fledgling town, which had been cut off by flood and suffered a four-month grog drought.

When *Gemini* arrived, Bourke's two publicans, Mr Sly and Mr Kelly were waiting. Mr Sly, 'a Yankee', asked for an axe, a cask of rum was broken open, and drinks all round were on Sly.

'About an hour afterwards Bourke was a perfect pandemonium. Everyone wanted to fight . . . There was jubilation in Bourke, and it lasted about three days,' Pickhills told Bean.

Bean called the *Jandra*, the paddle-steamer on which he travelled from Bourke down to *Dunlop*, the 'Dreadnought of the Darling'. A local gave him this description of the boat and it appealed to the young journalist's military turn of mind. When he looked at the little Dreadnought, which he called by the pseudonym of *Yanda* in his original edition, she did conjure up 'a warship of sorts – a certain dimly remembered gunboat that one had seen as a child steaming in bright colour amidst smoke and shell and dervishes up the centre page of the *Illustrated London News* to the relief of the unlucky defenders of Khartoum . . .'.

This Dreadnought was

> . . . clean as a new pin; like a British steamer ought to be. Her deckhouse and upper works were painted with the same speckless, rich buff as those of a P. & O. mail steamer. Her rail was a neat black. The two huge gig-lamps staring like the eyes of an owl from either side of the bridge were polished as bright as a jeweller's window.

The *Jandra*'s owners were the Brown brothers, Captain Walter and his brother Herbert. Bean initially 'camou-flaged' them as the 'Jones brothers'. Also on board was a ten-year-old steward, 'The Imp', Ern Bentley of Bourke.

The little Dreadnought had a 'saloon' and four cabins, each with two bunks and wood panelling reminiscent of 'a little wooden cottage, and painted white'. The skipper 'never left the wheel, except to snatch a cup of tea at midday . . . Beside him in a cage was a white cockatoo, which had been his shipmate for years and years – ever since one evening, passing under some overhanging river gums, they had heard a quarrel in the gum leaves above them, and a featherless, helpless outcast had flopped on to the deck. It was part of the skipper's religion that he never had a meal but he gave that old shipmate a part of it . . .

> The cockatoo was given an almond whenever he wanted it – on one condition. He had to use the proper formula in asking for it. It was not enough for him to say, 'Cocky wants an almond'. It was held common politeness that he should address the skipper or his brother by name first – 'Mr Brown!' It was not a big price to pay, considering the reward. But it was a fad of that cockatoo, except in his happiest moods, to pay it under protest.

Just before dozing off on his first night on the river, Bean heard 'a husky whisper'.

> 'Cockywansanalmond!'
>   Silence.
>   Husky voice: 'Cockywansanalmond!'
>   Deep voice: 'No.'
>   Husky voice, after consideration: 'Cocky-wants-an-almond.'
>   Deep voice: 'No.'
>   Husky voice, after a long silence: 'Misser Braown.'
>   Deep voice: 'Yes? What do you want?'
>   Husky voice: 'Cocky wants an almond.'
>   Something tapped on to the floor of the cage, and there was silence for the night.

'Cocky' was famous in his own right. According to entries in the multi-volume history of Bourke, he lived until September 1928. The old bird, nearly as featherless as when he fell out of the nest and met up with the Captain, was at least 40 when he died. He got a special mention in the Captain's obituary several years later, lauded as a 'great favourite on the river steamers' and a 'splendid talker'.

The original *Jandra*, Bean tells us in a later edition of *The Dreadnought of the Darling*, was cut down and used as a barge for another riverboat, *Nile* (also owned by the Brown brothers) to tow.

But the *Jandra* lives again, in the form of a namesake which takes visitors along the river. Bourke is now advertised as 'home of the *Jandra* Paddleboat'.

Russell Mansell, a big local fruit producer, built the modern boat, which has the paddle wheels of the old *Nile*. It was quite a feat. After a trip on the *Jandra*, we call in at the Mansell orchard to hear the story.

The Mansell family came to Bourke in 1982 from Mildura. Russell's grandfather had been one of the first settlers in Mildura, with the famous Chaffeys. Russell had decided to move because there was not enough land to go round the family. He spent several years travelling around looking for suitable fruit-growing country, before settling at Bourke.

When the locals were planning the exhibition centre they talked about buying a boat. Russell's brother, who was interested in paddleboats in Mildura, checked one out there, and warned them off it.

'So I said I'd build a paddleboat. It took me five months [in 2000]. I had a lot of co-operation from the waterways people. I initially built the boat in my head. Then my house architect in Mildura did a plan.' His day job imposed a timetable: the shed where the *Jandra* was under construction was needed as a coolroom when the fruit ripened.

It cost $5500 to get *Jandra* inspected by the authorities to pass muster as river-worthy. When he saw the boat the waterways inspector from Sydney could hardly believe his eyes. The boat has now been bought by the Exhibition Centre for $450,000; the Centre operates it.

Like Bean's *Jandra*, this boat is 77 feet long but its width is 22 feet, while hers was 19 feet. And today's boat has a steel, not wooden, hull, and a modern engine rather than the boilers which used to be fed by wood, chopped and sold by men along the river.

Mansell's *Jandra* was the first paddle-boat at Bourke in nearly 70 years. It has no material from the old boat. So why wasn't she called the *Nile*, in honour of the paddles?

'The Nile is synonymous with Egypt. The *Jandra* is synonymous with Bourke – there's a *Jandra* station, a Jandra restaurant,' Mansell says. The local high school magazine is called *Jandra*.

The new *Jandra* has two captains, and one of them is a woman. John Mahoney, who moved from Newcastle for the job, had 40 years in Australia's merchant navy before he got this gig. He was an able seaman in those days, sailing to Korea, Japan and India. It was sailing the Darling, however, that brought him a captain's certificate.

Jack Buster, the local big cotton grower and a driving force of a great deal in Bourke, knew of John through Mahoney's son.

'Jack Buster rang me and asked me what I was doing. I said I was retired. He said, "How would you like to operate a riverboat?"'

To get his captain's qualifications he had to do 240 hours with another captain. John then trained co-captain Julie

Martin, who was born and bred in Bourke. Julie's last job had been as a bar attendant. 'This beats pulling booze for drunks. I wasn't working – I jumped at this job. I love it,' she tells us as she cradles the big wheel. Julie is the first ever female paddle-boat captain wholly trained on the Darling River; she had to do 1800 hours.

The *Jandra* runs three cruises a day, and is available for night trips. But these days, even when the water is good, a boat can only go a short distance down the river, because of the weir.

In early 2003, the *Jandra* was nearly high and dry. For four months she couldn't run. As we chug slowly down the river – the only passengers, apart from one couple – Julie shows us pictures of the depleted river when you could walk across the Darling at some points.

The Brown family's old house still stands, hugging the riverbank. When we are first in Bourke, travelling heritage officer Barbara Hickson has just done an inspection of the dilapidated building and takes us round it. John Brown, father of Walter and Herbert, started in the riverboat business at Echuca and owned the paddle-steamer *Florence Annie*. Another son, Francis Brown, became a well-known bush poet.

Francis wrote 'The Last of the Darling Dreadnoughts', about the *Nile*, which was destroyed by fire in the 1920s.

> But never again shall we hear at the dawn,
> As the wild-ducks fly ahead,
> The splash, splash, splash of her paddle-wheel,
> As out from a timbered bend she'd steal
> To straighten her barge on an even keel,
> With a load from the *Dunlop* shed.

The old house, called *Lynwood*, is topped by a 'widow's

walk', the look-out for the boats. In 2002, $31,000 was allocated from a NSW heritage program to restore it.

When we look at it again in 2003, almost nothing has been done. The rivermen's house is again fighting for its life, and its place on the Darling's bank. The council wants to have it moved. It might have been there more than a century, but now it interferes with the town's levy bank, it seems.

I ask people in Bourke whether they know any relatives of the Browns, but the family has long since disappeared from the area. They were so central to Bean's journey, and he was clearly so impressed by them, that failing to find any trace leaves a gap in our story, but I despair of filling it.

Then, when this book is almost finished, comes a small miracle. An excited Ann McLachlan rings from the Bourke Library. Pattie Hall, a niece of Walter and Herbert, has seen a reference in the *Sydney Morning Herald* to the book on the Bourke cemetery and written to Ann for two copies.

'I am 92 years old & the only remaining granddaughter of Captain Brown [Walter and Herbert's father]', Pattie writes to Ann in a firm hand, adding, 'My mother Annie Francis and her sisters were regularly despatched from their home in Melbourne to act as temporary hostesses on the boats and my Aunt Alice told me it took her 3 weeks to travel from Melbourne to Bourke.'

When I contact Pattie, who lives in Sydney, she is a goldmine of information not only on the Browns but also on the Bean connection.

She directs me to a 1956 *Bulletin* article by her late cousin Ken Barratt, following the reprint of *The Dreadnought of the Darling* (in which Bean had given the *Jandra* its proper name and also named the Brown brothers).

Walter and Herbert came from a respected and wealthy family that lived in Melbourne; the children were sent to the best schools. Their father John, although known as 'Captain Brown' wasn't actually a captain but the owner of the boats and a trader. Hard times came in the 1890s and Brown lost everything and moved to Sydney, but Walter and Herbert (neither of whom married) continued in the trade, based at Bourke.

'The picture Dr Bean paints of them is substantially true, even though Herbert has written a few pithy contradictions in the margin of his presentation copy,' wrote Barratt.

'When Dr Bean remarks to the effect that to the skipper's mate (Herbert), the Rivers were his whole life, Herbert annotated, "He likes the Rivers like the devil likes holy water".'

'Where Dr Bean comments that the skipper's mate was snatching a quiet nap "as usual," Herbert writes, "Lies, All Lies"; but I'm afraid that comment is slightly exaggerated. The Browns, as I knew them, were never people to kill themselves with overwork.'

Pattie tells me her daughter has *The Dreadnought of the Darling* first edition with these annotations, and she will ask about it. In fact, she turns up another, equally interesting copy of the book. The inscription reads, *To Capt. Brown and the Skipper's Brother from CEWB (in remembrance of the best trip he has yet taken). London Nov. 20, 1911.*

Bean was impressed by the 'considerable' black beam wharves at Bourke, a tiered structure built to serve the dramatically changing levels of the river.

> The river just here at the Old Port has risen within memory to forty feet . . . and the wharf is built so that

the steamers could lie alongside it when the river was low, and rise gradually alongside of it – should they care to do so – till the river was a banker.

Already, however, the river trade was declining, although Bean held out hopes for its future. Some crews still signed on for voyages of from six to ten weeks that ended at the sea where there were 'real sailors and strange English and new oaths and incomprehensible languages.'

Maybe once a year a big steamer from the Murray was able to make it all the way up to Bourke.

But the small steamers, whose home port it is, now run only a few hundred miles up or down the centre of Australia at the most. And for the present, and until the river is locked – as, of course, it some day will be – the great black wharves of the Old Port, with their three white cranes stretching out their necks high over the river, are something of a white elephant.

The white elephant was to become whiter as the years passed. Bourke's old wharves were pulled down long ago. By the 1920s the river trade was dying. Rail and increasingly motor transport were more convenient and certainly more predictable than a capricious river. Wool could have to wait up to two years in Wilcannia for the river to become navigable. The last boat came to Bourke in the early 1930s, after a long decline of the trade. In the 1990s, a replica of the wharf was built.

In one of those ironies of modern life, if you don't have a

car, it's harder to get to Bourke than it was in 1909, when there was the railway as well as the river (when the water was high enough). The trains have stopped. Now there's only a bus and a very expensive air service.

— 16 —
The Once Great
Dunlop

Dunlop is a magic name, and it is the station at the heart of *On the Wool Track*. Getting entry to it provided the biggest challenge of all the journeying Margaret and I undertook, but we knew that unless we could do so, we'd miss the place at the essence of Bean's classic.

In the early 1900s this great property on the Darling stretched over a million acres. One fence ran for 43 miles in a single direction. *Dunlop* and neighbouring *Toorale* were in a huge parcel of land secured by Samuel McCaughey, who was the quintessential expansionist. McCaughey moved on from the comparative security of large Riverina holdings to the far horizons of the Darling, becoming the first man able to claim he owned a million sheep.

McCaughey built two grand houses – country versions of the gracious homes to be found in Sydney and Melbourne – way out in this tough, inhospitable country. A 22-room house was erected at *Dunlop* in 1886, with stone quarried nearby. When fire burned the interior soon after, it was rebuilt using the same walls. *Toorale*, constructed a decade later, had 27 rooms. McCaughey lived at neither, preferring his Riverina properties as residences. The wonderful *Toorale* house was for Louisa, a favourite niece – her husband Matthew Robinson managed this and later all of McCaughey's properties.

Robinson and Tom Vincent, the *Dunlop* manager with whom Bean stayed, eventually went into partnership and bought the properties. Tom Vincent's granddaughter, Patricia Standfield, who now lives on a property at Grafton, spent her early childhood at *Dunlop* in the 1930s, when her father managed the station for his father. Although she was very young, she does recall the vastness, the horses, the Chinese market gardeners and that 'everything revolved around wool'. Tom was 'a very hard man – a very strong boss. He ran the place very efficiently.' Pat's father Val Vincent later 'told me about the historian who visited *Dunlop*. Dad gave me *On the Wool Track*. He said, "there is a bit of history in here you might like to read".'

When he was there, Bean found both a factory and a wool 'township'.

At Dunlop, about a mile up river from the homestead, stand some half a dozen large buildings. The four largest are unmistakably factory buildings, enormous grey iron sheds, which are kept humming for two months in the year with the industry of from one hundred to one hundred and fifty men. They shear the wool with the plant in one great shed; scour it with the machinery in a second shed; dry it on the green and press and pack and dump it with the machinery in a third; store it in a fourth; and, when there is water in the river, keep at least one steamer making continual trips to Bourke and back as fast as ever she can get away with her cargo. If there were a custom-house on the river bank the trade return from that one little port in a good year could not show much less than from £20,000 to £30,000.

Today, *Dunlop* is not even marked on the touring map. The vast run has been reduced to 2200 acres surrounding the old homestead and shearing shed.

In his book chronicling today's shearers, *Shearers' Motel*, Roger McDonald recalls Bean's travels in these parts. McDonald says of his fictionalised hero:

> Six months before, when he asked the owner of Gograndli Station why his NRMA road map didn't show Dunlop Station . . . when every other station in the Western Division, large and small, was marked, the cocky had an explanation: 'Isn't that the one they gave to the Abos?'

They didn't, of course. But what's left of the once-great *Dunlop* run has turned in on itself, hiding its memories from prying eyes. Bernie Murray, the present owner, doesn't encourage curious visitors. The property is definitely not on the burgeoning tourist circuit, though many people, especially the eager local historians for whom it is virgin territory, want to visit.

After toing and froing with Bernie over the telephone, Margaret and I feel our efforts are an equally lost cause. Then, as so often in the West where everyone knows everyone else, a helpful local steps in. We've reached the nearby township of Louth and are wondering what to do when our host at Louth, Robyn White, offers to make an attempt.

Even then, the phone call to *Dunlop* doesn't sound hopeful and, resigned to the idea we're unlikely to get to *Dunlop*, we go off to inspect the famous monument in Louth cemetery (of which more in a later chapter).

We're still wandering the cemetery when a vehicle hurtles up the road in a cloud of dust. It is Robyn telling us she's had a call back and we're to ring *Dunlop*. The summons comes: set out from Louth in 15 minutes. We have the feeling we've climbed our own small Everest.

While *Dunlop* is now tiny, the wider Murray family owns a string of places along this stretch of the Darling – including *Trilby*, *Idalia*, *Bellsgrove*, *Tara*, and collectively they produce a lot of the district's wool.

Bernie Murray's grandfather bought *Dunlop* in the 1930s, completing his purchase when he acquired 268,000 acres, including shearing shed and homestead, in 1937, the year Bernie was born.

The Murrays have been along the Darling since the 1860s, when Andrew Murray established the Shamrock Inn. In the era of travel by horseback, coach, buggy and on foot (later by bicycle), inns dotted the Western lands. All that remains of this watering hole, on the property *Newfoundland*, which we visit another day, are a few stumps and bottles.

Not far away, on the banks of the river, is Andrew Murray's well-marked grave. He has a spectacular water view. Matthew McCorkle's wish is 'to be buried beside

Uncle Andrew', whose grave stands apart from a family cemetery that is still used. Bernie Murray sold the last big slice of the original *Dunlop* country – the property *Delta*, on which he and his family had lived – in the 1990s, and moved into the McCaughey-built homestead, with 18-inch thick walls and spacious rooms, where his father and grandfather had lived.

The traveller to *Dunlop* must keep a careful watch to the left, driving from Louth along the gravelled road (hazardous at dusk because of kangaroos) towards Tilpa, for the name stencilled on a gate that's usually padlocked. Bernie has promised he'll unlock the gate for us, but when we arrive, it looks solidly closed. We sit in the car, waiting for him to come.

And sit, and sit. Surely, after all this, something hasn't gone wrong again? After an eternity it dawns on us to take a closer look at the padlock. It has been unlocked – and draped over again. At last we're on our way to the house.

For all his reluctance to let in strangers, Bernie is intensely proud of the *Dunlop* heritage. He tells us about Dick Smith arriving years ago in a helicopter with a team who filmed the place for a documentary.

We sit on the verandah that looks out onto a little court-yard, enjoying a beer in the hot afternoon. Bernie's hospitable, if provocative. The shotgun on the table is surely there for effect, a prop of the 'hard man'.

Bernie takes an age to roll his smoke with cigarette paper (not the *Sydney Morning Herald*!) and tobacco. Finally, after thoroughly sussing us out, he asks whether we'd like to look around the property, and we step into the past.

These days the famous big wool shed, with its 45 stands

(the last with a big 45 on it), sees only a few sheep – the neighbours sometimes shear there – although it remains in good repair. Its modern engine kicks over at once.

On one pen is scratched a date in 1897, and the letters NY – an American shearer perhaps? In and around the shed are steam engines, an ancient wool press, and wool tables from the early days. Close to the riverbank are some remains of the old scouring plant.

In 1888, *Dunlop* had the first complete clip shorn by machines – 200,000 sheep in 12 weeks. It had been a test of strength between shearers and bosses – initially, the shearers refused to use the new-fangled handpieces and set up camp across the river. This was to be one of many industrial clashes in the Bourke district, where unionism spread strongly.

McCaughey was an innovator and the previous year, *Toorale* had become the first wool shed lit by electric light.

After we go round the shed, and sit for a while on the bank of the Darling, we try to keep Bernie's vehicle in sight by its cloud of dust as he drives at high speed back to the house.

Bean described *Dunlop* as 'a great stone homestead with a pretty garden and pool in front of it', where '[e]very sort of fruit, from strawberries to bananas, grows about the house'. Bernie's cousin Pat Le Lievre, who owns a property nearby and lived at *Dunlop* in the '40s and '50s, remembers the pool from her girlhood but it is long gone. The present circular front garden has been there since before the Murrays. But Bernie speculates its palms would be a century old. The garden is full of fruit trees, including a banana tree, and vegetables. Pat (whom we meet in Canberra a while later) recalls the fruit. She, her mother and her siblings had moved there after her father left home. 'We'd come from a property further out that had bore water; you couldn't have citrus trees. It was wonderful to have fruit to pick at *Dunlop*.'

We walk through the house, which is much better preserved than most of its contemporaries in the West. We don't dare to ask if we can have a closer look, so it's a matter of glimpses here and there. It's getting late, and parts of it, including rooms that seem to retain a trace of the formality of times past, are shrouded by the failing light. Unlike most properties round here, *Dunlop* is not connected to the main electricity; it still uses a generator.

Dunlop has seen really sad times. Norah Vennell, a friend of Margaret's who lives in Wagga Wagga and is a relative of the Murray clan, has told us how her mother Noreen, diagnosed with cancer, had gone to *Dunlop* in the 1940s to live out her last days with her sister Mary. The nuns from Bourke came to give help and comfort. Even so, caring for someone terminally ill so far from help could only have been a terrifying experience.

More recently, Bernie's son Jamie was killed on the property when his motorbike hit kangaroos. He lies in the family graveyard at Newfoundland.

Across from the *Dunlop* house, past an enclosure where the ubiquitous feral goats are held and fed before they are marketed, is a large building, built of stone that, like that used for the house, was quarried on the place.

We already know this building, which is glowing wonderfully golden in the late afternoon sun. It's amazing to see it so well preserved. It was the station store, the contents of which Bean listed in meticulous detail. He catalogued nearly 150 items – and 'much more also' – ranging from calico to cartridges, castor oil to coconuts.

The building has seen no trading for many decades but it's a treasure trove of relics of the past. It's dusty and derelict. How easy to imagine, though, this busy spot when the station buzzed.

In the way that one remembers little things, Pat later recalls to us the many tins of salmon put away there; the family, who were Catholic, would often have a salmon dish on Fridays.

We follow Bernie, our way lit by a torch, careful where we put our feet. This country has carpet snakes, which are not poisonous, but it also has the more deadly variety. In the half light we can see old saddles and bridles, large boilers, cases of baking powder (Bernie, who takes quite a shine to Margaret, insists on giving her a tin of the baking powder – it now has a place of honour in my kitchen), soap by the boxful, a commode packed away in a container (which Bernie displays with special delight).

One room in the store used to be the office; its pigeon-holed cupboard is still there; letters could be posted through the slit in the door.

Dermie Murray, Bernie's cousin and Matthew McCorkle's uncle, who lives with his wife Ruth on the nearby *Bellsgrove*, remembers the *Dunlop* shearing of 1942, and the well-stocked store.

'It was very, very dry. Things were going to hell in a handcart as far as the war was concerned. Singapore had fallen. Darwin had been bombed. The Japanese could have been on Australian soil anytime. Tobacco, tea and sugar were severely rationed. For all that, the shearers went on strike because one chap was using a machine comb that was a bit wider than the others.

'There were 12 shearers, so there were 25 in the team. The Expert had a piece of cardboard tacked up with two and a half inches ruled out, and he had to put every comb on it to see it measured.

'There was quite an amount of stuff in the store. The family was able to help the shearers out. [But] after the shed cut out, the cook showed his appreciation by tipping what was left of the sugar, rice et cetera into one bag. It wasn't a happy camp. I think it was the lack of tobacco.'

The world had changed a lot in the decades since Bean's time. But 'the Boss' – as distinct from 'the boss of the board', the man in the shed who actually oversaw the shearing operation – still reigned supreme.

Pat recalls 'grandfather coming from *Bellsgrove* to *Dunlop* for the annual shearing. It was always an occasion when the Boss arrived. 'It was a little bit like royalty coming – everything was spick and span for the Boss. He'd go to the wool shed and perhaps have a sleep on a bale. But he was there.'

Dunlop will never see another 'Boss', nor indeed a 'boss of the board.' Some of the younger Murray relatives would like to buy the property one day, and open that great shed to the public. For now however, it remains one of the most private places in the West.

~ 17 ~
The T on the Gum Tree

Up river from Louth, at *Toorale*, manager Tony McManus has an early edition of *On the Wool Track* on his shelf.

His mother found it for him in a Sydney secondhand bookshop. He, like others, has searched without success for the big T that Bean, travelling past in the river-steamer *Jandra*, observed cut into one of the trees on the Darling's bank, a landing spot for picking up wool and unloading provisions for *Toorale*. As Bean wrote in *The Dreadnought of the Darling*:

> [T]he great T ... with a broken notice-board and a trench made by the sliding down of hundreds of thousands of pounds' worth of wool bales, is the only mark of the port at which the great station ships its wool – Toorale, eight miles back, depends for its water on the Warrego. Dam after dam has been thrown across the Warrego at various places up its course.

These days one of the *Toorale* dams, put there by McCaughey, is irrigating a cotton crop. Unlike *Dunlop*'s livable and still lived-in homestead, the old *Toorale* house is a disintegrating shell. Bean described this house as 'the finest homestead in all the West', and the visitor can still imagine what it was like in its glory days.

Standing in what has become a ruin, you marvel at the remnants of the luxury and grandeur of the past – and changes of circumstances.

When we're there, there's a dead snake hanging on the back verandah – a verandah so carefully constructed that each of the floorboards was moulded to fit precisely the curves of the ripple-iron wall.

Ninety years after *Toorale* was built the National Trust, following an inspection, described the house as 'a remarkable example of a large Western homestead of unpretentious appearance yet with an interior of surprisingly sophisticated details'. In the large central courtyard, which once had coloured glass ceiling panels, the jackaroos would gather in the early morning for their day's orders.

Wallpaper, with an elaborate leaves-and-fruit frieze at its top, still adorns an entertainment room. In the old times, the family occupied the front of the house; it's said no one was allowed to step beyond the courtyard, off which ran corridors of rooms, unless invited.

Close by is the modern homestead, where the McManuses live, with its functional big sitting–dining–kitchen area. Michelle McManus often cooks for the jack-and-jillaroos. Beside the house is an equally modern school building; the McManuses, with four children, have a governess, although when we're there, their eldest son is soon to go to a Sydney boarding school.

Sixty kilometres south-west of Bourke, *Toorale* now

belongs to Clyde Agriculture, a private company that is part of the British based Swire group, which proclaims its 'ethos' is 'always taking the long-term view'. Clyde has 14 pastoral properties – all but three in NSW – totalling more than 1.5 million acres, and six cotton farms. *Toorale*, one million acres in Bean's time, is now about a quarter that size.

Some years ago it had shrunk to about 70,000 acres; it has been gradually expanding again. In normal times, it shears some 35,000 Merino sheep and grazes 1500 cattle. Clyde, which has owned *Toorale* since the late 1980s, has invested heavily in a new wool shed, yards and fencing. The old homestead hasn't been so lucky, although the company tried to get heritage funding to 'mothball' it. Heritage experts estimate it would cost $1 million to restore.

As well as its livestock, *Toorale* (when the seasons are good) grows about 3000 acres of cotton, the 'new wool' of the Bourke district. The grazing and cotton sides of *Toorale* are managed separately.

Clyde is both the biggest wool producer and the largest cotton grower in these parts. And around Bourke, cotton (when weather permits its growing) has now supplanted wool as the biggest earner.

In contrast to the bigger station staff in the days when *Toorale* was a 'wool town', the property now runs its grazing operation with a staff of four – manager, overseer and two jackaroos.

Contractors come in for shearing, lamb marking and some of the mustering. The shearing contractor from Hay brings about 25 people, including up to 14 shearers – *Toorale* supplies another eight for mustering and yard work.

The sheep, which must walk from as far as 30 kilometres away, start their trek just after Christmas, for a shearing beginning the second week of January.

'We shift them a paddock a day, waterhole to waterhole. They move five kilometres a day, then have a couple of days rest,' says Tony.

His eldest boys sometimes take part in musters, which are done by plane and motorbikes. Horses have virtually disappeared from this country. The McManus boys 'can't ride a horse well – they can sit on one'.

Two sheds run simultaneously, one with eight stands and the other with six. If necessary, portable equipment can be taken to the outer paddocks if dry conditions make the walk too difficult. It can take up to a month to cut out, producing between 600 and 900 bales depending on the season. In a drought, shearing can be over in about a fortnight.

In Bean's day *Toorale* would have had up to 46 shearers, matched by a similar number of men to handle the wool. Like *Dunlop*, *Toorale* had its own scouring plant – we see the bits of equipment are still scattered about. Some of these came from *Dunlop* years ago when that place was sold.

The huge old *Toorale* shearing shed, built in the 1880s, is still standing but only just. Tony McManus drives us over to see it.

It was in this shed that Henry Lawson had a brief sojourn, picking up wool, during the few months he spent around Bourke in 1892–93.

At *Toorale*, according to an account of Lawson's Darling experiences,

[f]or the first time, Henry Lawson experienced life in the western shearing sheds with a group of toughened men

from the bush. Never before had he seen sheep shorn on such a large scale, and the experience stimulated his senses. He spent hours taking notes and jotting ideas for future writings.

Lawson apparently never picked up the blades, or one of the 46 new-fangled steam-operated machines to shear a sheep.

When we later visit Cobar, we run into Gloria Jones who, as an infant some 60 years before, lived on a *Toorale* outstation, where her father worked.

Gloria is a modern 'old timer'. A few years before she'd bought the Presbyterian church in which she had been married. She set up an arts and craft shop there, with a bed-and-breakfast in the former manse.

From her youth Gloria had remembered 'a big old house with date palms in front'. She thought it was in Bourke, where she went to live with her grandmother after her mother died. One day a woman brought a painting of the house into the shop, and told her it was *Toorale*.

'It's always been in my mind,' she tells us.

18

The Shearing at
Toorale

Sadly, *Dunlop*'s wool glory days are over forever. So I went to *Toorale* which, like *Dunlop*, has so much history and romance about it, to watch modern shearers at work in the West.

Machines had already taken over from the blades well before Bean was on the track. The mechanised shearing handpiece is one of Australia's great inventions, though it is little talked about today. It was developed by Frederick Wolseley, and widely demonstrated in the mid-1880s. *Dunlop* in 1888 had 40 Wolseley stands, and was the first large machine shed.

If Bean went into the main *Toorale* shed today, the scene would not be unfamiliar from that at *Dunlop* in 1909. The shearer is dragging his sheep from the pen, in the same way as his forefather did, and, with great rhythmic strokes – if he's good at his job – is stripping off the wool, where it lies on the board like rippling white custard for only an instant, before a young rouseabout gathers it up and carries it to the skirting table. And now, as then, 'the process of peeling, particularly with such a remorseless, irresistible implement as a shearing machine is always a fascinating process to watch'.

The modern observer will stand, as Bean did, 'dreamily spell-bound as the shiny brown forearm steered patiently over wrinkle after wrinkle, buried sometimes well over the wrist in the wool through which it ploughed . . .'

As his eyes moved from the shearers to the rest of the shed, the modern Bean would notice some changes. A small but symbolic feature in the shed might strike him first. Some of the rouseabouts are women. Once, women were more or less banned from sheds. The superstitious might have thought they brought bad luck but mainly it was a matter of the bad language and all that. This is where the phrase 'ducks on the pond' comes from – shearers used it to warn each other women were around so language should be minded. Now a lot of women, including quite a few New Zealanders, are 'rousies'. Some are wives or girlfriends of the shearers. But, even today, you'll go a long way to find a woman shearer. Their absence is not so much because of discrimination, as the extreme physical arduousness of the work.

The observant Bean would also quickly note that a lot fewer shearers are at work in the modern shed. A dozen stands is a big shed today; 50 stands were not uncommon in the back country then. He would understand immediately why most shearers in today's shed are wearing harnesses, and perhaps wonder why it took so long to invent it. 'When the men bent down over each new sheep,' Bean wrote, 'you could almost hear their backs creaking, cre-ee-eaking like doors on rusty hinges.'

When morning 'smoko' arrives, and the shearers and

rouseabouts tuck into the cook's fare, Bean would be thoroughly familiar with the routine.

Bean brought to his descriptions of the shearers the same romantic view he had of the wool industry generally. He also understood that shearing and shearers encapsulated many of the struggles and cross currents in Australia at the start of the 20th century.

To describe the process, he wrote,

> is to give no conception of shearing – which is a long diplomatic relation between strong men, a mixture of genial autocracy, red republic, cross-currents, undercurrents, deep arguments, deeper silences, tact, pitched battles, real friendship, frank hostility. To describe a shearing shed as a place where they shear is the poorest description in the world.

On the Wool Track gives a graphic picture of the troupe of shearers who moved in waves around the sheds a century ago, on their ubiquitous bicycles.

> Have you ever seen the galahs eating across the face of a paddock, lined out like a fan, grubbing as busy as bees, the birds on the flank that is eaten out always flopping across and tacking themselves on to the flank which is entering new country? That is the way, each year from July to November, the shearers come across New South Wales. And the sign of them in these days is their bicycles.
>
> It is true some still come on the horses, some in sulkies, some on foot. But of late years the bicycle has

spread through the country as fast as the rabbit . . .
The shearer sets out on these trips exactly as if he
were going from Sydney to Parramatta. He asks the
way, lights his pipe, puts his leg over his bicycle, and
shoves off . . . If he is city-bred, like many shearers,
the chances are he starts in a black coat and bowler
hat, exactly as if he were going to tea at his aunt's.

Many in today's industry are what are called 'suburban
shearers' – in the 'inner' country they commute daily to the
job. This has been made possible by good roads – although,
paradoxically, they can make for more travel.

'The big trend has been away from shearers' contract
teams living in shearers' quarters and staying on properties,' says Duncan Fraser whom Margaret and I meet on
his property near Hay. It has advantages all round – for
the shearers and for the property owners – when shearers
can work within a day's travel of their homes in country
towns.

Shearers routinely used to have to spend most of the year
away; those willing (or having) to put up with this life were
often the more footloose types. And, especially in the days
when the union was strong, even smaller properties were
forced to spend quite a lot of money keeping up shearers'
quarters which were in use for only a few weeks each year.
These days too, shearers often are multi-skilled, spending
some of the year in other jobs. Farmers' sons pick up extra
dollars shearing; some men drive grain headers in the
summer and shear in winter; a shearer might double off-
peak as a roo shooter. Out in the Western Division however,
the stations are too remote for the 'suburban shearer' to

return home at night. The teams here still come on an expedition rather than an excursion.

Toorale uses a contractor from Hay, Andrew Morrison, and I arrange to travel the 600 kilometres with him. Bean noted that the contract system was increasingly in vogue. The advantages were much the same as now. 'Instead of a squatter having the trouble to engage shearers and manage them, there were certain contractors who would do the whole work for him – paying rouseabouts and all the rest – at so much per sheep.' Yet some grudged the money: '[S]ome big Western stations, which for a time had employed contractors, were again shearing for themselves in order to save the contractors' profit,' Bean wrote.

As everyone familiar with big shearing operations knows, food – plentiful and well-cooked – is at the heart of things. Andrew piles huge quantities of supplies into a trailer van before we set out from his Hay home.

Wife Kaye estimates these will last a week. Seventy loaves of bread, 60 kilos of potatoes, 40 kilos of sugar, 300 eggs, a box of lettuces, and that's just the start. 'The way we work it out,' says Kaye, is 'a round and a half [of sandwiches] per person per sitting, and there are ten sandwiches in a loaf. Two smokos a day equals three full sandwiches.'

Kaye used to cook for years in shearing teams, though she insists she doesn't like cooking 'at the best of times'. What the shearers eat varies according to who's in the team but mostly with the weather. *Toorale* will be hot, and a lot of fruit goes up.

Kaye stays at home but three Morrison children pile into the back of the four-wheel drive. The eldest, Ryan, a university student, is to be one of the rouseabouts in the shed.

Young Hannah has travelled with her father whenever possible since she got out of nappies. Andrew, who started shearing at 16, has been a contractor for 15 years; he sold his business to a shearing services company several years ago. In 2002, his part of the company business made him the biggest Western Division contractor, with his team shearing about 600,000 annually and crutching 400,000. For the Morrisons it's been a family enterprise; Andrew's father started the business. Andrew gives the impression contracting is a pretty difficult job.

Only about 5 per cent of his men are union members; 'a decade ago it would probably have been 5 per cent that weren't'. Good shearers, he says, can earn $60,000–$70,000 a year; for this, they need to be able to shear around 200 a day. But these are the top of the range. When a union shearer hears this figure, he says tartly, 'If a shearer is earning $50–$70,000, then the award is being breached by seven-day work and even so, this is not the typical yearly salary but an exaggeration upwards.'

We set out north just before 4 pm on Saturday; in the hours that follow, Andrew is constantly on the mobile, talking to his men, teeing up transport for some of them. Things have come a long way since Bean's wonderful description of the bicycle that 'looked like an overloaded towel-horse' laden with billy, pannikin, water-bag and other necessities. But transport seems one of those perennial problems, with shearers sometimes needing a ride or a shed team often short because of cars breaking down. Most of our journey is on sealed roads but closer to Louth the road is dirt.

We roll up to the shearers' quarters just after midnight.

The *Toorale* homestead is in darkness, and Andrew obviously has no intention of disturbing the McManuses. I spend my first night in the quarters, where there are two beds to a room, thin foam mattresses, a bright light, and an overhead fan. It's basic. As Andrew tosses me some thin sheeting, I feel a mild surge of gratitude to the union which fought for the conditions in shearers' quarters.

A few years before Bean's journey the *Shearers' Accommodation Act, 1901* was passed, setting out the sleeping and eating conditions for sheds where six or more shearers where employed. Accommodation buildings had to be separate from the shearing shed, and at least 50 yards from it. Sleeping quarters couldn't be used for cooking or serving meals. The Act went into considerable detail: sleeping and dining rooms had to have sufficient light, flooring had to be of approved material, and 'proper cooking and washing vessels' provided.

The shearers had to keep the quarters clean, and not do any damage, or they'd lose wages or could be sued. In the early 1900s, racism was legislated in the pastoral industry; where 'persons of any Asiatic race' were in the shearing team, separate sleeping and dining facilities had to be provided for them.

Andrew and the kids unload, and go off to a nearby cottage. Most of the gang haven't arrived yet. I find my way in the dark to the shower and toilet block, wondering about snakes. When I get up in the morning the huts' area seems deserted and I walk over to the homestead.

On this Sunday morning at *Toorale*, a neighbour, Doug, is helping Tony McManus and the jack-and-jillaroos (these on motorbikes) to muster the sheep. The Western musterers of a century ago wouldn't recognise the modern sound of the bikes, but the plaintive voice of the flock hasn't changed since the days when there were just men, horses and sheep. Author Katharine Susannah Prichard, writing in 1906, gives a wonderful description of the sound of sheep being brought in for shearing.

> The cry of a moving flock in the distance is like the sound of a multitude in distress, some throng of people voicing their wrongs and wretchedness, serfs praying for freedom and mercy, sorely pressed by grief and anguish.

At *Toorale* this 2001 season is poor (the next will be much worse) and with the drought some of the sheep are debilitated to the point of collapse, unable to move or unwilling to do so (the musterers call the latter 'sulkers'). These are tossed into the back of a ute. A few, the worst victims of heat and weakness, die before they get to the shed. No doubt it was always thus. Yet you can't help wondering whether the rhythm of nature has not been disturbed. When animals were moved by men on horses rather than on bikes or in utes, things were more in sync. The horses and their riders knocked up only marginally less than their charges. However you increase the technology, the sheep and the cow can only walk as fast as they ever did.

By Monday morning, everyone's in place: sheep, shearers, cook. Andrew is in top gear, here, there and everywhere.

In the main of the two sheds, Andrew is the modern version of the old 'boss of the board', running around, eyes and mind on all aspects of the operation. Everyone in the shed is moving fast, especially the rouseabouts, as they pick up the wool, 'skirt' it to remove the daggy pieces, take it to the various bins (one each for fleeces, bellies, locks), and sweep the 'board'.

Horses have found their place usurped but there's still full employment for dogs. One shearer has his tied up beside him; others wander at will, ready to push the sheep up into the pens from which the shearers grab them. A tiny pup (a Christmas present) is tethered on the side, asleep.

Only seven shearers are working in the main shed; one hasn't turned up (at the second shed that day, two of the expected six shearers are missing – they've had car trouble). Four of seven are using back supports.

Fans whirr, but the day is relatively cool after an overnight thunderstorm (often the temperature is in the 40s at shearing time). Properties in the district are in desperate need of rain. The night before, when the downpour came during a children's party at Louth, the kids danced in the rain, soaked to the skin. Alas, the storm was only a tease.

Morning smoko arrives, Andrew the delivery man. Pizzas, toasted sandwiches, cordial, tea, coffee, bacon slices. The cook is already receiving compliments. The whole shed suddenly falls silent. Some eat while squatting on the 'board'. The dogs get scraps; the tiny pup is given its freedom.

There are female rousies in the team. John, the wool classer from western Victoria, tells me the girls make better rouseabouts; they're 'more particular', while male rousies want to be shearers or something else. Kiwi girls are thought especially good; they're bred to the sheds. Later in the day, a friendly New Zealander girl hands me a broom. I sweep along with them, but I'm thankful she hadn't thought of it earlier. You have to be quick and it's better to be fit.

I'm also told that rousies, who sometimes come from the local dole queue, can be flighty. The year before at *Toorale*, a couple of boys packed their gear and disappeared into the night at 3 am.

Back at the shearers' quarters Marg the cook, with always an eye on the time, is flat out – and panicking. Already she's exhausted her supply of 30 tins of canned fruit. Seven tins have gone into jelly alone.

Like the shed, the kitchen is driven by the clock. Marg needs to have lunch packed when Andrew arrives to take it to the second, more distant shed (those in the main shed will drive over to the quarters' dining room for theirs).

Marg, who's from Hay, has only been cooking a few months, mostly for Andrew's shearers. Before that this mother of six drove her own taxi, but there was no money in it. Her 'cook's offsider' is husband Dave; eight-year-old grandchild Dean is along for the ride. Marg and Dave plan to dash away the coming Saturday to see another, newly born, grandchild; they'll leave after tea and be back, after a round trip of hundreds of kilometres, in time for Sunday tea. 'Otherwise it might be three months before we see our little grandson,' Marg says.

In the modern outback shearing operation, a good flow of quality food, plentiful and on time, is as important as in Bean's day. It's more catch-as-catch-can with 'suburban' shearing, where the men may bring their own packed lunch.

A bad cook today won't get another gig. Still, the cook's fortunes aren't quite as hazardous as when they had to win a ballot. 'Their names are put up at the meeting – men tell what they know of the reputation of each,' writes Bean. 'A vote is taken, and after it one cook settles down to earn anything up to £5 a week, for a couple of months. The others pack disconsolately, and wander round the country on a precarious hunt for another shed.'

If the shearers were picky, a bit of bluff could sometimes work. Shearers Bean met told of one brawny cook who went on the front foot from the start.

> At the first dinner he marched into the hut with his sleeves rolled up and the knots on his arms well displayed, and planted the dinner decisively on the table.
>
> There's your tucker, gentlemen,' he said. 'You can have a piece of that or you can have a piece of the cook.'
>
> He folded his arms and waited. It was the tucker they choose.

Now, as then, the routine is as gruelling. Marg and Dave are up each day at 4 am; they get to bed around 8.30 or 9 pm. In between it's non-stop. The quarters has a kitchen, separate eating area, three fridges (one not working, one for the 'boys' beer'), and a freezer. 'It's quite a good kitchen – a lot of bench space. One of the better set ups. The air conditioning is a great bonus. Normally we don't have air conditioning and fans.'

The big cool room is also 'a luxury', but there's no dishwasher. 'I've never ever come across a dishwasher,' says Marg. 'Only me,' Dave interjects. Marg carries her own pots and pans and other utensils. 'We're running short of knives and forks out here. Not often you cook for so many – usually 20 is the limit. I haven't been bringing knives and forks, but I think I might have to go to a $2 shop and get some.'

Shearers are fussy when it comes to their food, Marg says, 'some more so than others'. A recent lot were particular, but Andrew has told her these ones aren't. 'We'll have to wait and see,' she says, but she's never had a complaint yet. Nor will she, if the test is variety and quantity.

On the breakfast table each morning are sausages, bacon, chops, eggs (she varies daily how these are done), spaghetti and tomatoes. Lunch is mainly meat and salad. 'I cook a couple of legs of cold meat each day for lunch. Each night of the week, there is something different: apricot chicken, a roast, cutlets, spaghetti bolognese if they have a mincer on the place. This place has one – they don't usually.' She plans to buy her own, which she says will cost her $800–$1000.

Like the cooks, the shearers travel with their own equipment, and it's not cheap. Jim White, from Cobar, working in the second *Toorale* shed, estimates it costs $2000. A survey by the Australian Workers Union found that typically a shearer spent about $2750 a year on tools. Two handpieces total $1100; combs are $38 and Jim says you need 16 of them, 80 cutters are $5.70 each. Usually Jim will need eight combs a day and 20 cutters (which are sharpened or 'ground' during the day), but here it's more – 16 combs and more than 80 cutters – because the sheep's wool is full of black soil.

Roger McDonald is the modern Charles Bean in his vivid portrait of today's shearing team, although his descriptions are particularly of Maori workers. Much of his story is set in the Western Division, and his main character is 'Cookie', who is only too aware, on his first job, at 'Leopardwood Downs homestead to the far northwest of Bourke' that if 'the shearing team didn't like him they could sack him'.

Much has changed in a century, but McDonald's description of today's shed would resonate with Bean as much as it would with Andrew Morrison:

> A shearing shed was a special kind of factory. It stood idle, empty, most of the year, cloaked in mysterious ruin . . . Like any factory the working shed had a clock, a pattern of work-flow, individual and team production targets. It was an assembly line functioning by deleting the raw material . . . There was a simple formula in the shed: keep the wool moving. Everyone knew it – shearers, classer, rouseabouts, presser, the owner and his helpers. The cook as well. The forces at work on the shearing team were as deceptively smooth as the forces operating on a pool table. Nudge one ball and another reacted.

— 19 —
Modern Bards Celebrate
an Old Romance

We first hear about the village of Louth when we are making inquiries about *Dunlop*. It is only when we get there, however, that we understand how special is this little place that has fewer than 40 permanent residents. Anyone who wants to experience the Darling country must go to Louth. It has a monument that's a technological marvel and an annual race meeting attracting thousands which is a must in the area's social calendar. And it has been immortalised in Australian literature by Henry Lawson.

Margaret and I go there on our way to *Dunlop*, and I'm back there a couple of times afterwards. One of them is a special trip just for race day. The stories about the Louth races have proved irresistible, and the event doesn't disappoint.

When Bean sailed past Louth on his way to *Dunlop*, the town had already caught the attention of Lawson, who wrote a witty piece called 'Louth, on the Darling'. Lawson writes that he didn't get to the place, despite rouseabouting at nearby *Toorale*. But he could imagine it, 'especially on a Sunday afternoon' with a primitive steamboat, the 'usual pub' with warped and cracked weatherboards, 'and half-a-dozen men standing at the end, by the uncertain chimney, playing pitch-and-toss, and one or two others sitting on their heels against the wall and spitting in semi-circles . . .' In Lawson's mind, the men would be 'dry-rotted' like most else about the place.

Louth was already past its prime when Bean described it.

> We saw two hotels in Louth. Besides those there were a post-office, a school, a police station, a store, about a dozen pigs, 150 goats, and a blacks' camp. It is not a town which moves very fast. They say that a Sydney man walked down the street at Louth and was arrested by the policeman for riotous behaviour.

Since then Louth, like many places in the West, has shrunk. Today, Shindy's Inn has a monopoly, and the McCorkles' wedding was the first the little local church had seen in many a year. The impressive old post office that Bean observed is today a B&B. It has been restored by Robyn White and her stockman husband David. Robyn, who's originally from Adelaide, has been a woolclasser and stock-woman. Now, with her elegant old building, she's a decorator and an inviting host.

Margaret and I become, by chance, the first guests at Robyn's B&B. We've been told she's starting it so, after what passes for a picnic lunch under the bridge spanning the Darling, we walk across the road to book into our accommodation. Robyn looks a bit surprised when two women clutching dirty plates appear on her doorstep. The B&B is actually still a few weeks off opening for business. But she takes us in anyway. When we come to leave in the morning, she absolutely refuses to accept any payment. After all, she says, she hasn't set up business yet!

Those who live in town mostly have jobs on, or own, properties out of town, or are retired. The town empties as the Louth workforce gets off to an early start in the mornings.

Louth is officially a 'village', one of half a dozen around this area, and it has all the spirit of intimacy that term suggests. Being a villager means keeping an eye out for those around you, and behaving in a neighbourly fashion. Wally Mitchell, who has property out of Louth but lives in town, says that if anybody goes to Cobar they'll come back with ten copies of the Sydney papers and distribute them, without expecting any payment for them.

What's unique about Louth is its extraordinary Celtic cross in the cemetery. The story of the monument is a metaphor for the hardness of this country, and the endurance and ingenuity of its people. It is also a romantic story of the Irish spirit that remains strong around this part of the Darling.

Louth was founded by Thomas Andrew Mathews, and named after the Irish county in which he was born. When he came to Australia, spurred by gold fever, Mathews left behind his wife, Mary Devine; it was five years before he was reunited with her and their children. After living in Bourke, they settled at Louth, where Mathews created the town, which quickly became a port for the river steamers and gained him the title 'King of Louth'. Mary ran the public house Mathews built, called the Dan O'Connell. In 1868, when she was only 42, Mary died.

Mathews ordered from a Bendigo sculptor a giant pillar

and cross to commemorate Mary. The structure, built of granite mined at Phillip Island off Victoria, was brought up the Darling by the riverboat *Jane Eliza*. But the boat got stuck in a low river at Tilpa, where it remained for two years. Mathews had the monument carted overland by dray. When it arrived at last, extremely late, Mathews' third wife is said to have hosted the celebration.

The cross, on top of a 7.6 metre pillar, reflects the setting sun, so that it becomes a ball of fire, and shines onto various parts of the village, according to the season. On the August 15th anniversary of Mary's death, its reflection beams directly onto where she lived.

So precise and intriguing is the monument's positioning that a few years ago a student from the surveying department at Melbourne University did a detailed study of it, producing a paper full of the most complex calculations. The question he pondered was: who'd have had the expertise to place the monument so that the minerals in the granite would shine on exactly the right spot to mark the day of Mary's death?

One explanation is that a surveyor may have set up the orientation of the cross before the sculptor – who came from Bendigo for the occasion – erected it. Or perhaps the ingenuity of a river captain is the answer. As the researcher writes, with so many boats stopping each year at Louth, 'any one of the captains of these boats would have had the expertise and knowledge to perform the necessary measurements and calculations'.

This 'monument fit for a queen / The most impressive headstone seen / In the river country and all surrounds' has inspired a CD of song and poetry, *Fire Stone*, by Bourke's bard, Andrew Hull and singer Tonchi McIntosh. It gives Mary Devine and Louth a deserved place in Australian folk legend.

The lyrics and verse tell a tale of love and struggle, and of a man who felt he must eschew emotion but who left a tribute to his partner that was built to defy the passing years. In the songs Mary Devine, a pioneer from the 19th century, comes to life for us in the 21st century.

Andrew, the songwriter–poet and Tonchi, a singer who is also a songwriter, have an ambitious dream. They're trying to bring the bush tradition up to date, and especially, to collect and tell the stories from around the river. They've called their project 'River Road'.

Andrew, whose family has been in Bourke for several generations, works as a contractor who levels ground for irrigation. His second life is writing and painting. His comfortable Bourke home is filled with his art work and he has a studio–workshop in a room down in the back garden, complete with computer, paints, sound equipment and a few bottles of wine, presumably to help the creative spirit. When politicians come to Bourke, Andrew gets an opportunity to write some rough verse and deliver his lines at community functions. He's composed verses about, and recited them to, John Howard and Simon Crean. It's his writing about the river and the land, however, that sends a wider message.

'I just fell into the poetry. I want to contemporise our region, instead of it always being remembered through Lawson and Ogilvie,' he says. 'Lawson's writing is fantastic, but I just wonder about the relevance of us raving on about a hundred years ago. The ballad will become fixed in the 19th century if we don't make contemporary stories about contemporary people.'

When I catch up with Andrew in Bourke he gives me one of his cards, 'Andrew Hull: Renaissance Man'. Well, yes, they were a bit of a joke, he says. Maybe not a 'renaissance man', but it's not so fanciful to see Andrew as a modern-day cast of the scribbling bushmen of a century ago who contributed to that bible of the outback, the *Bulletin*.

Tonchi, who divides his time between Melbourne and Bourke, is of Aztec Indian descent on his Mexican mother's side; there is Irish in the family on his father's. He was brought up near Bourke, imbibing early from his father's bookshelves the old bush ballads, and he has a strong feel for the country. 'My favourite place in the world is this huge big plain outside of Bourke,' he told one interviewer. 'It is about 30 kilometres across with not a single tree on it. I like to . . . lie on my back and totally relax in the vast expanse. At night time I like to look up to see the whole sky . . . I can just let my soul go.'

Tonchi tells me part of him wishes he'd been born a hundred years ago when all the things the great writers wove into their yarns were happening. 'And then I realise they're happening now.'

Hearing tales of the area put to song inevitably starts those in the audience remembering stories they know personally or have heard told. After Tonchi and Andrew perform the Louth songs at the Port of Bourke Hotel one Sunday, a man comes up with a modern tale – well, half a century or so old – that might find its way into their music one day.

A shearer had set out for the season, leaving behind his

pregnant wife. A while on, the man was stranded and delayed by floodwaters. A note eventually arrived for him with the supplies, saying he had a baby daughter but his wife had died in childbirth. Grief-stricken, the man headed off on the long sad journey home, camping for seven nights before he reached his destination. When he finally made it, despair turned to relief and joy when he found both daughter and mother were alive and robust. It's a story that captures how uncertain life can be in the back country.

—

Come one weekend in August, between three and four thousand visitors flock to Louth. Light planes line up like an aerial flotilla on the strip, and at night time the race course becomes a sea of tents. The Louth races – which in 2003 won an award for excellence – are worth a very long trip to get to them. Margaret isn't coming this time, and I wrestle with how to travel from Canberra without making the excursion several days long. Eventually I hitch a ride from Sydney on one of the planes that Clyde Agriculture has chartered for visitors they're taking. At the Port of Bourke Hotel it's a long and noisy night, as some of the younger race-going crowd get down to serious pre-meeting celebrations.

Next morning I meet up with Sally Bryant, journalist on Bourke's *Western Herald* and one of the extended Murray family. I'd met Sally on our first trip to Bourke, when she'd appeared to interview *me* about what I was doing there.

After a coffee at the local bakery we set off for Louth. Sally's a woman of the West; her family had a property between Louth and Wanaaring. She's also a woman of the world. In other lives she looked after the Sydney house and dogs of the late David McNicoll, well-known journalist on the *Bulletin*, and she was a groom for Prince Charles's polo horses, a job from which she has good memories and plenty of stories. It was 'magic', she says, exercising young horses around the grounds of Windsor Park in the snow. Not so magic, perhaps, when one of three horses she was taking back to a field got away; Sally turned round to see the Queen, surrounded by corgis, watching her predicament.

After she returned to Australia Sally lived in Sydney, but became homesick for the outback. A job came up on the local paper, and here she is, five years on and in her early 40s, reporting and photographing everything and everybody – and today, the Louth races.

Being a local reporter out here has its own rules. Small-town journalism is a very different kettle of fish from the trade as practised in the capitals, where the journalists are well separated from their subjects. Here the journalist is a part of the local community, and possibly related to a significant slice of it.

'You know which stories you can write about and which you can't,' Sally tells me as we fly along the unsealed road. 'A lot of the tenets of journalism you can't apply. Some stories you can't touch.' The paper reports crime, but doesn't 'splash' with it on page one. 'We are not there to make money out of someone's misery.' And it doesn't run endless stories about the drought, because after all, 'people know about it. What's the point?'. All this is just how things are; Sally was annoyed when a while back a TV reporter from the city claimed the local media wouldn't tell the hard stories.

'In a place like Sydney people don't know who your parents are. In a little town like Bourke people have very long memories. I have this dream of writing a book – but I'd have to go and live somewhere else.' (When we talk Sally is already a bit restless for new challenges – a few months later she changes jobs, becoming a local 'community facilitator' which means trying to get a better deal from government for Bourke and making sure programs are the right ones for the area.)

As we near the race course Sally assures me, 'I'm related to most of the gate – they'll trust you.' She'd already warned me the dressing is 'Ascot at Louth'. It might be the backblocks but many of the women are in elaborate finery, ready to greet friends they mightn't have seen since last year. Others are in very casual country gear. Here are multiple communities in one, bound together by the outback and the occasion. There's a tent and formal lunch put on by Clyde Agriculture. In another part of the course several veterans of the bitter wide comb shearers' dispute, and later internecine union politics are cooking up their meat over a fire. As I roam the betting ring, where punters are laying wagers on the big smoke races as well as the local field, one of the men recognises me from an earlier encounter, and takes me over to his mates. Among them is John Morgan, secretary of the Shearers Union, which broke away from the Australian Workers' Union. Sitting on camp chairs around the fire, they relive the dramas when the AWU used to chase them out of the sheds.

Later, enjoying a drink at one of the outside tables, covered with a neat white cloth, which looks over the course where the last race will soon start, I fall into conversation with

Heather Dalgety, who is the doctor on duty at the course for the day. She reminds me we'd met a few years before when I travelled through Bourke with John Howard; at that time, Heather was agitating on behalf of country doctors.

A Scot who trained at Aberdeen, Heather came to Australia 13 years ago on a 12 months' working holiday, and stayed. The Britisher fell in love with the Australian bush. 'It's very exotic . . . red dust, gum trees, the sky goes on forever. And people are very honest, open.'

Her outback sojourn started with a few years at Walgett, then she moved to Bourke to be her own boss. It took a while to be accepted by local colleagues. There are several doctors in Bourke and these days a good roster system; nevertheless the doctor's life is hard out here, and 'you can't sell a practice for love or money.' She loves the peace and quiet of the outback life, where 'you are embraced by a small community'. The flip-side is that when you're in a high-profile job 'you live your life in a goldfish bowl.'

Her partner Paul is a local, so Heather is firmly ensconsed in the community. But one day, they will face the big decision about education for their young son. 'We'll probably be here until our boy goes to high school. Then you face the choice of staying here or going to somewhere like Dubbo or Mudgee.' But not to the bustle of the city, she insists.

I hitch a ride back to Bourke with Heather and Paul. We leave after the last race, which is when Heather's official course duties finish. The barbecue and music will start later on.

It's set to be a big night in Louth, and, from reports of the shenanigans of previous years, not quite as genteel as the day.

Henry Lawson would have approved. 'Our attention was first directed to Louth by a letter to the *Out Back Advocate* . . .' he wrote. Condemning the goings-on in the village, the letter-writer reported 'the sounds of a fiddel and the scufling of feat dancing from one of the howses and, what is more a comeic song'.

Lawson's sympathy, he had to confess, was 'inclined towards the wrong parties'.

> They could find a ray of pleasure, then, even there;
> when the drought and rabbits were ruining all the land,
> and when the Unionists sadly shouldered their swags and
> tramped away, penniless and hungry, from the hopeless,
> one-sided fight they lost.

— 20 —
Sale of a Bride

Visitors to the Bourke cemetery can see an old tin hut that once served as a mosque for the local Afghans, the camel drivers and traders that were so vital to the inland. The hut, moved a few years ago for safe-keeping and now in the small but prominently marked Muslim section, faces Mecca, with several marked and more unmarked graves of Afghans nearby. The corrugated iron mosque came from the garden of the Perooz family. We'll come back to their story.

Camels and their Afghan cameleers were still indispensable wheels of the West in the early 1900s, bringing supplies and modest luxuries to towns and stations and transporting loads of wool from them. On the road near White Cliffs Bean came upon 'a long string of camels, tied nose and tail, with two bales of soft goods or groceries on each, one on either side of the hump, and a slender willowy Afghan all gentle curves and blue holland walking patiently at their head.'

The remote outback depended on their services, but racism and the pressure of competition bred White resentment of the 'Afghans' – a term which covered cameleers generally, not just people from Afghanistan but those from the adjacent area of India (most of which is now Pakistan). The camels upset horses, which led to incidents. Sometimes at the Bourke railway yards the cameleers were attacked by the teamsters. The bullockies who lost out to a tougher transport team were bitter about those who threatened their livelihood.

Bean was a man of his times. So we find him writing that

> . . . one cannot help feeling a great weakness for the bullocky. He is the man of our own race, and with all his roughness often a very simple and lovable one. He served this country first, and served it well, and it was not his fault if the camel beat him.

During his time in Broken Hill, Bean and a companion went for a stroll to the big camel camp. The modern reader shudders at his language; he was 'anxious to inspect the benighted heathen in their own hovels – and perhaps get a photograph or two both of the camels and the drivers'.

But a 'tall dignified man, with strong military features cast like a Crimean veteran's' told him not to photograph the cameleers. Instead he took Bean for a camel ride where the young journalist got 'the Afghan side of the question'.

'Afghan think honour and re'gion above everything,' the man explained.

'Dear me – what a very unprogressive nation!' thought the Sydney passenger.'

Camel camps were on the outskirts of Western towns and, Bean records, the police used the rivalry between different 'castes' in the camps to help them trace prohibited Asian immigrants.

Sale of a Bride

While he shared his era's pride in the white man, Bean had a gentle dig at his own countrymen's double standards.

> 'Curious beggars, aren't they?' said a railway official to the Sydney passenger, who was anxious for information. 'Rum idea that about "caste". We can't exactly understand 'em. One man won't have anything to do with another because he reckons he lowers himself. It seems foolishness, doesn't it? – but there's some very decent fellows amongst them, too . . .'
>
> 'Do white women ever marry them?' asked the Sydney passenger.
>
> 'Well – not many,' was the answer. 'They'd sort of lose caste with other white people, you know.'

On our travels a century later we hear the story of a white woman who did marry a cameleer. When we try to find families around Bourke who trace their ancestry back to the Afghans, leads keep petering out. We are told many had intermarried with the Aborigines. People suggest names, but our inquiries usually come to nothing. Then we are told the story of Myrtle Barnes, who in 2003 was well over 100 and in a nursing home in Cobar (unfortunately not well enough to talk to us).

As a 13-year-old girl, Myrtle Dee had been sold for the equivalent of $20 to an Afghan called Morbine Perooz, then in his early 30s, from Bourke. According to Myrtle, who taped some oral history, her mother arranged the marriage, against the girl's wishes. Her mother also put her age up to 15.

The pair were married in Nyngan when Myrtle was 14 and Morbine in his 30s and for half a century Myrtle found herself living between two cultures – symbolised, perhaps, by the name of her only child. He was called Juma, reflecting his father's heritage, but he was known as Jim, an adaptation to local conditions.

It must have been hard for the child mother. MP John Cobb gave me a flavour of the dual pull when he paid tribute to Myrtle in federal parliament just before her 105th birthday in February 2004. 'Morbine took their son to the Afghan mosque at three days of age. Even then Myrtle displayed her strength of character and strong will when she subsequently took her son to the local Presbyterian church and had him christened . . .'

In his 80s, Jim wrote a few pages about his parents. Morbine, born in what's now Pakistan, had served in the British army before he came to Australia in search of his brother, who was working on the cane fields in north Queensland. Myrtle's father was an Englishman, 'a black sheep of his "noble" family sent out from England on a remittance,' who had a general store in Tilpa.

Morbine had a transport business in Bourke, training teams of camels to pull wagons and Myrtle and Jim sometimes went along on the trips.

After motor vehicles took over in the 1920s, Morbine sold his remaining camels. The Peroozes had a fruit and vegetable garden; later he built a small store. Morbine died in the mid-1960s, in his 80s; Myrtle continued running the store for years, and remarried. (Her second husband was European.)

In 1990, a writer for the *Australian Geographic* encountered Myrtle in Bourke; she 'still wears her hair in a plait down her back, the way her Afghan husband liked it'. The *Geographic* writer saw the mosque standing like 'some oriental garden shed' in the Peroozes' house in Hope Street.

Morbine's granddaughter Marilyn lives on the NSW central coast and teaches music. She remembers her grandfather was quite religious, very quiet, with a penchant for lamb curry. When Morbine stayed at his son Jim's home (Marilyn's father), 'he complained that my mum, Jean Perooz, didn't make the curry hot enough. One night Mum put in extra curry powder, Dad sneaked in extra curry and then Morbine came through the kitchen and added even more curry powder. In the end the curry was too hot even for Morbine's taste but he ate it with great difficulty because of "honour". Dad couldn't eat it and I just howled and refused to even try.' Marilyn also remembers Morbine and his friend Adjune having 'hours of conversation in Pakistani about the politics of Pakistan and India of the 1950s – Nehru [first prime minister of independent India] and Jinnah [founder of Pakistan]'.

Like so many later migrants, Morbine wanted his son to have opportunities. 'As hard as his life was, he was adamant my dad had the best education,' Marilyn says. Her father became an expert in radio and set up a station which broadcast in the 1930s from his parents' home. A history of Australia's cameleers records that 'Juma's voice and the strains of a Caruso or some local Bourke talent brought pleasure and welcome company to many lonely stations and tiny outposts.'

War's coming meant the end of the private station, and Juma joined the Australian airforce, serving overseas.

The cameleers have gone and their descendents do not form any distinct community. They have blended away into the white and Aboriginal communities. But the hardy camel survives and, in some cases, adapts. The modern camel has joined the tourist trade, and even the film industry.

Along the road from Broken Hill to Silverton we drop in at the Silverton Camel Farm. It's a bitterly cold day, and a few camels are sitting stoically in their yards, waiting for business that today may not come.

The owner is away but Billy, who works there as a casual, introduces us to Johnny Cake and Paddy who, he says, worked on the movie *Burke and Wills*.

The camel farm's animals have come from the Northern Territory, where wild camels are rounded up by the station owners. You can buy a promising young camel for about $500–$550, and he will take about a year to train.

Billy assures us it's just like educating a horse. People often give camels poor character references but Billy will have none of it. 'I've been on horses most of my life. Camels are a lot better than horses – a lot easier to get along with.' They're gentle and not bad tempered, he says, and if you go about the training the right way they won't buck.

Every evening these get let out into a 15,000-acre paddock; each morning a motorbike is used to round up a few, who come in and wait for the customers. Compared to the old days, it's light work for a camel.

— 21 —
A Garden in Need of Watering

Anthony Pease designs houses for the suburbs of Melbourne. They are environmentally friendly and mostly built of mud brick. He'll have three on the go at a time.

Not very unusual – except that Anthony works from his home on the banks of the Darling at Wilcannia.

His old house, built around the 1870s out of the local sandstone, has a spectacular water view down to the bridge. In the days of the paddle-boats it would have been like living on a busy street. Now, there is just the flowing and slowing of the river to watch.

Passing through (twice, according to his expenses) on his 1908 journey, Bean found Wilcannia 'a pretty town, thanks to the heavy pepper trees that grow in avenues along its streets'. It was, he said, 'probably the chief coaching centre in New South Wales'. From here the mail coaches fanned out in many directions through the back country of the state and into Queensland. He discovered an incredibly busy little post office; each week it dealt with 67 mail bags coming in and going out, as well as private bags and about 250 parcels.

The traveller who arrives in Wilcannia today – often ignoring well-meaning but misguided warnings not to stop there – is confronted with a sluggish town that sends conflicting messages.

Big elegant buildings in streets still attest to a proud past, when it drew wealth and hope from pastoral and mining riches. But what is today an overwhelmingly Aboriginal town is run-down and listless. There are few shops. In 2003 we find what was a sizeable general store on our first visit is now just a burned shell. The craft centre closed ages ago. Even the pepper trees are sparse, many of the old ones killed by termites.

The first time we were in Wilcannia, we knocked on Anthony's door 'on spec'. We were looking for his friend, Karin Donaldson, a potter and painter who has her studio nearby. Karin was away, but Anthony took us to her place. We came away having bought some of her pieces, which capture wonderfully the contours of the land. Then Anthony gave us morning tea on his front lawn.

When we pass through Wilcannia on a later trip to Broken Hill, we decide to find out more of these two city-siders who've adopted the town, and in turn have been adopted by a place that, on first blush, isn't an easy spot in which to live.

As soon as we appear, Anthony remembers us. Never mind that he and Karin have just farewelled Sunday lunch guests and that the day is rapidly headed towards evening. He just asks, in his hospitable way, as though he'd been expecting our visit, 'Will I put on the kettle?'

The kettle is a billy, boiled outside. The kitchen sink is on the edge of the back verandah. Not even a window pane stands between washer-up and an outlook for which, if it was 'close in', near a city, people would pay huge dollars.

Anthony, who studied architecture at the Royal Melbourne Institute of Technology, first came up here from Melbourne 18 years ago. He knew Karin, and he'd spent time in Alice Springs and far north Queensland.

'I felt at ease here pretty well straight away. I saw this house from the old bridge, and I said to Karin it looked like a nice spot.' Later she rang and said 'that house you liked is up for sale'.

Every couple of months Anthony goes to Melbourne to meet clients and look at sites. 'Most of the work I can do from home. I email sketch plans. Communications have made a huge difference to me here – in some ways you can be on an equal footing to someone in New York.'

As we look at the hardly moving river in the dying light, it's a bit difficult to get your mind around the concept of New York equivalence, but Anthony presses on with his point.

'I used to miss coffee shops and bookshops. Now most bookshops have rationed their stocks to fast-moving items – I can find more on the internet. I still like a nice cup of coffee if I'm travelling, but it's hard to find. I certainly don't miss the traffic and the aggro. I suppose I get a bit jaded with the materialism of the city, because it is on a lot of people's minds.'

It's cheap living in Wilcannia; 'the overheads aren't great'. His Melbourne clients seem to recruit themselves; his name gets round by word of mouth.

He's come to feel part of Wilcannia, and puts quite a bit of time into his duties as a local councillor. There is something more that grips him to the place now. 'I've seen a generation grow up, to 18-year-old kids.'

Karin arrirved from Sydney more than 20 years ago, with friends. She was a lay member of a Catholic community in Redfern who came, several at a time, to help a priest who'd been posted to Wilcannia. But why she came, she says, is less important than why she stayed, and that has much to do with the local Aborigines. Quite simply, her heart was captured by a generation now virtually gone.

She met people 'who were the last generation of Aborigines who were fully employed in the pastoral industry. They had led dignified, independent lives. They were in touch with their country. I fell in love with the whole lot of them – I fell in love with the cultural landscape and the outback landscape.'

In Redfern she'd already experienced the caring side of Aboriginal culture. When she'd had a miscarriage, she drew consolation from the understanding some of the women showed. One woman, whose children had been taken by the welfare authorities, saw something like that in Karin's loss.

The local Wilcannia Aborigines were different from the dispossessed people she'd encountered in Sydney, because they were in their own country. 'I saw something in Aboriginal culture and the Aboriginal heart that I could learn a lot from. When I came out here and saw those people, I thought, "Wow, this is a big learning curve for me."'

For years Karin has been doing oral histories with the Aboriginal people, many of whom have connections in various other Western towns – people they often visit. It started when she heard wonderful stories from an old woman with whom she used to fish. Realising what great material was there, she consulted oral history experts, although diffidently. 'I said, "I'm a painter"; they said, "whatever you were before, you're an oral historian now".' Karin has already been involved with a number of Aboriginal people in the book, *The Story of the Falling Star*, in which she recorded one Aboriginal legend, and there is another book coming.

From the people she's learned 'a whole way of being'. She describes it as a 'heart culture'.

'Even though at present a lot is in disarray functionally, there's something about the heart of Aboriginal people that's very touching. They haven't lost their sense of kinship. They relate to life from their hearts.'

She gives an example. 'People want a new house. They don't want to have a house like this and do it up.' She gestures round the old verandah. 'They get a new house – then something critical happens in the family somewhere else and they are willing to walk out of the house they've longed for. It has to do with people and relationships – you can walk away from material things. It's wonderful – I couldn't do it myself.'

But over the years Karin's now-trained eye has seen a sad picture unfold. At first she heard plenty of stories of good times, although the rough shanty dwellings might have looked like hard living to outsiders.

'Up to the '60s everyone had jobs. A lot of people came here when the Menindee mission closed in the late 1940s. They built shanties on the river. It sounds like paradise – people look back to that as a sort of golden age. Men had jobs, kids were going to school, families lived economically independent lives and there was deep community bonding.

'In those days people weren't depressed. Every Saturday the "top end" – the people nearer the bridge over the river – played the "bottom end" at rounders. They'd have a claypan dance every Saturday. Old Bert would play the gumleaf. Just imagine: by the light of the fires, dancing, and music on the gumleaf! Anyone aged from the 40s up will talk about these things with great nostalgia.'

Now all is changed. 'It's the third generation of 80 per cent unemployment. The energy level, the depression, have got worse. One of the hell things about Wilcannia is the lack of things for the kids to do.

'The kids don't have a sense of "the world will open up for me". There's virtually no work. They haven't seen their parents and grandparents work. You have no model of getting up and going to work.'

Out here, Anthony says, 'you hear little kids saying, "When I grow up and go on social". And that's what happens.'

When a bright local kid goes away for further education, it can be traumatic. Their schooling is likely to have left them poorly prepared. And when they come back for holidays their friends will probably take the mickey out of them. All the life and peer pressures are pushing them just to go on the dole.

Karin believes it's not necessarily a matter of getting people into jobs. 'If you had a vision of how you could build "community" in the town, people could get a lot of energy and life just from doing community-building things.'

She illustrates her idea with a story she's heard of a 19th century explorer 'invited by Aboriginal people to a corroboree. It was light when he got there, and everyone was sitting in a semi-circle doing tasks – the women were cooking, the men were making boomerangs. They were being entertained by a great story-teller, and rocking with laughter. Then the full moon rose and they painted up and had their corroboree.

'I thought, what a brilliant image of how to live! Aboriginal people can't go back to that, but they could find a new way to create that sort of rich community life.'

As well as from Karin, we'd heard the nostalgia for earlier days from two local women we'd met the previous year.

Tricia Kemp, of Aboriginal descent, was brought up in Wilcannia and worked as a preschool teacher there when we met her in 2002. But she's spent more than 20 years away, teaching school and early childhood education in Sydney, lecturing in Aboriginal Studies at the University of NSW, and heading the Aboriginal and Torres Strait Islander centre at the Australian National University.

We talked to Tricia on her front verandah too, only this verandah looked across to the store that she owned (the one we saw burned and blackened on our next visit).

'When I was a girl the Aborigines had awful living conditions but they didn't think them awful. They lived in humpies. They'd built them, and they were spotless. The men who worked on the pastoral properties were smart and clean – they epitomised the stockman. A lot of the Aboriginal girls would do domestic work. They felt good about themselves.'

And Gloria King, a respected elder of the Barkindji, the local Aborigines of the river country, and a former preschool director who retired in 1996, told us that when she was young the place was completely different. 'There were only a handful of Aboriginal families living here then' although individual families were very large. 'My mother taught us about our culture and language. This is where our community has gone wrong. People have no idea of where they're coming from, of their culture. They disrespect their elders and others in the community.'

There is a tragic irony in local Aborigines' looking back to these better times, for their memory is partly a mirage. In 'Lament for the Barkindji', written in the 1970s, Bobbie Hardy recounts the decimation of their society over many decades starting in the 1800s. Many were forced into the 'demoralising' life of the reserves; the towns 'provided an excess of evil influences'. Yet there were some whose spirit survived; those, often of mixed blood, 'who lived the free life of nomad workers in complete self-sufficiency'. Perhaps it was their spirit that had been passed down, to the times remembered by the old people Karin interviewed.

Karin doesn't despair, though most observers probably would. Rather, she describes things as being 'at a difficult stage. There are a lot of problems that need to be named clearly. There's virtually no one with the energy to address it – there is so much pain in facing it all.

'A lot of tribal things have gone for ever. The last initiated men have died. That's irrecoverable. But that's not to say that ceremonial life has vanished. It's possible for people to start new ceremonies.

'It's not to say people are in no man's land. Aboriginal people are in their own country, with their own mob. There is a network of Aborigines in Western New South Wales. There is a network of warmth for Aboriginal people. There are lots of problems but no Aboriginal person will ever live in a ghetto and no Aboriginal people will ever live alone.

'The kids today are very different from the old people. The old people spoke their language and had knowledge of the country. But the heart culture is still there. They haven't become materialistic – the kids are still relating from their hearts.'

Karin has to run off. She's expecting a group of Aboriginal people who meet for tea and cake. They are part of a Pentecostal church which has got quite a few of the local Aborigines off alcohol and into more meaningful lives. Soon she's back; the gathering's in someone else's home and would we like to go over?

We drive to a nearby house, where we meet 34-year-old Darren 'Horse' Whyman, and his 25-year-old wife Marsha. The place is crowded with the six children of 'Horse' and Marsha, including year-old twins, and other visitors. Kids are being fed; cups of tea are handed around.

'Horse' – the nickname comes from being a fast runner on the football field – was born and bred in Wilcannia, and works as an Aboriginal education assistant. The church has transformed his life. 'I had a lot of problems – money and alcohol and gambling problems. I thought I would give it a try.' It remains a constant struggle, however, for him to keep on the straight and narrow path.

About 30 Aboriginal adults and 30 children are part of the church. Its philosophy is tough love, and it appears to be working. Karin admits she was cautious originally about the fundamentalist aspect, but she's now an admirer of the obvious results.

The driver of this small miracle is Pastor Scott Lamshed,

of the Assemblies of God, helped by his wife Kathy, who is part Aboriginal. Scott, in his 30s, knows the remoter parts of Australia. Born in Darwin, he grew up in Tennant Creek, and worked for a machinery company, the Northern Territory government (as an accounts clerk) and a meatworks before becoming a pastor. He tells people to come to the church 'as you are and let the Lord deal with the issues that have to be dealt with'. But those who sign up find themselves in a demanding schedule to help the Lord along.

'I believe people should be in church whenever the church door is open,' Scott says firmly. This means attending on Wednesday and Friday nights, prayer meetings at 6 am on Wednesday and Friday mornings, and a service on Sunday.

The Lamsheds arrived from the Kimberleys six years ago. As they drove towards Wilcannia, they received all the usual bad reports. These were exaggerated but still, the situation was pretty grim.

'There was chronic drug and alcohol abuse, domestic violence, child molestation. Up to 30 or 40 kids at a time would be on the street petrol sniffing,' Scott recalls.

He says that drug and alcohol abuse has been cut by half, and child abuse has been brought out into the open and reduced. There's still petrol sniffing but only six or seven kids will be seen on the street now.

Some Aborigines – but he doesn't kid himself it's anything like a majority – would like to see a 'dry' community at Wilcannia. When he took 24 locals to the Kimberleys, 'we went into dry communities – they said, "wouldn't it be good for Wilcannia to become a dry community?"'

That won't happen any time soon but Scott would like the town to go on the front foot. 'It needs some positive advertising to promote Wilcannia, with some local Aboriginal people to say, "This is a good place to stop."'

Like many of its individuals, however, the town battles with itself. In 2004, there was a huge and dreadful brawl between two family groups; it left one man critically injured and the citizenry of Wilcannia shocked and exhausted and frighteningly aware how fragile is any progress they make.

Wilcannia had 3000 people in 1880, two decades before Bean was there. With 13 hotels it was called 'the Queen City of the West'. The road sign on the way into town says it has a population of 1000, but the 2001 census found only 697 souls, of whom 446 were indigenous.

In its heyday, 30–40 coaches passed through every week. The place was crowded with people (including Afghans and Chinese) and animals, and in the background there was always the busy river.

'Wilcannia stood, a lusty, raucous urchin with red dust on its face,' a local history says. But the 'urchin' had aspirations, and in the later 19th century invested in the future by putting up the grandest of buildings, which make the town an historian's delight.

The Anglican church was finished in 1882, constructed of white freestone quarried locally. It was here that in 2002 'Horse' and Marsha wed, with all their friends there, the bride in a dress Kathy helped her choose in Broken Hill – and, Karin says, looking like a fairy princess.

The white sandstone hospital has been restored. But it doesn't have a doctor. The locals rely on fly in, fly out medicine. Contrast 1879, when the hospital was built; the town was well served with medicos. That year, someone with a dash of wit wrote, 'Our new doctor has arrived from England. We now have two doctors. Will the cemetery, therefore be more embellished?'

In today's Wilcannia there are two motels, in place of the 19th century bakers' dozen hotels. The wonderful Athenaeum building, once a library, is now the local telecentre. When the Athenaeum was opened in the 1880s, there was a grand procession of the Orders of Oddfellows and Druids in full turnout, who were met by the Masonic brethren.

One of those likely to have been there was Charles Dickens' son Edward, who was active in the Masonic Lodge and a luminary of the area.

Two of Dickens' sons came to the West. Alfred Dickens managed a station in the Barrier country, and Plorn (as Edward was called) arrived to work on *Momba* just as he was about to turn 17. Later he went on to be manager of *Mt Murchison* and bought a share of *Yanda*. When that went bad, he went into a stock and station partnership with his brother in Melbourne but returned to Wilcannia and ran his end of the business from there. He became secretary of a group set up to fight a land bill before the NSW Parliament. The group made a short run pitch for secession, on the grounds that Sydney knew nothing of the area. Edward became Wilcannia's member of the NSW Parliament, fighting on the familiar issues of land, water, railways and rabbits.

Writer Thomas Keneally plans to make a novel out of the story of Edward and Alfred, which is recounted in Mary Lazarus's *A Tale of Two Brothers*. Keneally has travelled the West for his research; as he went, he read Charles

Dickens' *Great Expectations*, which has an Australian connection – the convict Magwitch, who is redeemed by pastoral wealth in Australia, as the Dickens boys never were.

Keneally visualises the young Edward arriving at *Momba*, little more than a boy. 'He dreamed of being a pastoral man all his life,' Keneally says, but success always eluded him. Edward was a racing and cricket enthusiast (he organised a station team) but according to Keneally 'one gets the impression of a certain amount of genteel scrapping from place to place'.

A local government official tells us that Wilcannia is 'the graveyard of good ideas. People come here, and then go. Things are set up without a lot of thought and then fail.'

The unemployment rate is high, but at the same time there are jobs unfilled. It's hard to get and keep shire staff. When we were first here people were talking about a project to grow roses, irrigated by the waters of the Darling. But it has failed to get started.

Tricia puts it well. 'This town is just like a garden that needs watering. We have so much to offer. Basically it comes back to employment and self-esteem.' Neither should be beyond a town with such a rich heritage.

— 22 —
'The Farthest Town'

When Bean arrived at White Cliffs the highly unusual opal town was already seriously on the slide from its 1899 peak of 2500 miners and perhaps 4000 people. Indeed this was a time of a big exodus; in 1907 and 1908 more than 2000 people departed. Bean records that the place had 425 miners. Prices were low for the grades of opal that White Cliffs was producing and Lightning Ridge was set to supplant it. At the turn of the century, White Cliffs boasted two doctors, seven general stores in town and two others nearby, three confectioners and two bakeries, three barber shops, three drapers, two solicitors, and four billiard rooms. In 1899 the school had 134 children; soon after a convent school opened.

At the town's height there were four cricket clubs, several libraries, and bands and choirs. Processions were popular and visiting stage companies came in to perform. A local history records that in 1901 the Centennial Hall, despite seating 600, couldn't accommodate all those who wanted to see lantern slides of the Boer War.

Today White Cliffs relies on the flying doctor, the school

has less than 20 children, and it's wise to do your shopping before reaching town, unless it's opals you're wanting. There's a roadhouse general store, but the internet cafe has closed down from lack of business.

Despite its decline, Bean could still write that White Cliffs was 'the world's opal field'. But, after it got another hit with World War I, it became almost a ghost town for several decades, until it started a modest revival in the 1950s. Now tourism is its lifeline of survival (25,000 a year). Also – believe it or not – quite a few people, who've previously come for holidays, like to move here when they retire.

'It's almost a retirement village for a lot of people,' Ross Jones, a former tour guide, tells us. Ross was 'pushing a pen' in the Victorian public service before he first visited White Cliffs in the mid-1960s. He saw the possibilities for tourism and moved there in the later '80s. The living is easy, he says (unless you happen to need a plumber or electrician).

Bean called this 'the farthest back town of any size in New South Wales', and that's how it feels today, except it's now a tiny town, with some 200 people. The modern White Cliffs is classed as a hobby mining field. There are perhaps 30 miners in winter (half of them from out of town); only four or five would depend on mining for a living. But White Cliffs still sells opals to the inveterate travellers who get this far and to some buyers further afield. The town only gets mail three times a week and a delivery of videos and library books once a week. But the internet provides new opportunities.

Graeme Dowton, who trades in opal products, advertises internationally and uses email for orders. 'I export directly to clients overseas. I polish [the opal] myself. By doing the extra work and polishing, you get five times as much.'

Opals have been like gold in spurring the efforts of men. The beautiful stone comes in various hues and values and, as Bean writes, it is 'full of all the colours of the sunset, of the Australian sunset, from the fire of the setting sun, through the pearl of the clouds, to the exquisite lemon and green and blue of the very farthest and faintest little patch of sky'.

'Opal mining's like an addiction. It's like gambling or alcoholism,' the driver of a tourist bus tells us. He's just brought a group to the Underground Motel, where Margaret and I are staying. 'You never know whether you're going to get $5 or a million dollars.' (You'd be waiting a while for the million dollar find at White Cliffs.)

Margaret buys a pendant from an old miner. The man is trying to sell his residence and shop, on nearly five acres, for $150,000. He's offering the stock on top of that, at a 45 per cent discount. A new owner would have to like a building made entirely of bottles.

Apart from its opals, White Cliffs is most famous for its 'dug-outs', comfortable underground residences and, in some cases, showrooms for opals or art. There are about 120 underground houses – prices range from $25,000 up to $85,000 – compared with about 10 houses above ground. People can't get a mortgage for a dug-out – because it is not freehold title – but there are moves to change that. Many dug-outs are holiday homes of people from Victoria and elsewhere, and quite a few are not finished. Locals pick up a few dollars by showing visitors through their homes. Some dug-outs have rendered walls; in others, the house-holders can mine their living rooms.

Graeme (who drives us out to the stations) says that he's always finding little pieces of opal ('nothing big') in his dugout. Mostly, he fossicks more conventionally. 'If I have a good hole, I'll take the kids to work. They can have a scratch round. There are not many jobs you can take your kids to.'

There are lots of unregistered vehicles whizzing about White Cliffs' steep stony roads, but who's going to come out and check? We take a picture of the stern notice at the cemetery gate warning you not to bury a body there without permission. In 1901 White Cliffs had six constables. Now there is no policeman. 'We don't have any crime to speak of,' says Ross.

Diana and Ray Hoffman have faithfully restored in 1890's style the police station – the oldest building in White Cliffs – which still has outside it the 'lock up' that saw busy days.

The Hoffmans' story is not atypical. They first visited in 1975, a spur-of-the-moment thing. 'We were on a trip to the Flinders Ranges [in South Australia] with friends and at Wilcannia we saw a sign to White Cliffs,' Diana says. They detoured, liked the place, and returned every year. Then in 1988 they moved up permanently from Sydney and took over the store, though neither had a small business background. (Diana had been a science teacher and Ray worked for a shipping company.) They've never done any prospecting, beyond the occasional bit of 'noodling'(sifting through dirt or dumps for opal). 'We came because we really like the outback,' says Diana.

Otto Rogge, who is in his 50s, also moved in to White Cliffs step by step. A nature and landscape photographer who sells his pictures all round the world (as well as photographing the White Cliffs school kids and doing other local work), Otto migrated from Germany in 1971, working at first with Kodak and then studying photography at the Royal Melbourne Institute of Technology.

He started visiting White Cliffs, and in 1991 bought a share in a dug-out. Since 2001 White Cliffs has been his home and his base, from which he travels within Australia and abroad. He averages five weeks overseas a year in a line of work that has taken him to Antarctica and the Amazon. An advertisement featuring his computer image 'Kangaroos jumping over Ayers Rock' won an award for the most read ad in New York.

For Otto, isolated White Cliffs is perfectly convenient for his work. 'We've got all mods and cons now – the satellite connection to the internet, which is the most important for me. I supply the picture libraries, and they do the distribution, with the main buyers being in the US, Britain, Germany, France and Canada.'

But, even though the technology permits it, why would he choose to live here? 'I needed a dramatic change – to concentrate on my own work. It's so different to anywhere else – that's what attracted me.

'I've travelled in outback America and I found a lot of people did the same thing – they moved away from a city and opened a gallery. Things are cheaper here – a gallery in Melbourne costs an absolute fortune.' And, 'I love underground living. I can get away from the heat and work undisturbed.'

What's hard to imagine if you've never been here is a town without lawns (except for a little patch behind the hotel). At a conference once, when women were complaining about having to mow their lawns, the woman from White Cliffs piped up, 'We rake rocks.'

And you don't see too many new trees coming up in White Cliffs. They get eaten by the goats.

The tourists who come in their busloads are lured by the opal story and the mystery of this place with houses dug into the hills. When they arrive, they marvel at the natural beauty of the vast outback sky, which seems so much wider here. Visitors to the Underground Motel troop up the hill to watch the sun coming up and going down. As the red ball sinks below the horizon, a pink glow merges into the blue sky, becoming like the smoke of a benign fire. We're there in mid-summer, when temperatures are regularly in the 40s, but the air this night is just pleasantly warm. A slight rustle comes from a soft breeze gently blowing through the leaves of a couple of trees. Melancholy music floats out from a dug-out nearby. There's a feeling of timelessness, almost other-worldliness, about the deepening evening.

'It's God's country out here, I reckon,' Graeme says. But he thinks he'll have to move by the time the children get to the serious stage of their schooling. The family hasn't decided where they'll go. 'Somewhere I can retail opals. It gets in your blood. That would give me a chance to keep coming back here.'

— 23 —
'A City Girl in Central Australia'

As we'd neared White Cliffs, a large unsignposted homestead had aroused our interest. Inquiring about it in
town, we were told this was *Tarella*, home of the Kers. The
station has one of the richest pastoral histories in the
district, but we find it special because it launches us into an
unexpected literary adventure.

Bean's brief mentions record only *Tarella*'s hardships. He
noted that beyond the Darling 'the first rabbit was reported
from *Tarella* station . . . in 1884', and listed the disastrous
fall in sheep numbers – from 105,000 on the 700,000-acre
property before the turn-of-the-century drought to 27,512
in 1907.

When we call at *Tarella* on our way to Menindee, we find
plenty from the past but no hint of rabbits as we drive
towards the impressive stone homestead, built in two
matching blocks separated by a broad lawn of buffalo
grass. One block contains the kitchen and large dining
room; the other has the lounge, bedrooms and office. The
absence of a covered walkway between them is not an
inconvenience in a place where it hardly ever rains.

'A City Girl in Central Australia'

From the ceiling of a verandah hangs a light from the Victoria Hotel, where Bean stayed both on his way to White Cliffs and when he was travelling back to Wilcannia. A century ago, when the Quins and their eight children lived at *Tarella*, the station, despite its remoteness, had plenty of visitors, and there was the occasional ball to which guests travelled great distances to dance until dawn on the large verandah.

Bruce Ker, whose father came to *Tarella* in 1951, generously shows us round his collection of records of station life in the late 19th century, including big volumes that name individually the bullocks on the property and their places in the team. He also has many old books, left over from the days when the station had its own travelling library. Bruce's mother, knowing the history of the property, added to the collection a novel by Tarella Quin, who was named after the property and became quite a noted author of her day.

But *Tarella* station nurtured the budding talent of a much more famous Australian writer. Katharine Susannah Prichard – whose books would in later years be widely read and acclaimed – came here in the early 1900s as governess, aged in her early 20s, in pursuit of her lifelong interest in adventure and romance.

From *Tarella*, she wrote a series of stories that blended fact and fiction, which were published in *The New Idea* under Prichard's name and the general title 'A City Girl in Central Australia: Her Adventures and Experiences at "Back o' Beyond"'. (By the second article, this had become 'Her Ups and Downs . . .') The stories, describing life at *Willara*, are written as letters from 'Kit' to her mother. The first of these, 'The Coach-Ride to *Willara*', describing the three-day coach journey from Broken Hill to *Tarella*, got her into trouble with Mr Quin, because the fiction took over from the fact.

The story portrays a lone young woman in rough company, who apparently was saved from possible misadventure by the timely intervention of the coach driver. The only other passengers for the first leg of 'Kit's' journey were 'two wretched-looking men on the box' and inside, 'a disreputable tramp, who was tipsy, and sprawling, half-asleep, on one seat.' With the trip underway the tramp, 'filthy and evil-smelling as an animal', leered at the girl. As things got worse, finally Billy the driver, whom Kit saw as her knight,

> threw his reins to one of the men on the box. He got down and grabbed the Irishman by his dirty red beard, and dragged him out of the coach. The road was stony, the beast too drunk to stand. Billy kicked him a bit, and gave him a bang on the head when he tried to get up. His horrid face was bleeding, his mouth full of sand. He spluttered and roared like a bull.

In her autobiography, *Child of the Hurricane*, Prichard confessed that her 'romantic imagination' had run away with her. In fact, she'd travelled with the family; the old Cobb and Co. coach had been engaged for the occasion, and the driver was a 'sober respectable middle-aged man', not a reckless and dashing cavalier.

Her other regrets were that she'd referred to the Aborigines as 'niggers' and portrayed her pupils as being rough and ignorant as young savages, rather than 'three sedate little girls', an elder sister whom she taught English and

French, and a grown-up daughter who had lessons in drawing and painting.

There was a further complication at the station. Prichard became keen on the owner's red-bearded son who 'looked my ideal of an Australian stockman', only to be warned by 'Red Beard's' father that he was engaged to someone else. The 'ideal stockman' morphed into the hero of the 'Letters'; a trip to White Cliffs 'suggested opal as the subject for a novel'. Years afterwards she visited Lightning Ridge; her novel *Black Opal* also wove in Red Beard and recollections of her earlier time in the back country.

Despite the element of melodrama, much of what Prichard wrote in her Kit 'letters' was based on fact, and she found *Tarella* a bountiful source of characters and tales of outback life.

Based on the notebook she kept at the time, Prichard's 'letters' paint the Western squatter as

> a king, and nearly a million acres is not such a meagre little monarchy . . . A station reminds one of those feudal holdings the history books tell of. The Boss-King commands, and lo! windmills arise, tanks go down. The Homestead is the Boss' castle – it is known by the men as Gov'ment 'Ouse.

When she was there, *Tarella* had more than 50 men employed, with their huts scattered around like a village. It also had 'all the adjuncts of a township', including a store that stocked everything from dungarees to peppermints. The property already possessed a telephone; in the house she found 'a magnificent library' and plentiful water for a bath, even if its colour was that of red-dust. A Chinese gardener lived in 'the most picturesque of bough huts' and '[s]ometimes the Celestial wails in Chinese, singing over his work.'

We know from elsewhere that the Quins once had to postpone a ball when a low river stopped the needed food and other things arriving. Prichard does not mention any hitch with the ball she describes in one 'letter' (and also her autobiography), for which guests arrived on Wednesday and stayed until Friday. Even today, it is easy to imagine it.

A verandah roofed in with pink blossoms and white muslin caught among the branches, for all the world like wisps of mist in an orchard, where almond and apple trees were blooming, was where we danced. The lamps dropped from the roof like huge pink flowers. The lights flickered and swam in the polished floors.

The next day there was a tennis tournament and that night a fancy dress dance, at which Prichard was a Spanish dancer. But her performance – at the request of the host and hostess – led to a fight later, when one of the men said something 'Red Beard' resented.

Prichard, displaying the talent that would later shine so brightly in her writing, captures the back country's landscape, its 'eternally blue' skies and 'sunsets beyond word-painting', as well as the spirit of its people.

The shearers who arrive on their 'bone-shaking bicycles' are paid £1 per hundred sheep. 'Chords' of the shearers' character are 'music and drink – the fiddle, whisky and funny stories. Back-country men go great lengths for a joke. There is a splendid bond of loyalty and affection between

Here we are at *Reola*, (Margaret centre) with our driver, Graeme Dowton.

A convention centre for sheep: despite its isolation, the huge *Reola* shed is a tourist attraction. The Brown family is enthusiastic about the New Merino.

The poet Dorothea Mackellar, who wrote the well-known poem 'My Country', was friendly with Bean, who later helped get her work published in Britain. Bean started his *Wool Track* research by visiting *Kurrumbede*, owned by Sir Charles Mackellar, Dorothea's father.

The great Darling.

Bourke, the town with iron windows.

Jack Buster, one of the
Americans who
pioneered cotton-
growing in the West,
and a larger-than-life
character.

'So that was the Dreadnought of the Darling! Well, when one looked again, she did remind one distantly of a warship of sorts.' *C.E.W. Bean*.

Modern *Jandra* captain, John Mahoney. He'd sailed for 40 years but only became a captain when he came to the Darling.

Skipper Walter Brown's cockie 'had been his shipmate for years and years'. The bird lived to at least 40, dying in 1928.
Courtesy of the Australian War Memorial, Neg. P02751.002.

Lynwood, home of the Browns, is part of the Darling River heritage, but fell into neglect.

Andrew Murray established the Shamrock Inn close to the Darling in the 1860s. He now has a spectacular water view.

Pattie Hall, niece of Captain Walter Brown of the *Jandra*, with the copy of *The Dreadnought of the Darling* that Bean sent to the skipper and his brother, 'in remembrance of the best trip he has yet taken'. *Courtesy of Judy Weir.*

The store at Dunlop 'is really a big general store, with a stock larger than is carried by many stores in country towns'.
(*C.E.W. Bean*)

This photograph was taken by Bean and appears to be the Dunlop store from the river side.
Courtesy of the Australian War Memorial, Neg. P02751.003.

Henry Lawson worked as a rouseabout at the *Toorale* shed but he never shore. The shed now sees only the ghosts of the past. Bean would find much familiar about the modern *Toorale* shed, although he would be surprised to see the woman rouseabout.

Andrew Hull (forefront) and Tonchi McIntosh are modern lyricists of the West. *Courtesy of Darren Clark.*

The extraordinary monument at Louth. A mark of a husband's devotion to his wife, although by the time the monument got up the river, T.A Mathews had married twice more. *Courtesy of Darren Clark.*

them. Mateship they call it, and it makes a rugged strain of poetry in the grim prose of their existence.' Even so, the shearers maintained their elite status; the rouseabouts, Prichard observes, had their separate quarters and their own cook. When the rouseabouts went on strike (at least according to the 'letters') she and the girls of the family offered to help in the shed 'if there should be any need,' but it doesn't seem to have come to that.

She heard plenty of stories of the bad times. 'Yet one can't altogether despise a place that gives £29,000 in a good year, even though those years are few and far between.' She heard too, of men lost right' out west, where the country was nothing but sandhills.

> When stockmen come across skeletons, the bodies of men who have perished of thirst in this relentless country, they are dry like mummies, with knees drawn up, and arms sticking into the air.

And she was also told about those *Tarella* rabbits to which Bean referred.

> 'You can't imagine, Miss Thing-a-me-bob!' the Boss said to me, 'what they're like – the rabbits – when they're bad. Last summer they were just like a carpet everywhere, a writhing mass. You couldn't walk without treading on them. The plains were just moving. The children used to knock them down with waddies. When we poisoned a tank, in one night there'd be 33,000, dead, round it, by the morning. They were piled up to be carted away and burnt. The stacks were as high as the mulga.'

Back on the Wool Track

Mr Quin was one of the veterans of the district, and *Tarella* had many tough drought years. 'I admired the gallantry with which the old man lived on the edge of disaster; but then, too, I was sometimes astounded by his pretensions,' Prichard says in her autobiography. One evening, from the end of the long table, he told her it must be interesting for her to have come into a literary family.

> With my background, Father's life-long work as a journalist, and daily discussions at home on books, poetry and art, it seemed absurd to consider this a literary family.
>
> But I remembered that a married daughter had once had a book published, and that another daughter was writing fairytales.
>
> 'Very,' I contrived to say meekly.

The young Prichard's six 'letters' record many of the same sights, characters, experiences and stories of the harshness of the land that Bean does, but in them and her autobiography she fills in sides of station life that do not appear in his account. At least at *Tarella*, because it was so close to White Cliffs, there was not such a feeling of loneliness as at some of the other stations. 'Opal-buyers, priests, businessmen, agents travelling between Wilcannia and the opal fields, often blew in for dinner at the homestead.'

Indeed, dinner in the Quins' time at *Tarella* was something of an ordeal for the young governess 'with the family ranged on either side of a long table, and usually several guests, on their way to one of the isolated stations or distant townships'.

242

Bean's and Prichard's accounts of shearing at a big station have much in common. And, while Prichard may have taken some literary licence with her account of the gallant coachman, Bean also portrayed coach drivers as always concerned about the ladies in their temporary care:

> [W]hen you travel by a Western coach, the driver on that coach is your host . . . At the stages he will probably get down and see how the lady passenger inside is getting on, and pass a few cheerful words to each of the others – exactly as the captain of a P. & O. mail steamer goes the round of his passengers.

— 24 —
Mining the
Art Market

The long building seems to loom out of nowhere as we drive from Wilcannia to Broken Hill, though we should have been looking for it.

'Topar Hotel, half-way house from Wilcannia, is the one landmark on a plain as flat and nearly as bare as a soup-plate,' Bean wrote.

Today's building is not the old one, which was on the other side of the road. It is, however, just as good a place for a stop and a yarn as the hotel was when the coaches came by.

Owner Colin Harvey has been 13 years at the hotel, which is a sort of hybrid establishment for the truckies, tourists and other travellers who pass through. There are half a dozen rooms out the back ($28 a single; $60 a double); a cafe-bar with a pool table for entertainment; and petrol bowsers in front.

And you'll get plenty of lively stories here, for this is the country of extremes. 'In Cyclone Steve three years ago, we had nine inches overnight. It was like a big lake,' Colin tells us. More often it's blowing than raining, however.

'There was a bloke one night sitting over there' – Colin gestures to the corner of the cafe – 'we couldn't see him eating his tea. When he finished his tea, his hair was red. And we couldn't see the fuel pumps and asphalt outside.'

It sounds just like the dust storm Broken Hill had the year before Bean's visit when, according to a contemporary description, '[i]ndoors it was impossible for people to find their way from one room to another. Windows could not be distinguished so absolute was the darkness outside. Women were terrified.'

Colin comes from Broken Hill and used to have a trucking business. With all the lifting the work got too hard for him; the hotel business looked, if not a doddle, at least as though it would be a fair bit easier. It didn't turn out that way. Heavy lifting was just replaced with a lot of running in and out to attend to the customers pulling up for fuel. He's had the place on the market for a couple of years, at an optimistic asking price of $350,000. The offers, so far, are more modest. This is not the sort of small business that's in high demand.

—

The mining areas girdle Broken Hill as the traveller drives in, almost overshadowing it, although most of them now are worn out. The first impression is of a city neatly kept and kempt and, given its inhospitable geography, surprisingly green. Even a century ago, the city's residents aspired to greenness; 6000 trees were planted in the city's several parks and streets. But an acute shortage of water parched the city, and sometimes its people. This has now been overcome and for today's grassy grounds and shady trees and gardens, thank the Darling, at least in part. A pipeline brings water 100 kilometres from the Menindee Lakes to Broken Hill. Its coming transformed life for this city that once had to recyle bath water.

Bean described Broken Hill as 'the great metropolis', with excellent shops and hotels, and race meetings to which went 'a population of a country about the size of Great Britain'. In 1908 Broken Hill had about 30,000 souls, making it one-third larger than now. The city centre had, in the words of a modern writer, a 'vitality manifested in the thrusting, grimy, and argumentative years before World War I'.

Like many places in the outback in those days, people there (or at least the men, in a majority of course) liked a drink. Within the city boundaries, there were 61 hotels, and another 11 in the immediate area; but here, also, in a city with a high proportion of Methodists, was a strong temperance movement. Employment in the mines was at a high. In 1907 a record 8820 men were employed in mining, and the city's steam trams carried two million passengers.

In the year of Bean's visit, Leonard Samuel Curtis published a history of Broken Hill, which he nicely described as 'a youth of 24 years', and 'the Second City of the State' and, more questionably, as 'one of the wonders of the world', although 'not the place one would live in from choice', with the summer heat, 'those dreadful, blinding dust-storms', the never-changing outlook and tumble-down tenements as well as the 'deficiency of social life'.

Nevertheless, it had handsome buildings along streets named after minerals, the hotels stayed open to 11.30 pm, and, if Bean had been there on a Saturday, he'd have observed the bustling scene that comes to life in Curtis's description:

> A human mass throng the street, taking possession of the roadway, and sway to and fro, listening to the Bands, Street Orators, Salvation Army, Cheap Jacks, &c, that are to be found at every street corner . . .

Residents of this city were joiners and activists, and not just of unions; it had a plethora of sporting, benevolent and church organisations.

Bean described Broken Hill as 'the capital of all New South Wales across the Darling', but observed that NSW had 'allowed it to be turned into a sort of back station of Adelaide'. This was because the first railway came from Adelaide to the nearby South Australian border, and linked into a small and very profitable private railway, rather misleadingly called the Silverton Tramway. Bean's visit to Broken Hill was to examine the competing claims for railway routes to the far West but it wasn't until the 1920s that a rail line connected 'the Hill' with Sydney.

In the 1890s Mark Twain, travelling on a train from Melbourne to Adelaide, met a judge from Sydney, on his way to hold court in Broken Hill. To get the 700 miles from Sydney to the Hill, the judge was travelling more than 2000 miles by rail via Melbourne and Adelaide. As Twain explained, Adelaide

> threw a short railway across the border before Sydney had time to arrange for a long one . . . The whole vast trade-profit of Broken Hill fell into Adelaide's hands, irrevocably. New South Wales furnishes law for Broken Hill and sends her Judges 2,000 miles – mainly through alien countries – to administer it, but Adelaide takes the dividends and makes no moan.

The Adelaide-versus-Sydney pull on Broken Hill echoes to this day. When we're there, people are arguing about where the TV news should come from. The Hill had been getting Adelaide news, but now Sydney newscasts are being beamed in – only as a trial, we're assured. Opinion is split on the relative merits. (By late 2003 Sydney news is confirmed to stay.)

There is also division over which time-zone Broken Hill should be in. It operates on South Australian time, and the business people like that. But public servants and others who have to deal with Sydney would prefer to be on eastern standard time.

Appropriately, the sheep men were in at the start of mining here. The ore body was found by Charles Rasp, a station hand on *Mount Gipps* station. In 1883 he persuaded six other men associated with the station (including two who had a dam sinking contract there) to put in money as a syndicate to take out leases.

Bean tells the story of Rasp and his colleagues, and the ups and downs of the early years. But he wrote before the social sequel; anyway, he might have been too fastidious to recount it in the graphic detail that Geoffrey Blainey does in *The Rise of Broken Hill*.

Rasp's German-born wife Agnes, a former waitress from Adelaide whom he married within three years of his great mining discovery, was an inveterate social climber. After Rasp's death in 1907, she sought a new husband in Europe, and became engaged to Field Marshal Baron Richard von Eisenstein, German ambassador to Vienna.

> He apparently had agreed to marry her to preserve his family's honour – she paid the enormous debts of his son

> – but the sight of that buxom fifty-six-year-old dowager as the marriage day drew closer made him more anxious to preserve his own honour. In her presence he blew his brains out. Mrs Rasp must have now seen the danger of a long engagement; without much delay she married his aide, Count von Zedtwitz . . .

Alas, the count was killed in the war.

Repeatedly in its history, Broken Hill has lived as a town on the edge, its future in doubt. In the later edition of *The Dreadnought of the Darling*, Bean says he was told in confidence when he was there in 1908 that 'the town had but a short life ahead of it' because the mining would peter out. This pessimism about the ore body was premature.

Nearly a century later, however, Broken Hill has no choice but to face the fact that its future – and nobody who visits will doubt it has one – cannot rest on mining. It seems, however, remarkably well-prepared; rather like a company that, finding demand for its product shrinking, turns to new lines. It has been seriously working up its tourism industry since the 1970s. And a now much slimmed-down city is living, to a considerable extent, on its art, which gives it special pull as a tourist attraction.

Galleries abound in Broken Hill itself, and at the nearby picturesque former mining town of Silverton (which was already well past its brief glory days by 1908). The Hill's city art gallery, established in 1904, is the second-oldest in NSW.

In a note written some years ago for the book *Art of Broken Hill*, then governor-general William Deane quipped, 'I understand that today there are more art galleries than there are hotels in the city.' The art book's listing names 24 in the Hill and Silverton, and that's not all of them. Pro Hart, Jack Absalom, Rob Wellington and Peter Browne are among the best-known names but the guide features more than 30 Hill artists; generally their work reflects the nature of the inland landscapes and has distinctive qualities.

One of the secrets of Broken Hill's success is that this art industry has enough critical mass to attract tourists and buyers in significant numbers. Famous for the 'Brushmen of the Bush', and with many of the artists on the spot with their work, Broken Hill and Silverton are places where visitors can be autograph hunters as well as viewers and buyers.

If art has been replacing mining, miners and others working in that industry have become artists and craftsmen. Pro Hart was once a miner. For some people, necessity has driven reinvention of themselves. Standing among the historic buildings that have become galleries in Silverton is a large tin shed where Andy Jenkins works in his 'Coin Carvery'. Andy was retrenched in 1982 from the mining industry, where he'd worked on the geology side.

What he did was turn his hobby of carving jewellery and decorative pieces from coins into a full-time business, setting up in Silverton in 1990. About 90,000 people come to the Carvery annually, he says, although he admits he doesn't make a fortune. 'I can live quite comfortably from the proceeds and have a holiday at the end of the year,' he tells us, as we peer into his show cases, and he produces some of his rarer coins.

Apparently you can't just decide to carve up the currency to earn a crust. 'It took two and a half years lobbying to be able to cut the coins up,' Andy tells us. He says he has a letter signed by Paul Keating, then treasurer, to allow him to do it. 'As far as I know, I'm the only one in Australia to do what I do. The main problem was that they didn't like me doing it with the current stuff. I've permission to destroy Commonwealth property – the sixpennies. But with the dollars, I can't cut them up and sell them. I copy them.' He also carves pennies, dated between 1938 to 1964, gold-plates them, and sells them for $150 a pop. When we were there he had a good supply of pennies to be going on with – 8000 had come from one estate.

Broken Hill is a service town for the great outback around it and two of the services, the School of the Air and the Royal Flying Doctor Service are tourist attractions in their own right. At the Flying Doctor we're shown around by Becky Blair, whose husband is the 'flying padre' (the American couple's story is told in chapter 7). Unlike modern flying doctors who don't actually work the controls, John's both pastor and pilot. Unusual to find an American in such a job? When the position came up, not one Australian applied.

While Broken Hill looks busy and prosperous, the town is still in flux. Only one mine is operating. This had been expected to close soon but talk now is that it may operate until about 2020. There's a suggestion of re-opening another and calling it after Rasp. Broken Hill 'is in the process of moving from a mining economy to a mixed economy,' Jim Leary, acting general manager of the city council tells us. 'It hasn't weaned off mining at this stage, but at least it's moving in that direction. It's like any community that wants to reinvent itself – it's a painful process.'

The nature of employment is changing. It's harder these

days for males to get jobs, as employment shifts to occupations that usually have high proportions of women workers – health services, education and hospitality. There's also a shift from higher-paid jobs – miners earned well when unionism was strong – to lesser-paying ones.

Older people are staying. Where is there to go when you've lived out here all your life? Anyway, with Broken Hill shrinking, house prices are low. But younger people are leaving. The population, which peaked about 35,000 in World War I and had a second, slightly lower peak in the 1950s, is now about 20,000 and falling at an annual rate of about 3 per cent. But the fear, expressed in a city history in 1988, that its population could fall to 15,000 by the end of the century proved another overly gloomy assessment about the outlook for this very durable little city.

The new Broken Hill has plenty of spirit but it's long since ceased to be a militant union town. Bean arrived shortly before one of its several huge industrial confrontations.

The bitter 1909 five-month lockout further radicalised an already militant community. The workers, who 'won' that year but paid a huge price in employment and hardship, were led by Tom Mann, one of the big names in the Australian and British labour movements; during the turmoil, Mann was charged with (and acquitted of) sedition.

A few years later, when Bean was reporting from Gallipoli the valour of fighting Australians, opposition to the war was increasing in Broken Hill, where a volunteer who later won a VC was stoned as he boarded the train to go off to war. In the 1916 conscription referendum, Broken Hill recorded a 70 per cent 'No' vote, much higher than the 52 per cent national vote.

Broken Hill is still a Labor town, but some of the old symbols have long ago lost their substance. In Argent Street is what seems today the quaintly named Barrier Social Democratic Club. This was set up a century ago with one of its objectives to educate people in the principles of 'social democracy'. Membership in those days had a special exclusivity; applicants had to give an undertaking to vote for Labor candidates. Today's 6000 members only have to pay their $6 annual fee, for which they'll get a free meal for their birthday and 50 cents off every beer.

One of the city's finest buildings is the Trades Hall, with its impressive painted ceiling. Circumstances have drawn the once sharp teeth of the union movement that occupies it. The last big industrial stoush was in the 1980s. Where early last century nearly 9000 men worked the mines, there are now about 350 employed, 'from the general manager to his dog', as Eddie Butcher, official with the union that covers the miners, puts it. Of these 163 are in his union.

Butcher is a third generation miner. He retains his faith. 'Broken Hill is still one of the most prospective metal areas in Australia. My belief is that it could still be going as a mining centre in the next century if technology changes and they go down deeper. I say this because of the numbers of companies which hold mining leases in the area and are doing exploration drilling. They're even drilling in the old rubbish tip!'

But Butcher's son is neither in mining nor in Broken Hill. And even if mining continues longer than anticipated, it will be neither extensive nor labour intensive.

Which brings us back to art, and one of the entrepreneurs of modern Broken Hill. We run into David Tunkin and his wife Barb when we go in search of paintings by Rob Wellington. Wellington is an artist much of the style of the ever-popular landscapist Hans Heysen. Pictures by Wellington, who also sells from a dug-out in White Cliffs, have become extremely popular and sell well. Horses are his speciality, and I'm a sucker for horses.

Barb and David have Red Sands gallery at Broken Hill, and another at Silverton. When we arrive, it's out of hours, but we knock on the door anyway. It opens onto a packed treasure trove of local paintings and imported furniture, ornaments, jewellery, clothing and knick-knacks. The Tunkins live in the big old house – originally seven bedrooms and five bathrooms – but the gallery is rapidly crowding out the personal space.

David, who was brought up in Adelaide, came to Broken Hill rather reluctantly. Coles posted him here in the early '80s to manage its store. 'I thought, are they sending me to the end of the earth?' He planned to stay only six months. But the unexpected happened. 'I fell in love with the place.' An extension of a year then turned into a choice between staying with the company or staying with Broken Hill. He left the company.

He likes what seem more genuine friendships, and the (relatively) slower pace of life here. 'I was a fairly fast-moving person, and I could afford here to slow down and still be keeping up with other business people. In the [big] city it was go, go, go. This allowed me to have time with the family – and do the work. And five minutes and you're in the bush.'

In the slow lane, David has been involved in a radio station, Hungry Jack's, a limousine operation, and a funeral parlour, as well as art selling. David and his wife got into the art business about ten years ago when they bought the Silverton gallery of artist Peter Browne. They love travelling, which fits nicely with the importing side of the business.

Their galleries carry a wide range of artists' work, with Wellington and Browne their staples. Most of it is sold to tourists from other parts of Australia; a minority goes to overseas visitors and locals from the Broken Hill area. David believes the art scene will continue to expand, albeit much more slowly than the surge of the last 20 years.

The same qualities of scenery and climate that have made Broken Hill an art centre also attract the filmmakers. Up to a dozen TV commercials are filmed each year and over decades scenes in feature films (such as *Dirty Deeds* and *The Adventures of Priscilla, Queen of the Desert*) have been shot around the region. During our visit there's a lot of talk about the possibility of Baz Luhrmann's *Alexander the Great* using the location, but it seems a pipe dream. Two film officers are attached to the local tourist information centre; they're a first point of call for filmmakers, and will send images of the area, or go out and take digital pictures.

As Margaret and I spend an enjoyable two days in this pleasant, if mini, 'metropolis', I remember a previous brief but memorable visit to Broken Hill more than 30 years before.

I was travelling with Malcolm Fraser, who was federal education minister, and we flew to the Hill on our way back from the Northern Territory, where he'd been inspecting Aboriginal schools.

Fraser and his party were taken down the mine. All except me, that is. The company management said it was strictly 'males only'. They wouldn't listen to argument. I was given a cup of tea and a rather turgid book about the mines.

My report in the *Age* at the time quoted a mines manager, a Mr Connor, telling me, slightly apologetically, 'Sorry, we didn't realise one of the press party might be of the female species . . . Traditionally, no women are allowed underground . . . In the Cornish mines in England there's still a superstition about women going underground. They say that if a woman goes underground a man will die.'

Mr Connor assured me they didn't believe this in Broken Hill, and indeed an exception had been made for the wife of the Victorian governor of the day. One problem was there wasn't a place where women could change into overalls. 'When female geologists come, I have to kick some males out of the underground manager's change house, put a big notice on it and get it policed, because otherwise someone will barge in . . . Traditionally, it's like a male army establishment – you'd probably have to alter a few things if you had females going down there constantly.'

I was told by a Broken Hill woman – I've forgotten who now but presumably someone who kept me company while I waited for the men to come back – 'This is a man's industry and a man's town – women are suffered where necessary but believe me they are not relished.' In those days, there was still discrimination against married women working.

The Hill has come a long way since then.

— 25 —
The Maidens of Menindee

When Bean arrived in Menindee in 1908 he described the town as a

> collection of a few one-storey hotels and public build-
> ings, a dozen or two bare weatherboard cottages
> waterlogged in a rolling sea of sand . . . as imposing as
> a dust-heap and as orderly as a scattered fishing-fleet in
> a heavy storm . . .

With his mind on railway routes, he lamented what might
have been – 'a big busy town where the experiment of
Central Australia – the experiment of irrigating the Darling
banks to supply a big, rich, high-priced market close at
hand – might have been tried'. This could have been
Menindee if 'the Government had built seventy miles of
railway'.

Perhaps Bean was a little harsh on Menindee, according
to the standards of the times. Sandra Maiden, fifth generation of a Darling River family, has done a history of the town.
Sandra, who now lives in Western Australia, married into the

Maiden family, which has deep and broad roots around here; she is also related through an earlier generation.

In response to my queries about the town in the early 1900s Sandra (who describes herself as 'a fan of Bean'), sent back this description:

> Menindee was a fairly vibrant town at the time of Bean. [I]t had a vibrant jockey club, busy commercial atmosphere, two churches, Anglican and Roman Catholic; with dedicated groups of followers and fundraisers.
>
> There was a small private hospital and at least two doctors, something that had gone by the wayside by the end of World War II. In a sense Menindee went downhill with the coming of the motor vehicle. So Bean would have seen it in its better days as far as commerce and social activity were concerned.

Yet, unlike many small towns, Menindee is holding its own. Although the town itself has a population of less than 400, the wider area is home to nearer 900 people. The Menindee Lakes and Kinchega National Park bring tourists, and the lakes provide water for a thriving fruit and vegetable industry.

Sandra Maiden's 'busy commercial atmosphere' has been replaced by a total of 26 people working in retail, property and business services. Menindee has three policemen and a central school. In place of the two doctors, there is a visiting flying soctor service on average three days a week, supported by local nurses. One hundred and fifty nine people in Menindee identify themselves as Aboriginal. The unemployment rate is about 12 per cent, not high for small towns around this area.

We arrive after a 150 or so kilometre drive from Wilcannia along a serviceable though unsealed road rather than, as Bean did, from Broken Hill along a track through sandhills. Before reaching the town we stop to look at the spectacular lake view. It's hard to imagine where you are, as you gaze at this picture postcard scene. It's like a beach with attitude, with all these skeletons of dead trees rising out of the water. This extensive lakes system, building on the natural lakes, was constructed many years after Bean's visit. It has enabled the Menindee area to become the fruit and vegetable-growing irrigation oasis he hoped for.

Menindee is a hop and a step, for these parts, from Broken Hill. Right on the Darling, it's as dusty and outback as these towns come. Yet drive a few kilometres out, and you will be in what Menindee calls 'Sunset Strip', a lakefront resort that seems a curious surprise when you come upon it. Apart from the locals, this is a leisure spot for people from Broken Hill.

One of the delights of our journeyings was finding people with a direct link to the Bean trips. It's like discovering specks of gold when fossicking on an old mining field. In our case, it's human gold, people with direct connections back to a past that's gone but still, when you start to scratch the surface, remarkably near. We were to have such an experience in Menindee.

There was one bright spot for the weary traveller who had rattled into town on the Broken Hill coach, that night drawn by four horses and a mule and running very late. In a postscript to the 1956 edition of *The Dreadnought of the Darling* Bean wrote of the kind host and hostess who, with their new wedding-present tray-cloth and breakfast set, once and for all changed the Sydney passenger's outlook on Menindie [the old spelling of the name].

When he wrote this 1950s postscript they were 'still associated with the Menindie Hotel'.

Like Bean, and many other strangers arriving in this small neat town, we immediately go to the Menindee Hotel. It's said to be the second-oldest hotel in continuous operation in the state, but it has a much stronger claim to historical interest. It was here that Burke and Wills stayed on their ill-fated expedition to the Gulf of Carpentaria. Part of the hotel was destroyed by fire in 1999, and the place had to be rebuilt. The 'Burke and Wills' room is gone these days; today's tourist must make do with a drink in the 'Burke and Wills' bar.

When Bean visited, the expedition was within living memory, and relics were of great interest. He heard the story of the camel shoes that the expedition left by the Pamamaroo lake from a 'Mr W. Maiden', who had gone through the country a few years later. A shoe could be viewed at the Albemarle Hotel.

In 1860, when the expedition passed through, the hotel was run by Tom Pain, credited with founding the town a few years before. When Burke and his expedition deputy Landells had a dispute over Landells' desire to take on rum for the camels – leading to Landells resigning and Wills becoming deputy – the hotel was the beneficiary. Burke sold the rum to Pain for the pub, Sandra's history recounts; in return, Pain said he'd cash Burke's cheques and offered accommodation.

We reach the town on a hot day; we're having a drink in the hotel lounge when Noeline, the present licensee, comes in. We tell her we're after some history; she says we must go and meet her grandmother, so we drive round to the home of Florence Maiden, and come a step closer to Bean's 'kind host and hostess'.

Florence's late husband, William Lewis, was born in January 1909; his parents, William Edward and Ruby Laura Maiden had married in February 1908. In that year William bought the hotel – which had been in the family since 1890 – from his father, also called William, who had the station *Maidenville* and no doubt was the 'Mr W. Maiden' who told Bean the story of the camel shoes. Years later it was said in his obituary that 'what Mr Maiden could not tell about the Darling country is not worth knowing': he used to take visitors to the Burke and Wills campsite a little way out of town. One can visualise the eager journalist soaking up his tales.

William Edward and Ruby Laura were the young couple whose hospitality made such a difference to the weary traveller.

Florence tells us her stories over a cup of tea. She came to Menindee in 1924; her father was a bridge builder and by then – long after Bean's exhortations on the matter – railway bridges were being put in. The Menindee bridge was finished by 1927. In those days, there was more social life in Menindee, including balls and two-day race meetings. Florence tells us her father-in-law, despite his trade, never touched beer, which perhaps accounted for his unresponsiveness to complaints from drinkers after barrels that had come from Parkes were left sitting for a long time in the sun.

Later we go to see Florence's daughter Greta in her house at Sunset Strip. Greta too has plenty of memories of her grandfather, whom she recalls being always at the hotel. He was a real connection to the old days, to Bean's era of pre-motor transport. 'He used to tell us that when he drove the Governor to Mossgiel, it took a week in the rain in the sulky. But he never mentioned meeting Bean,' Greta says. She's familiar with the name because of the mention of 'Mr W. Maiden' in *The Dreadnought of the Darling*.

A piano that Ruby used to play is still in the hotel, and the hotel is still very much in the family. Noeline is Ruby's great-granddaughter. The hospitable couple lie side by side in the local cemetery. They both lived well into old age, dying in the early 1970s, Ruby at 84 and William at 93. Sadly, a while after we spoke to her, Florence died too; her grave is in front of theirs.

And there the story of our encounter with the Maidens of Menindee would end, but for a chance conversation weeks before this book went to the printer. As we're doing last minute checking of the Menindee chapter, one of the researchers muses, 'I wonder if Sam Maiden is one of that family.'

Samantha Maiden, a journalist with the *Australian*, works in an office close by in the Canberra Parliament House press gallery. As I rush off to find her, I can't believe I failed to make what now looks like such an obvious connection. Sam is from Adelaide, the city with a natural link to Menindee. Yes, she says, the Menindee family is related. 'They own a pub,' she adds vaguely, then quickly gets into the spirit of the hunt.

Next thing, Sam's grandmother Laurel Maiden, who's

almost 89, is reminiscing to me about when she and her husband stayed for a week, more than 50 years ago, with quiet William and outgoing Ruby at the old-fashioned hotel ('it wasn't the Hyatt'). She recalls a big family table in the dining room and all the station people coming in for lunch. Suzanne Maiden, Sam's mother and a professional genealogist, bombards me with details by email. It turns out that the great grand-niece of the young couple has been across the press gallery corridor all the time.

— 26 —
The Secret of *Kilfera*

On his first trip to the West, to report for the *Sydney Morning Herald* on the arguments for the competing railway routes, Bean had himself driven by buggy over 200 miles from Menindee to the small town of Ivanhoe.

It was just out of Ivanhoe, after this character-forming journey, that he called in at *Kilfera* station, a huge property which that year (according to the records of the time) ran more than 32,000 sheep, 1050 cattle and 100 horses.

Some years earlier, *Kilfera*'s sheep numbers had been even larger and its shed, one of the biggest in Australia, had the incredible number of 82 shearers, and shore 7000 to 9000 sheep a day.

In 1908, the manager lived there with his mother and sister in a homestead that lay beside a dry lake, a house Bean found 'delightful with its garden, its cosy old-fashioned living-rooms with snug cushions and armchairs and the invariable oil lamp beaming on a table littered with modern books'.

Bean describes as 'typical of the West' the way he came to be introduced to the small social circles of Ivanhoe, a town that was '[p]erhaps in the loneliest part of all New South Wales'.

Early one evening, the Sydney passenger

had come, after driving all day through empty country, to a long, low, white house with a garden in front of it facing out over the plain.

He left the horses looking over the garden fence and went up to the front door and knocked. A lady came to the door; he told her where he was bound for and asked if he could put up there for the night.

She told him to put his things in the spare room, and he was taken in there and then and made a member of the family for the time being.

Later in the evening the manager came in from his work; and he, next morning, took the Sydney passenger some miles on his way into the township and introduced him to the people there.

The station manager introduced him to the hotel keeper who, thinking he might like company at his meals, in turn introduced him to the schoolmaster. The station manager and the hotel keeper introduced him to the store keeper, who asked him to Sunday dinner.

The manager, having done what he considered his duty by a man he had never seen or heard of until six o'clock the night before, drove back home.

For Bean, the hospitality he received from *Kilfera* was typical of the 'simplicity and generosity in the life out back' which was 'bound to have its effect on the city life too, if for this reason only, that the Australians of the cities – especially the younger ones – have a wholehearted admiration for the man whom quite rightly they make their ideal – the Australian of the bush'.

We found the son of the generous *Kilfera* manager. Walter Sheaffe, who lives in Wagga Wagga, tells us his father Roger was manager at *Kilfera* in 1908. Roger was still a bachelor then and, although we could find only his name on the electoral roll of the day, his mother and his sister Isabella would have been the ladies to whom Bean referred.

Roger, whom Walter says was 'a very quiet person who loved the land and liked telling stories about things that had happened in years gone by', married about 1911, and the family was still at *Kilfera* when Walter was born in 1914. 'My mother went 130 miles by buggy into Hay to catch the train [to Sydney] to have me and my twin brother,' says Walter, who was born in March. 'The jackaroos drove her from one property to another in the cool and she rested at the properties in the day. It would have been a three-day trip. My father got a telegram to say twins had arrived – he thought someone was playing a joke.'

It was a drought year and when mother and babies arrived back, the milking cow had died. The only available milk was from wild goats. 'The overseer and my father went out and ran down the wild goats.' Walter lived at *Kilfera* until 1916 or 1917, when the family moved to another property.

Walter gives us a photo of the *Kilfera* homestead taken in 1912. It shows the fence that Bean's horses looked over when he jumped down from the buggy in search of a night's accommodation.

The fence has long gone but the old *Kilfera* house is still there, slowly disintegrating, victim of the harsh climate, white ants and the inexorable passage of time.

Clive and Fay Linnett, today's owners, lived in that house until they put up their modern transportable one beside it. The shearing shed of earlier days was burned during industrial troubles in the 1920s.

In 1994, there was a poignant reminder of that year in which Bean called at *Kilfera*. Three elderly sisters arrived from South Australia, accompanied by their not-so-young nephew. Laura Phillips, 93, Myrtle Maloney, 85, and Doris Hart, 83, were seeking the tiny *Kilfera* graveyard where in 1908 their two brothers – one a baby and the other eight years old – were buried. The Linnetts had suspected that one spot in the cemetery contained an unmarked grave, but they couldn't be sure.

The Linnetts take us to see the little cemetery and give us the name of this family, and in 2003 the nephew, Fred Sharon, 77, sent me the story of the grave, now marked by a plaque, that had remained in his aunt Laura's memory for a lifetime.

George Alder, an earthmoving contractor, who sank dams and constructed banks, was on *Kilfera* with his family when his sixth and youngest child, Henry Isaac, died on March 23, 1908, aged just seven months. Henry had been a weak baby and succumbed to the hard living conditions. Then, as so often happened in those days out here, tragedy again hit the family. Their second child Walter died of lockjaw (tetanus) before medical help could be brought.

Fred describes the family's return. 'Upon arrival at the *Kilfera* homestead the eldest sister, Laura, who was only about nine years of age when the family left *Kilfera*, indicated precisely the direction and distance to the cemetery . . . 86 years had elapsed since the funerals.

'We located the site complete with the buried wire netting enclosure, the corrugated iron name plate, plus a horseshoe from Walter's pony that was placed there at the time of the funeral. After clearing the site we laid a base and the plaque.

'The weather was very inclement and unpleasant the following day but . . . the three sisters placed two red roses at the site. This was quite an emotional moment.' In their simple message on the plaque – *Remembered by their sisters Laura, Myrtle and Doris* – the sisters finally got to say their goodbyes near the end of their own lives.

Clive's brother Bob, who now lives in Wagga Wagga, recalls the *Kilfera* house as 'very liveable. In the kitchen there was a brick oven – we used it for a wood box. We used the old wood stove in the winter – it was next to the oven. There was a big long room where they used to eat. The old homestead was the hub of the whole business.' His family obtained the block in the 1950s, when Bob was a boy.

In '56 the big flood came, and they had to ride horses to get to and from the homestead. The youngsters used thick pieces of wire to kill snakes on the levy bank as they came out of the water.

Bob was taught by the district's travelling schoolman, Alex Fraser. This 'travelling school' had been set up at Ivanhoe in 1914. At first the teacher went round in a horse-drawn van, which carried school equipment, and had accommodation. He'd spend some days at each property, leaving behind work to be done. In the 1920s the transport was upgraded to a car.

Remarkably, from its start to its closure in 1949, this school only had two teachers; Fraser was schoolmaster some 34 years.

'Alex "Schoolie" Fraser taught my father. There were seven boys and three girls in the family – he taught them all. Their maths was good, and they had beautiful handwriting. I was the last one to be taught by the old fellow – and the only one of the next generation of Linnetts.

'Even though he would leave me six weeks' work, I spent most of my time out mustering and riding my grandmother's race horses. Then I had to rush to catch up because I was frightened of him – he used to use the cane.' Later Bob moved on to Ivanhoe school. 'I was in the first class and just about ready to shave.'

In Bean's time the back country was something of a magnet for villains, but it also entrapped them: '[i]t is curious how difficult it is for a man who has committed a crime to escape in that country . . . Everyone that sees him will remember him for years.'

Not much had changed when Bob was living there. 'The back country attracts colourful people. They want to get away from the law [but] strangers attract attention. You would hear of a robbery on the radio. You could tell the tracks of a strange car, and you could just ring the next town – they never got away.'

One day when he and his father were at *Kilfera*, four dirty-looking men turned up, saying their car had slipped off the road.

'Dad said, "I don't like the look of them blokes – we'll get them off the place."' The men's Holden had no keys in it, and no luggage. 'We had an early model landrover, and we got them on the road. Dad said, "Don't look back" and we dragged them all the way to Ivanhoe to the police station.' They were relieved to see the policeman in the garden.

— 27 —
Hospitality in a
Western Town

Ivanhoe, on the plains way out beyond Hay, is modest by anyone's standards. Its official population at the 2001 census was 273 and falling. Five years before the census had recorded 322 souls.

The town's name is a little special. How many outback places are named after a novel? 'Ivanhoe' comes from Walter Scott's classic. George Williamson, a Scot who once had a store there, is credited with the naming, although there was already an 'Ivano' hotel.

Margaret and I drive to Ivanhoe one afternoon along an unsealed road, through wave after wave of red dust. It is like being in a bright red snowstorm.

'Ivanhoe is the hub of the roads in this part,' Bean wrote in his 1908 newspaper account of the rival railways routes.

A huge plain, a wide, straight road, 10 wooden houses, 70 people – it is the centre for a district half as large as Tasmania. But it has to bring the comforts of life from Hay, just now almost cut off by 134 miles of drought, for £8; or on camels from Wilcannia for £4.

271

The town appealed to Bean because its people were so hospitable. And he was charmed by an unexpected touch of the old world.

He writes enthusiastically about his Sunday dinner with the storekeeper, 'an Italian, I think, by descent'; this was 'the most delightful meal the Sydney passenger enjoyed in all his time in the West'.

> The table, the courses, the manner of their service, and especially the host and hostess seemed to belong rather to some refined, cultured country society in old Europe than to this village on the outskirts of the Empire. It will be long before the Sydney passenger will forget the delicious coffee his hostess gave him with the dessert.

The host was 'a well-read man, with all the quiet, thoughtful courtesy of these gentlemen of the Australian wilderness. 'I envy you the time you get for reading,' said the Sydney passenger, looking at a bundle containing a week's newspapers which had just come in.

> 'I don't get as much time as you think,' was the answer. 'Such time as I can spare from the counter goes mostly digging spuds in the back garden.'
> However, he did manage to get in his reading somehow – much more of it than most Sydney men find the leisure for.

So who were this intriguing host and hostess whom Bean does not name? (It's only in the later edition of *The Dread-*

nought of the Darling, where he talks about the couple, that Bean mentions the storekeeper's an Italian.)

When we get to Ivanhoe, we delve into a local history and identify the Villas. But the family has long disappeared from the district. It takes a while (Margaret as usual is the detective) to track down the story of Francesco and Antonietta Villa. When we do, we find one of the most delightful tales in the history of the West.

It's recounted in a little family account, *An Italian Heritage*, co-authored by the Villas' granddaughter, the late Gina Twigg.

Francesco Villa came to Australia in 1880 from the Lake Como area in northern Italy. He'd trained as a language teacher and spoke fluent English, French, Spanish and German. Apparently he migrated to Australia for health reasons. But why on earth Ivanhoe?

Family legend has it that a map of Australia was laid out in front of him at his home in Monza, Italy. A relative blindfolded him and Francesco said, 'Wherever my finger points, that is where I shall go.' He put his finger on Ivanhoe. A greater contrast – in lifestyle, scenery, and almost everything else – between Monza and this dusty town where he was to spend more than three decades can't be imagined.

After landing in Melbourne, Villa went to a local trading company where he ran into a young man of his own age, Maffio Rossi. Maffio was also from the Milan district, although the pair hadn't met at home. A friendship started that lasted not just throughout their lives but has bonded the two families to the present day.

Francesco and Maffio joined forces and became hawkers, supplying household and personal goods to outback properties. These were the travelling storekeepers of the time, whose visits were eagerly awaited by the people on stations and in the towns. Their wagon was painted, drawn by four horses and stocked with shelves of clothing, linen, boots, hats and the like. They journeyed through Victoria and later into NSW, where they introduced themselves to the manager of *Kilfera* station, to which they became frequent callers. A local Aborigine used to call out as they approached, ''Ere come the Hi-talian 'awkers!'.

After they'd established stores in Hillston and Ivanhoe the two, by this time in their mid-30s, brought to the bush the Italian sweethearts they'd left behind. Rossi went home for his wedding to Lucia, but Francesco waited in Australia for his bride, Antonietta. On the insistence of her father, the Villas wed by proxy (Francesco's brother standing in for him) before she set sail for Australia. Antonietta was in her 30s but such were the demands of respectability in the late 1800s, at least for an Italian father. When she arrived in Melbourne, the couple had a wedding at St Patrick's Cathedral.

The Villas lived in Ivanhoe, and the Rossis in Hillston. Eating Italian didn't become fashionable in Australia until about the 1960s but in Ivanhoe Antonietta – who had brought a maid, Paulina, with her from home – introduced the local women to these tasty dishes, including spaghetti and ravioli. Antonietta encouraged them to use tomato paste – she called it *pommodora* – which she made from home-grown tomatoes, and urged them to serve crusty bread and red wine with the dishes. No wonder she was treated like a celebrity by the men of the district.

Bean mentions the family had sent a daughter to boarding school in Sydney, 'half a continent away'.

All three Villa girls (there were no sons) attended the Convent of the Sacred Heart at Rose Bay. But when Bean visited in the winter of 1908, tragedy hung over the family. He doesn't mention it and maybe they didn't tell him, although that seems unlikely because the family were devastated.

In April their eldest daughter, Luigia, had died of peritonitis after a burst appendix. The girl was only 17 and had been preparing to sit for her matriculation. Luigia was talented and Francesco, who put so much value on learning, had insisted to the nuns she must have the chance to go further in her studies than the usual convent education. The school still has records of her prizes (and those of her sisters), and poignant accounts of her death. Afterwards, second daughter Elvira went home and may have been there during Bean's visit.

By the time Bean came through the Villas were long-term Ivanhoe residents. When there was a civic 'do' Francesco was chairman or a member of the committee, and often a speaker. On the day the governor visited Ivanhoe, Francesco gave the welcoming speech on behalf of the locals, after the dinner at the Ivanhoe Hotel. He was also the reliable score-keeper in the local cricket matches.

A few years after Bean's visit Francesco, nearing 60, sold his store and the Villas moved to Sydney in 1913. The Rossis had shifted there quite a while before. Maffio had a business importing goods from Italy, including marble, and had become a very prosperous figure in the commercial world. Francesco invested his money and spent his retirement reading his books.

It was the Villas' third daughter, Esterina, who fulfilled a dream Francesco and Maffio had shared over a meal at the

Ivanhoe Hotel before Maffio went back to Italy to marry Lucia. According to this rich family legend, they'd toasted each other and their future brides with 'a bottle of colonial wine', and Maffio had said how wonderful it would be if a marriage of their offspring one day brought together 'a friendship that has known the vicissitudes of creating a successful business in this new and wonderful country'.

In 1919 'Essie' married 'It' (Italo) Rossi.

I catch up with the rest of the Villa–Rossi story at another Sunday meal – lunch at the home of Theo Rossi, grandson of Franscesco and Maffio, in Northwood in Sydney. The family is as hospitable as when Francesco extended his invitation to Bean. They're absolutely familiar with Bean's description, and Theo's wife Mary jokingly worries that her food (apricot chicken) and coffee mightn't be up to Antonietta's standard. (I'm sure they are, of course.)

Francesco's home in Ivanhoe was a timber cottage surrounded by a wide verandah. The sitting room's horse-hair sofas had pretty cushions; candle-holders and family pictures were on the mantelpiece. The room was lit by colourful lamps, and Antonietta had brought out a floor rug from Italy.

The Sydney house where Theo and Mary have lived for more than 40 years is grand. Among the art work is a painting by Lloyd Rees, who used to be a friend and neigh-bour. The garden runs right down to the water, and the Rossis' big 'verandah' has spectacular views of the pleasure craft sailing on a winter's day. The high-rise of Sydney is shrouded in mist this Sunday – you have to look very hard to make out the skyscrapers. As we sit chatting about the past, the haze slowly lifts.

Theo, who turned 80 in October 2003, speaks only a little Italian, and most of that he picked up as an adult. But the Italian influence is here in this house, with its statues and European touches, and deep in the soul of Theo and his family including Mary, who has no Italian ancestry but knows the Rossi–Villa story backwards. Years ago, the Rossis drove out to Ivanhoe and *Kilfera*.

Theo contrasts his grandfathers; Rossi, the real businessman and the 'goer', and Villa, the reflective reader. 'Villa was never the big success Rossi was', but he was 'always more dashing and erudite'. He brings out a framed picture of the two men standing either end of their wagon. They've posed for the camera (did they have in mind an advertisement for their wares as well as a memento picture?). They're cheerful, jaunty, and snappily dressed – men of their new country, with a touch of the old one about them. Theo also has the wagon picture on a big carpet that used to adorn the family business in Sydney.

He remembers that 'both my grandfathers had swords. They'd brought swords to Australia – they'd both been soldiers. I traded Maffio Rossi's sword for a model ocean liner.'

Francesco, who died in 1935, often talked about the bush. 'He loved the country – he just adored the Australian outback,' Theo says. So did Antonietta.

The Villas never returned to Italy. In contrast, Maffio Rossi (who had been mayor of Hillston) visited regularly, was knighted by the Italian king, becoming Cavalier Maffio Rossi, and started the Australian–Italian Chamber of Commerce.

There seem to be no stories of Francesco and Maffio running into prejudice. But it was another matter for the next generation, and even Theo when he was young had a few bad experiences.

Italo – born in Hillston, educated at St Stanislaus College in Bathurst (near to Bean's old school) and, says Theo, as Aussie as they come – was detained by the military police in 1940, after Italy entered the war.

Antonietta by that time was well into her 80s and living with her daughter and Italo. On this day, 'my grandmother was doing some knitting. The military policeman even started to look through her embroidery bag'. Antonietta wasn't cowed, startling the man with a loud 'boo'. He quickly rebuked his elderly tormentor.

In one of the two court cases about Italo, a woman who'd been collecting for the Red Cross gave evidence that – when Essie Rossi had gone to get some money to donate – she'd seen in the house a statue of Mussolini on a horse, his arm up in a Fascist salute. Theo now has that statue. It is Apollo saluting the sun.

At one stage Theo went to the NSW Supreme Court to pick up his father. He recalls being told by a military policeman, 'He's Hi-talian. The only good Hi-talian is a dead Hi-talian'. It was a black contrast to the friendly greetings the 'Hi-talians' had received in the bush half a century earlier.

In a cruel irony, one of the places where Italo was detained was Hay, relatively near to Hillston and Ivanhoe; in another irony, Italo's brother-in-law, Colonel Coghill, was camp commander.

The situation did have the odd lighter moment. Theo, his mother and her sister at Christmas got permission to take Italo from the detention camp to the Monagetti Hotel in

Hay. Coghill, however, said the rules required that Italo had to have a military escort.

'I picked Dad up in his Oldsmobile. I was introduced to Sergeant Major Duffy, who had a tin hat and a rifle over his shoulder. We had a marvellous Christmas dinner, during which Sergeant Major Duffy proceeded to write himself off.' When they returned to the camp, Theo wasn't allowed to take the car up to the gate, so he let his father and the minder off a little distance away. 'Dad had to walk about 200 metres. Sergeant Major Duffy was having trouble with his rifle and his tin hat. Our last sight [as they went into the camp] was of Dad with the rifle over his shoulder and tin hat in hand escorting Sergeant Major Duffy.'

Even after all these years Theo burns with indignation at the injustice done to his father. He still has a letter from Italo's lawyer Howard Beale (later a federal minister) dated September 1945 in which Beale congratulates Italo for how well he bore his misfortune, adding 'I never had any doubt whatever that a great mistake had been made, and everything I have heard subsequently has confirmed that view.'

The affair had been all the more bizarre as Theo himself in 1940 was waiting impatiently for his 18th birthday the following year to enlist. He spent two years in the army, serving in New Guinea including Kokoda, and then two years in the RAAF. After the war Theo, who'd been christened Maffio (after his Rossi grandfather) Renzo changed his name by deedpoll. As a boy, at his Christian Brothers school he'd been labelled 'Dago'; now, after four years of war service, he wanted to Australianise his name. He'd been called 'Fio' as a shortening of Maffio, so he took as his new names Theo Richard.

It and Essie went on their first visit to Italy in the late '40s, but It pined to get back home. In the '60s Theo and Mary, who by then had eight of their 10 children, steeped themselves in the Italian heritage when the family had a year in Florence.

When Theo was in Italy another time, he saw the gazebo, looking down on Lake Como, where Francesco, in his soldier's uniform, courted Antonietta.

—

Today's spacious Ivanhoe store, 'Crisp and Halley', owned by the Whitchurch family, has seen livelier trading days. Clarrie Whitchurch, in his 70s and recently retired, tells us that in the 1950s it had 23 staff. Now his nephew Andrew and Andrew's wife Judi employ one other person there and a couple of casuals.

In those really good times, the big properties had recently been cut up into smaller blocks. My cousin Bill's property *Gladstone* was bought around then. In the early '50s wool was a £ a pound, and once more people in the West overestimated the country's potential.

With closer settlement, families were building homesteads and shearing sheds, and fencing their properties. They needed materials. The store sold almost everything; no, not 'almost' – Clarrie insists it sold the lot. 'It was a typical old store – everything from a needle to a haystack.'

You could outfit yourself and the kids, get your farm supplies and hardware, and stock up the family's groceries all under the one roof.

'We used to claim we served 1000 people in the district – in the town, on the railway, and on the properties,' says

Clarrie, who with his brother came to Ivanhoe in the '40s from an uncle's property nearby and started working in the shop. The owner, a Mr Crisp, encouraged employees to buy shares. Eventually the brothers bought the store. Business has been on the slide since the 1970s. Properties have consolidated again and the population has fallen. The roads are heaps better, allowing people to travel regularly for their shopping to bigger centres – the town of Hay or the regional cities of Griffith or Mildura.

The store eased itself out of fencing materials, sheep dips and other rural supplies. The wool firms were providing these on extended credit against the graziers' clip. Business was hit when the Commonwealth Bank left town. In the 1990s the store closed its drapery section, and gave up its Westpac agency. Today it's pretty much just a food shop and newsagent, as well as selling some general hardware. One of its two big interconnecting shops (where the drapery used to be) is used by local voluntary groups.

For Ivanhoe – and the Whitchurches' store – crime does pay. In some places people would be appalled at the idea of living cheek by jowl with a prison. But not in this struggle town. Established a few years ago a low security gaol, with about 70 prisoners, is a real boon, even if early hopes for the commercial boost it would give weren't quite realised.

'The gaol promised to buy everything we could supply,' says Clarrie. 'It didn't work out like that but we get a lot of money out of them.' The staff don't buy much locally – they drive away for weekends when they can. But the inmates send in orders for soap and shaving gear and lots of frozen foods, especially pizzas and pies.

Apart from the store, Ivanhoe has a cafe that also sells

fuel, two service stations, one with motel-type accommodation and the other with a caravan park, a hotel with a few rooms out the back, an RSL club, a telecentre and a vintage post office.

The gaol has come, but the railway's gone. And like many small towns, a lot of vitality has drained out. 'Life was really good in the '50s,' Clarrie remembers. 'We had lots of people in town, on the railway, and in the country. We used to have tennis, cricket and rugby league. The town, the railway and the country fielded their own teams in tennis and cricket. There was a lot of fun – it was a good place to live.'

What's it like now? 'Dead. There are not enough people to carry on the activities we used to have – and they are mainly elderly people. The young people have moved out for work and not come back again.'

The problem grabbed the attention of Sydney's *Daily Telegraph*. 'Ivanhoe bachelors pray for end to love drought' screamed a headline in June 2003. The *Telegraph* reported the town was 'running out of women'. The modern Ivanhoe has the highest proportion of males in NSW – 65 per cent. 'From Ivanhoe 200 km to Wilcannia, men outnumber women six to four,' the *Telegraph* reported, and quoted the laments of the local young men.

⁓

The Ivanhoe Hotel has modest accommodation for travellers. But its bar-cum-dining room is cheerful and friendly, and that encourages us to book in there rather than at the motel cabins. We make it our base for a couple of nights as we go round some stations in the daytime.

It's outside the hotel that we meet Jenny Farrar, from

Tooralee station. I'd heard of Jenny and her family from her sister Amanda Vanstone, minister in the Howard government. Amanda had stayed out here with her sister, and we'd chatted about the West.

I'd forgotten I'd told Amanda I would be travelling in Jenny's direction. So it's a surprise when she suddenly hails Margaret and me outside the pub. She's come in to cook that night at the hotel – a part-time job a couple of nights a week. 'Here, carry these,' she says briskly after the briefest introduction, thrusting various dishes of ingredients into our hands.

Jenny's a slimmer version of Amanda – bubbly, opinionated, and delighted to have company. She immediately rings husband Ian and son Charlie, who drive into town for the meal. We wash down the food with a couple of bottles of red and many stories. She and Ian have *Mossgiel* station as well as *Tooralee*, a total of 50,000 acres.

Jenny moved out here when she married Ian (who came from a property near Menindee) in the early '70s. 'We [girls] used to drive round [Adelaide] looking at whose utes were in town. I used to say, "You're mad, they've got hay in their hair" – [then] I was the only one who married one of them.'

She got into what passes for the hospitality industry in Ivanhoe by cooking for the RSL club. 'I've always liked the catering side of things. My father's family owned a couple of big hotels in Adelaide.

'The RSL club couldn't get a cook and they asked me to do it. I was a bored menopausal housewife. I said I would do it for three months – and I stayed two years.' She had a 'baptism of fire into the restaurant industry' when one of the guests of honour dropped dead at dinner. She gave up the job when things got busy at home, but later helped the hotel out.

As the Farrars speed off into the night they insist we come out to *Tooralee* for breakfast the next morning.

The visitor to *Tooralee* is in for a great surprise. After driving through rough and ugly country, the end of nowhere, you come upon a house in the most beautiful setting, looking out over a spectacular lake.

Jenny and Ian are brighter-eyed than we are after the late night. Breakfast is generous farmer-style. Looking out over the sunlit lake, this feels like country living at its best. The visitor can be lulled into forgetting the reality, but you can't if you live here, especially as drought deepens.

The area is too hard and lonely for Jenny, who wants to get away. She'd like to run a pub on the Murray, she tells us. At the time, I think Jenny and Ian won't leave. But a while later, I hear they have a business in Adelaide and one of their sons is running the property. Jenny explains when I contact her: 'We were looking down the barrel of no income, and we owe money. We just decided we couldn't live on Centrelink for two years.'

'Especially when sister Mandy's running it!' I can't resist pointing out.

Jenny and Ian had been hunting for a business for Charlie. They saw a little enterprise that delivers smallgoods to shops, hotels, small supermarkets, and military places on the Fleurieu Peninsula south of Adelaide. It seemed just the thing for the three of them, so they left Angus in charge in the West and moved.

Will they ever go back?

'We don't know. It would be unfair to saddle Angus with looking after that. He's 23 and half way through a pilot's licence.'

Jenny believes the value of Western land will lift, as people see they can, in certain conditions, raise fat lambs there and just maybe the wool situation will improve. 'If somebody offered us the amount of money we'd like, I'd murder Ian if he didn't take it.

'Probably if I was being truthful I'd say we wouldn't go back. But it wouldn't bother me to go back. Life out there [is] interesting , frustrating – and a very, very good learning curve.'

For us, Jenny and Ian bring alive Bean's observation that this country 'is the inhospitable home to a most hospitable people'.

From her new (temporary or permanent) home Jenny faxes me a poem written by a 'Pom' about his first impressions of Ian in the 1970s. It's called 'The Optimist'.

'We are both optimistic about life – as are most bush people. They are always looking out hopefully for the next rain that they know will come – eventually.' Typically, she adds: 'Come over and visit some time – we are three-quarters of an hour south of Adelaide.'

— 28 —
The Mystery of Mossgiel

I first interviewed Loma Marshall in the summer of 1990, when the temperature was 46 degrees and the red country radiated heat like a frying pan. I'd driven out to Mossgiel with my cousin Bill's son Red. He dropped me off at her house in the evening, after a five-hour journey from the 'inside' country, before he went on to the family's property near Ivanhoe.

I was to stay with Loma for a couple of days at the old decommissioned Mossgiel post office, on the plains where the Hay–Ivanhoe and the Hillston–Balranald roads intersect.

The next morning we set off in the blazing heat with a few poddy calves in the back of her ute to release them into the lignum. Unloading them seemed to me a massive effort. I thought I'd die, as I kept grabbing swigs from the water bag. The 60-year-old Loma was unflagging.

When I return to Mossgiel in 2003, this time with Margaret, to catch up with Loma, our conversation of 13 years before has been only slightly interrupted. 'The last of those calves turned up six years later,' she drawls laconically. Loma is not a woman who forgets much.

She's a one-off. So's Mossgiel, literally. Marked deceptively clearly on the map, it comprises one woman in one
dwelling. And that house has an intriguing and gruesome
history.

The West can be as savage on its towns as it is on its
people. We visited two towns, Mossgiel and Roto, that have
died within living memory. They've disappeared so compre-
hensively that, driving past, you'd never guess these had
once been flourishing communities.

In the 1890s, Mossgiel was a robust little town with aspirations. Old maps show the network of streets with the
grand names of the empire: Gladstone, Nelson, Victoria,
Albert, Waterloo. There were two hotels, two stores, a
tailor, the post office, two saddlers, two blacksmiths, two
butcher shops, a Chinese store and bakery, and a school.
The police station was manned by two mounted troopers;
the town was a Cobb and Co. change station. Wool was
sent off to Hay from the surrounding stations.

By 1903, the beginning of the end set in. The area was
gripped by drought. Mice invaded in plague proportions.
And typhus swept through, hitting every home.

The death blow finally came to Mossgiel when the
railway went through Ivanhoe in 1925. In the 1920s, many
houses were vacant and the town was doomed. Ida Long-
worth, now in her 80s and living in Newcastle, is one of the
few people with memories of those days. When I ring her to
find out more about the place, we step back through the
decades.

Her father was postmaster in the 1920s; the family lived
in this house that's now Loma's. 'I went there as a toddler.
There was a store, a hotel, a cottage hospital with a nurse,

a school house and a school but no school master, a church but no minister, and a community hall,' Ida says.

The hall was blown down by a cyclone. Church services were given by any minister who happened to be passing. Goats, which survived better than sheep in dry times, were everywhere.

'It was very much on the way out when we were there. It was a very lonely place,' Ida says. But she's got a soft spot for Mossgiel – 'being a little kid and running wild'. She didn't start school until she was eight and a half and her family had moved to Newcastle.

A few years ago Ida and her two sisters came back to have a sentimental look at the old post office, which had outlived the other buildings but acquired a certain notoriety. By then it had a ghost. Or is it two ghosts?

In her much-praised book *The Road from Coorain* Jill Ker Conway tells of her childhood on her family's station, seven miles from Mossgiel. By the 1940s all that remained of the town was the post office, remnants of a hotel, and a ramshackle hall.

At shearing time in June 1943, the Ker family hired 'Pommy' Goodman, a local eccentric, to help at *Coorain*. Pommy was a larger-than-life character, 'a middle-aged Englishman with a perfect Mayfair accent, one of the foulest mouths I ever heard, and the bearing of one to the manner born.'

A while later, Pommy took the job of postmaster. He operated the telephone exchange, listening into the conversations, and butting in when he felt like it. The post office opened and closed when he chose. At the telephonic hub of the district Pommy was, however, alone and isolated, and drank heavily. Ker Conway writes:

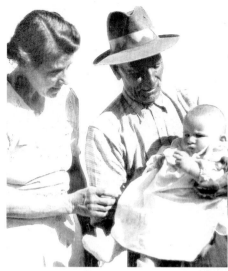

Morbine Perooz was one of many Afghans in the West. He bought a white bride who was only a child; the photo shows him with his wife Myrtle and granddaughter Marilyn.
Courtesy of Marilyn and John Abel.

This mosque, now in the Bourke cemetery, was in the yard of the Peroozs' house.

Anthony Pease and Karin Donaldson have put city life behind them to move to Wilcannia.

A light from the Victoria Hotel hangs from a verandah ceiling at *Tarella*. Katharine Susannah Prichard describes a ball at the station where a verandah was 'roofed in with pink blossoms and white muslin'.

The dug-out is the house of choice in White Cliffs.

'Topar Hotel . . . is the one landmark on a plain as flat and nearly bare as a soup-plate.'
(C.E.W. Bean), Courtesy of the Broken Hill Library.

The Trades Hall building's grandeur is a reminder of the era when mining was flourishing at Broken Hill and so was unionism. The former has declined and the latter has dwindled.

The Menindee Hotel has been in the Maiden family since the
1890s. Bean wrote that its just-married 'kind host and hostess'
(William and Ruby Maiden) changed his outlook on the town.
Noeline, the present licensee, is William and Ruby's great-
granddaughter. The town and the hotel still celebrate their link
with the Burke and Wills expedition.

The construction of the Menindee Lakes scheme transformed the area and provided Broken Hill with water and a leisure area. But in the recent drought the lakes virtually dried out.

Bean 'left the horses looking over the garden fence and went up to the front door and knocked'. *Kilfera* would have been little changed when this picture was taken in 1912; Roger Sheaffe, who drove Bean into Ivanhoe and introduced him around, still lived at the station. Today's *Kilfera* owners, Clive and Fay Linnett, lived in the old house for some years.

The Alder sisters made a sentimental journey late in the century to mark the graves of the brothers they had lost early in the century. *Courtesy of Fred Sharon.*

Maffio Rossi (left) and Francesco Villa started off with a well-stocked hawkers' cart. *Courtesy of the Rossi family.*

I found the grandson of Maffio and Francesco, Theo Rossi, and his wife Mary in Sydney; they live up to the old-style hospitality. Here they are with Theo's nephew, David Twigg, a great-grandson of Maffio and Francesco.

Francesco and Antonietta Villa brought a touch of European style to Ivanhoe. Antonietta introduced the local women to Italian cooking. Daughter Esterina is on the left and Elvira is on the right. *Courtesy of the Rossi family.*

Loma Marshall and
Billy Baird –
another two of the
great characters of
the modern West.

One morning, about three months after he left us, the exchange was dead. No one paid much attention, thinking that he was taking longer than usual to sober up. His first customer of the day found him swinging from the central beam of the post office, fully dressed in suit and tie. He had been sober enough to arrange the noose efficiently and kick the chair he stood on well across the room. I could never go there again without eyeing the beam and wondering about his thoughts that night.

Ker Conway's book came out about the time I stayed with Loma, but I hadn't read it then. A while later, when I came upon that passage, it gave me a start. From the description, it was almost certain the room where 'Pommy' died was the mail room – now the bedroom in which I'd slept.

I dined out for years on this ghost until, after my second visit to Loma, Ida sent me the reminiscences of another former local, Hope Walker, born in 1912, who grew up in Mossgiel. Hope's family lived in the residence of the then-closed public school. She has a different account of tragedy in the post office – a tale of unrequited love.

In the 1930s Rod D'Ornay arrived as postmaster. He was a man in his 60s, with a limp and a walking stick, and close about his family and background. Obliging to customers, D'Ornay lived at the post office, taking his meals at the hotel.

A community-spirited individual, he became secretary of the hospital board. He also apparently became infatuated with the nursing sister. The Sister, for reasons unknown, suddenly decided to go back to Sydney.

Very soon after, the postmaster did not appear for his usual breakfast at the hotel. Two men were sent to see if he was ill.

They found D'Ornay hanging from the fan-light of a doorway. Things were complicated by no one knowing how to work the telephone instrument board to summon the police, 31 miles away.

There was, apparently, a long letter in the post for Sister. Hope Walker says its contents were never revealed. I was able to verify the D'Ornay death through the official record, but wasn't able to find a death certificate for 'Pommy'. Curious, I wondered if Jill Ker Conway knew any more. She emailed: 'I can speculate, but that's all. In 1943 the war was at its height in the Pacific. There were no doctors within 70 to 100 miles, and for a brief time there was no police officer in Ivanhoe. So perhaps there was no one to issue a death certificate. In hot weather no one waited too long to bury someone.'

When I send Loma this story of the two deaths – she'd heard of only one – she writes back, in hand and style that would have delighted Banjo Paterson, 'Ha, didn't know was two hangings? in this old dump. Still can't see any rope marks . . . only marks in door crack where screw top bottles where opned [sic].'

Loma arrived in Mossgiel in the 1970s. Why would she want to settle in such a back of nowhere spot? Well, it was a place where you could get a house (with a history) for $1500. But she was anxious to expand beyond the house land, so she could grow feed for her animals. And that turned into a bureaucratic nightmare.

She was given a limited lease, but would not be allowed to take over the whole town. In a letter that was a triumph of caution over common sense, an official wrote to her: 'While it is conceded that the demand for land at Mossgiel is not high, experience in other Western Division towns has shown that long-term future demand is difficult to forecast.'

Loma originally comes from the Cann River area of Victoria. As a boy, her father had broken in horses for the gun carriages of World War I. Later, he had a farm, and was the 'powder monkey', doing the blasting in the road-building team. Other times he was timber-cutting, horse-breaking, fruit-picking, slaughtering and droving.

When her parents separated, Loma stayed with her father and went on his droving trips. She married twice. Her husbands (both of whom died) were drovers. Her younger years were filled with droving trips, riding buckjumping horses, and having two children. Once she settled at Moss-giel, she did jobs for the neighbouring stations. When I met her in 1990, she had recently taken up sheep crutching. Her place that year was a sort of domestic zoo. She had some 16 dogs, ten horses, 30 goats, two peacocks, a few calves, fowls, and one or two sheep. All were 'old tarts', while the ute was a 'touchy old tart'. Also living with her was Dave the horse-breaker, his charges laden with pans and bags to quieten them.

By 2003 the animal numbers are down. Death had claimed her favourite horse, a skewball called Elizabeth, on which she'd posed for me to take a picture during a fierce dust storm. She still keeps a picture of Elizabeth in the kitchen.

Dave is no longer there. I hesitate to ask about him. The area is gripped by drought. 'We've cut more sheeps' throats and shot more cows this year.'

But Loma is just the same, slowed only slightly by a botched hip operation after an accident with a horse a few years ago.

When I call up from Wagga Wagga to say we're coming, she laughs and laughs at the thought anyone would make an 850-kilometre round trip just to talk to her.

We arrive mid-morning. Loma's still amused, her bright blue eyes set off with generous dollops of blue eye shadow and a hat that's decorated with a sprig of artifical flowers. The flowers had blown through the fence of the cemetery. What a waste, she says, to let them just scatter about – and so she'd stuck them in her brim.

The cemetery is still in use. Only the dead multiply in Mossgiel.

Loma has staying with her Margie Moore, her friend from Morundah, near Narrandera, whose daughter recently died of an overdose. Margie says she needed to get away from nosey friends, so one day she just arrived at Loma's. A formidable woman with the brightest of red hair, Margie has been a shearers' cook, and she's soon in full flight with stories.

The women are waiting for Billy Baird, the 86-year-old mailman who twice a week rises at 4 am to do the run from Hay to Ivanhoe and back. When he arrives for his lunch, Loma clucks over him protectively, bringing soup.

Baird was born in Hay, growing up in the area during the Depression. His father had a few cows. Billy didn't go to school – 'in those days you followed the cows and milked the cows' – but he did go to war. Caught in Singapore, he was a POW for three and a half years, forced to work first on the Singapore wharves, then on the notorious Burma line and finally in Japanese coal mines. 'I've seen war from both sides. When you see little kids blown to pieces, it's not a nice sight.'

After he returned home, Billy took over his father's milk run; the herd of about 100 supplied 300 gallons of milk to Hay, Ivanhoe, Carrathool and Maude. A partnership with two of his five sons didn't work; they took over the milk production business, but eventually they went broke. Later 'one son shot himself; the other shot through'.

Billy went to Queensland, working for James Hardie Ltd at Wacol. 'They sacked me at 65, then I went on the pension.' Back in Hay, he took up the milk run, often getting bogged on what was still a dirt road. The road's good now, but the bureacracy is another matter – they're always on his tail about driving tests. He puts them off when he can. A few years back 'I drove for 18 months or two years without a licence. I got fined $400 or $500 for it.'

The night before, the refrigerated truck is loaded with meat, vegetables, milk and mail. Then at the crack of dawn – well before dawn in winter time – the bread arrives from Wodonga on the Murray and the Melbourne papers from Echuca where they've been sorted.

It takes up to four hours to get from Hay to Ivanhoe, dropping letters and goods at the station mail boxes along the way. Billy's only concession to his age is a sleep at the trucking rest camp near Booligal. The highlight of the trip is lunch at Loma's.

He and Loma are quickly into a set-to about the war in Iraq. Billy's against ('I've got nothing against Hussein, the Yanks are just as bloody mad about religion'); she's equally passionately in favour ('I reckon, get in there first').

But today Billy has something closer to home on his mind. Fresh tenders are being called for the mail run. 'The bastards want me to go to Broken Hill to be interviewed.' He'll drive as long as he can. 'I've got nothing else to do and I might as well keep doing it.'

Baird's become a legend; indeed he and Loma are minor media stars, in ABC programs and written up in *Good Weekend*'s 'two of us' column.

After Loma has posed, coy as a girl, for photos with Billy beside the mail truck, he's on his way.

Loma takes us to visit the cemetery. Later we look at the cards and pictures that crowd the walls of the old post room, and debate where the hanging took place. Loma is bleakly practical about life in a dreadful year, when it's 'feeding stock, penning up, cutting throats, mustering, shooting cows. Di Huntley [a neighbour on a station] has got to shoot her sheep that are down – I can cut their throats.'

Margie appears from outside. 'I think that old dog's had a heart attack.' Loma is surprised – the dog was all right the day before, she says – but philosophical. If its time to die has come, so be it. She just hopes the other dogs don't bother it.

A while later, Margie's back. 'I think you'll have to shoot that dog, Loma – it's in pain.' Loma doesn't hesitate. She picks up a rifle, and the two women walk out of the house. Margaret and I brace ourselves for the sharp 'pop'. Loma comes back and takes up the conversation without missing a beat.

− 29 −
The End of the Line

Roto station, about 40 kilometres from Hillston – a town on the Lachlan river, which forms the border of the Western Division – has a place among the great sheep runs of Australia's past. 'Oh we started down from *Roto* when the sheds had all cut out', goes a bush song '. . . we humped our blues serenely and made for Sydney town'.

Bean camped in the area in 1908, yarning with a bullocky 'at Fourteen Mile Well, on the boundary of *Roto* run'.

> The bullocky's team must have been somewhere near, enjoying themselves in the Roto grass, which was luscious and long. The bullocky was camped right under the well. His wagon, all sheeted in, showed vaguely like some huge rounded boulder in front of the fire. Behind, black against the sky, we could see the great winze of the well; and the low, long iron of the trough occasionally glinted in the firelight.
>
> Far away, like a cigarette end in the dark, a tiny spark showed where we, too, had camped for the night under a wilga tree . . . Our horses, too, were enjoying themselves on Roto grass.

Reading the words, we have to see *Roto* for ourselves, and once we get there we find, as in so many places, interesting wider stories.

Frank and Shirley Underwood, who came from Victoria and have been here more than 20 years, own the modern *Roto* station. Their spacious contemporary house is on the site of a homestead that went back to the 19th century, where the Underwoods lived until fire destroyed it.

There is no Fourteen Mile Well any more but a Fourteen Mile bore, near the northern boundary; traces of the old well have all but gone. The historic shearing shed, however, which already had had many years' use by Bean's time, is still operating. Today it shears only about 10,000 sheep (in a normal year), not 70–80,000 as it once did, and bikes, not horses, are used for mustering, although the Underwoods used horses when they had girls working on the place. Frank, incidentally, is full of praise for the stockwork skills of women in the back country. 'Girls do a miles better job than blokes. We've in the past employed some marvellous girls, but they are so hard to get today.'

After coffee and chat at the homestead, the Underwoods take us to see the large and still-solid airstrip that was built on the property during World War II. Although it saw few planes, this was part of a southern line of defence in case of Japanese attack; there were other strips at Bourke and Tocumwal on the Murray. The *Roto* runways are of a cement and soil mix and stretch 2.4 kilometres from east to west and 2.7 kilometres north to south. These days grain silos overlook the strip.

From the airstrip we drive on to an old Chinese well on the property. This is part of the remarkable story of the many

Chinese settlers who moved to these parts, of whom little trace now remains.

Frank says that, according to the stories that have been passed down, the Chinese came to *Roto* from the goldfields, and very many lived there. He has two old metal buckets that he believes the Chinese used, one for digging and the other for drawing water. A wheel would be suspended above the well, and the heavy bucket, which could hold perhaps 30 gallons, lowered. The bucket has a flap which would be forced open as it went down below the water line; the flap would close again as the bucket was raised.

During a bad drought in the early 1990s, the wind blew away a lot of soil and exposed the remains of the extensive Chinese settlement that was around this well. The area is called 'Chinamens', Frank says. 'We found the remains of where they had huts – they put in bed logs.' These were slabs of native pine laid on the ground for foundations, instead of using stumps. The Chinese went from the settlement out to work in various other areas.

The *Roto* woolshed, which dates from the 1860s and has horizontal logs, was built by the Chinese, as was the log section of the old homestead. They'd also ringbark and cut trees.

The role of the Chinese in these parts of NSW is an underwritten story, although more has been said of their presence in the closer-in Riverina country. One researcher who is gathering information on them is Barry McGowan, a historian and heritage consultant based in Canberra who has recently published a book on Australian ghost towns, including places in the West. When I contact him, he tells me he's unearthing evidence all through the area between Hillston and Cobar of the Chinese presence in large numbers and their extensive activities. These included, but went well beyond, their lush market gardens in the towns and on the stations, which, it is no exaggeration to say, a century ago kept much of the West supplied with fruit and vegetables.

The Chinese also worked in large teams, and they sank 'tanks' (dams) and did a lot of land clearing, with Chinese entrepreneurs organising contracts for work and settling on rates and timing. Many landowners were totally dependent on the Chinese for land clearing. Barry has told the story of the Chinese in various parts of NSW including the far West in a paper he presented at the Australian National University titled 'Ringbarkers and market gardeners'.

The picture he paints of the Chinese is one of 'labourers and gardeners . . . very much in charge of their own destiny,' and much sought-after by employers because of their industry and reliability. The Chinese had market gardens on the banks of the Lachlan at Hillston, and in the late 1880s there were up to 1000 Chinese in the Nymagee district where, for highly competitive prices, they cut scrub and ringbarked.

The Chinese have largely disappeared (although the West, we found, is well supplied with Chinese restaurants). Many, no doubt, moved on. And another explanation is to be found in a little book of memories of Nymagee where one author writes of the Chinese gardens, with more than 30 Chinese working under the supervision of Ah Hooey. Hooey drove around the town 'with his horse drawn cart laden, and sold his produce to the townspeople during the 1930s'. But 'as there were no Chinese ladies the colony faded'.

—

When we drive to *Roto* station, Margaret and I see that 'Roto' is also a town on the map, but it's the Underwoods who tell us some of its details, including the fact that the map is deceptive – Roto has disappeared.

They suggest we talk to Joe and Jean Wood, who lived 45 years in Roto town, and stayed to its end, so we go to Hillston to meet the last couple from Roto (a nice counterpoint, we think, to Bean's meeting the first white baby born in Cobar) before we drive through the ghost town by the railway line.

Joe, who worked on the railways for 34 years, was the last to operate the mail run out of Roto; after they moved to Hillston, Jean took the run over and did it from there. They share their recollections so we can imagine what it was like when we see the 'town' itself.

Roto was a modest but substantial settlement in the middle years of the 20th century. It was built around the railway, with maintenance workers stationed there, but a sawmill and a rabbit-freezing business also provided jobs. There was a post office-cum-store, a second store, and a school. Perhaps appropriately for a small railway town, the teacher lived in a converted train carriage. As late as the 1960s, the Roto school had more than 30 children, but by the early 1970s it was closed.

In the West, the fate of some towns, indeed whether they've lived or died, has often been determined by changes in transport routes or modes of transport. Wilcannia might have one day been a grand inland town if the Darling had remained a waterway. It was the coming of the railway to Ivanhoe that spelled the end for tiny Mossgiel. The ascendancy of road over rail was the deathknell for Roto.

Today, the traveller drives into Roto past a sign that, like some wayside Cheshire cat, is the face of a town that has been left with no substance. All that remains is a community hall, full of memories of when it doubled as a church and a centre for parties and even the Grand Roto Ball of 1956.

Roto was once a rail centre for sending away wool and receiving supplies for the stations around. In World War II, the town was a hive of activity when the nearby airstrip was being built.

The railway line still runs through Roto. But the trains don't stop there anymore; they speed past as if scorning a place that used to be vital to them, and they to it.

And what do you do when a town becomes surplus to requirements? In this part of the West, where buildings are mostly transportable, you cart it away – that is, those parts that haven't burned down, like the Roto shop and post office did, and the sawmill as well. And afterwards, you auction off the blocks.

Some of Roto town's buildings are scattered around the district. The railway carriage where the teacher lived is on another property; the school building went somewhere else. The Underwoods progressively bought up the town blocks. Roto town only waits for someone to remove the sign.

In the West the life and death of towns has been part of the normal cycle. With all the publicity about how country towns are shrinking and dying, it's easy to get the impression that it's something new, a product of a modern drift of people to the cities. But, from soon after the West was settled, it was always thus (although perhaps the difference is that it was not such a one way street – some towns were also developing).

The fate of many towns was linked to the fortunes of mines. Barry McGowan, whose speciality is mining history, says that while pastoralism was very important, the impact of mining was crucial in the development of many of the towns and roads of the West.

The story of Mount Hope makes the point. Bean's list of expenses for the 1908 trip shows an entry of 17 shillings paid to the Mount Hope Hotel. By the time Bean travelled through, that little township had already endured the best and worst of times. Copper mining saw it boom in the 1880s, with more than 1000 people and a goodly number of businesses. A fall in copper prices quickly had the town deserted. Then mining and Mount Hope revived for a while, only to have the cycle start over again.

Like the town of Roto, Mount Hope's appearance on the map can deceive the unwary. It does have a functioning hotel, but that's about all. When we stopped there one morning, we found a young couple knocking a little desperately on the door of the pub. They'd run their petrol low, assuming that they could get fuel at the petrol station that's near the hotel. Alas, it had closed down, and the couple had to persuade the hotelier to supply a can of fuel so they could make their next stop.

4

The Future

— 30 —
The Future of the Darling and its Land

Over tens of thousands of years, the Darling was a bountiful provider to the Aborigines. At the town of Brewarrina, a little upstream of Bourke, you can see the remarkably sophisticated approach they brought to harvesting the fish of the Darling. They constructed an elaborate set of stone traps or 'pens' in which to capture the Murray Cod and other fish that swam upstream. In a paper for the Royal Society of New South Wales in 1903 R.H. Mathews drew on the pastoral imagery of the time to describe the fish traps as operating 'much in the way that sheep are driven into "catching pens" at shearing time'.

The traps had their ends open towards the direction from which the fish came in spring or when there was a 'fresh' in the river. Men and women kept watch and when enough of the 'finny tribe' were in the 'labyrinth', big stones were used to close the openings.

The people then went into the pens and 'splashed the water with their hands or feet', moving the fish into smaller enclosures, for ease of catching. Particular families had their own traps, and others, apart from relatives when they came into the river area, were not to remove fish from someone else's trap.

Bean did not get as far as Brewarrina, but referred to the fish traps, 'a sort of curious network or maze of stones', without, perhaps, realising the extraordinary nature of them.

More vividly, he reported that a Scottish settler in the back country recalled the Darling blacks floating down the river 'in their dug-outs – a whole family party in one hollow log, gins, piccaninnies and paterfamilias'. With a fire burning on a bed of clay in the bottom of the boat, the family would be roasting a tasty fish meal.

The importance of the Darling to the Aborigines over thousands of years before white men came is obvious, and went beyond just being a rich source of a staple in their diet. Even today, however, the river is special for the indigenous people who live near it. The study of the impact of the 2001–03 drought by Margaret Alston and Jenny Kent found the drying up of the Darling near Bourke had a big effect on the town's indigenous residents. The river's spiritual importance meant 'the symbolism of the loss of the river has major cultural significance'. When the river started running again, this brought 'great joy'.

Before it reaches the dry lands of the Western Division, the Darling is a complex of nine or ten streams rising in the state's eastern highlands, supported in modern times by a series of catchment dams, and then passing through relatively well-watered areas. The Darling's catchment area relies heavily on rains coming down from the north. Consequently its flow is less reliable than the flows in other rivers originating elsewhere in the eastern ranges. Further downstream the Darling changes character as it moves into flatter and dryer country. On first encountering it, Charles Sturt was so impressed with its broad deep channel and the fringe of large gum trees that he described it as 'a magnificent canal', but realised that it was obviously subject to severe dry spells that could reduce it to no more than a series of waterholes.

Below Bourke, in all the West only two watercourses join the Darling, the Warrego and the Paroo; each is of such intermittent flow that only occasionally it reaches the Darling.

When on our travelling we passed over the Paroo watercourse there was nothing in it at all. The Paroo has been described as the last major free-flowing river in the Murray–Darling basin, and it has been the object of tussle between those who wanted to grow cotton in its upper reaches and downstream graziers. The graziers some years ago thwarted the cotton interests by buying up the water rights.

During our visits we crossed the Darling, or stood on its banks, at numerous points: including the towns of Bourke, Brewarrina, Menindee, Wilcannia, Louth, and Tilpa, and the properties of *Toorale*, *Dunlop*, *Jandra* and *Killara*. Its character and strength of flow is not markedly different from that noted by the early venturers who entered the country of endless horizon and glaring sunlight.

We were seeing it in dry times, but we heard first-hand stories of the great floods that can have those on stations balancing a load of groceries in a small boat. The river still has the potential to offer a feast or a famine, either breaking its banks to spread over its flood plains, or shrinking within its deep and steep channel until nature replenishes and empowers it.

The Aborigines lived in harmony with the river. Except in bad times, it supplied them well; even in drought its banks and flats were easier country than further out. They in turn treated it gently; their limited numbers and hunter–gatherer economy made few demands on the Darling or the other great rivers.

Nor indeed did the busy river trade of the late 19th century and early 20th century put great pressure on the rivers. It was the land, rather than the water that was becoming, in more modern jargon, 'under stress' at that time.

In the 21st century, the health and future of Australia's rivers have become a great national issue. The Darling is part of the general debate about the vast Murray–Darling basin, as well as being at the centre of the particular argument about the extent to which the irrigators should be allowed to draw water from the river.

In Bean's day, irrigation was one of the great hopes for coping with Australia's dryness, and even perhaps for fulfilling the dream of populating parts of the continent's semi-arid areas. A century later the trend in rural areas is depopulation and the emphasis has shifted to the costs and limitation of irrigation.

As the water debate gained momentum during the drought of 2003, I was among some guests of Clyde Agriculture who stood on the reconstructed wharf at the Old Port as David Boyd, the company's managing director, put the irrigators' case, before taking us to see the unplanted cotton fields.

He said it was ironic the argument should rage when, at least for Bourke's irrigators, 'there isn't any bloody water.

If there was no irrigation, the impact of the drought would be the same.'

David told his listeners that 'ecology has replaced economics as the dismal science. The ecologist is likely to extrapolate things to Armageddon.

'We have a Captain Cook syndrome going in Australia – [the idea] that Australia should be as it was when Captain Cook came. I would challenge that. I believe environments evolve – nothing stays the same. It's not valid to look back and say it should be like that. [But] looking at what's there now and taking a long-term view is very valid. If Australia has a distinctive characteristic, it's not so much one of dryness but one of massive variability. We have to conserve in times of plenty for the inevitable times of scarcity.'

The cotton growers have attracted a barrage of criticism, but they get some carefully qualified and perhaps unexpected support from Ben Gawne, the director of the Murray–Darling Freshwater Research Centre at Albury. Gawne makes an interesting comparison between the respective 'footprints' of sheep and cotton on the environment, pointing out that sheep have a low impact over a huge geographic area, while cotton has a high impact but limited spread.

Australia needs commodities that are capable of dealing with our 'boom and bust' climate, Gawne tells me. 'The cotton industry is more capable of responding to variation in climate, compared with sheep. [After a drought] cotton takes a year to respond, while rebuilding a flock takes a lot longer.'

In the case of the sheep industry, 'we've tried to impose an agricultural system that is attuned to a relatively predictable environment on an arid environment. Wool-producing sheep need a benign environment for a long period. We have to learn to say that we can't control the environment and ask, can we develop agricultural systems that are more flexible?'

One group that has become a major force in the national water debate is the Wentworth group, formed by eminent scientists in 2003. Peter Cullen is an expert in aqua ecology and a member of the group. He sees the argument about the Darling as a typical example of the tension between upstream and downstream users of the water from a long river. 'There's competition for water up and down the Darling,' he tells me. 'The pastoralists and towns who are dependent on Darling water are competing with the irrigators.'

Although the cotton growers at Bourke can only pump when the river is high – as David Boyd says – it does mean the users downstream get less. And the broader issue of the Darling's ultimate flow in support of the lower Murray is of concern both to irrigators and to South Australia as Adelaide's population is dependent on the Murray's water.

One major change to the Darling waterscape since the early 1900s has been the construction of the Menindee Lakes system, based on the area's natural lakes and completed in 1968. This gave a water supply to Broken Hill and Menindee, as well as supplying a small irrigation area. Because of the high evaporation the shallow storages are inefficient, but they have been important in allowing the development of the irrigation along the Murray and in ensuring the reliability of the supply of water to South Australia.

The Darling is a very different river to the Murray. Its

more unpredictable flows made it less easy to exploit in earlier days. Therefore it does not have anything like the current problems of the Murray; it is not so over-developed and the irrigation is more limited and its practices are better. However Peter Cullen stresses that we don't know enough about this river. 'We have got to understand the Darling a lot better,' he says, adding that we have the opportunity to do this before there is a crisis.

The use of water from the Darling is one challenge for the West; an equally crucial challenge is the viability of the West's pastoral properties. The years 2001–03 underscored the difficulties faced by station owners from recurring drought; increasingly, because of the limited options for using this land and the problematic future of wool prices, it is hard to be confident of making enough in better times to cover the bad years.

New beginnings being made by the families on neighbouring old Darling River stations, *Yanda* and *Jandra*, symbolise the two sides of the story of the Darling pastoral country today. These stations lie side by side along the east bank of the river, not far from Bourke. Both have rich histories stretching back into the 19th century, although neither has a fraction of the acreage it once had.

Bill Stonnill and his wife Marissa Vincent came to *Yanda* in 1990, soon after they married. *Yanda* has had many owners over the years, and it has taken its toll. One story has it that nobody has ever made any money out of *Yanda*. One who certainly didn't was Charles Dickens's son Edward, who lost badly when he invested in the property.

Bill came from the comparatively benign country of the Riverina, where his family has *Cocketgedong* near

Jerilderie; Marissa was a city girl, from Geelong in Victoria. It's been a challenge ever since the couple, then in their 20s, arrived; first wool prices plunged and then they were hit with three droughts. Now they've sold *Yanda* (70,000 acres) to become part of the Gundabooka National Park. By early 2004, Bill and Marissa had rented a house near Hamilton in Victoria's Western district; they'd been fare-welled by neighbours who were depressed to see the departure of another family from the district, and Marissa was about to move south. Bill was to wait until they found a buyer for their other property, which has 100,000 acres and is nearby. But that wasn't likely until there was some more rain.

Marissa explains to me how they made the decision to leave. Four years ago she and Bill took up 'holistic farming'; part of this approach is to set goals for 'farming, family and finances'. Bill and Marissa, who have two young children, found they could not reach these goals living on the Darling and so 'we either had to change the goals, or move.'

Life in this back country is extremely harsh, Marissa says, and she thinks it is this harshness that makes the people so 'fantastic'. 'Their friendships are honest, almost bare, because of the hostility of the environment. It's not an envi-ronment that welcomes you; it's one that you have to survive. This country is like the cemetery – a great leveller.' She's sad to leave the people but not sad about departing this land for the easier climes of Victoria, where they plan to buy a farm.

'A lot of people say you have to be born here to know how to run the country. I think you have to be born here to accept what the country imposes on you,' she says. It's country of 'no prizes and lots of badges'. She sees the Western District of Victoria as 'like a Ferris wheel where you can anticipate the ups and downs with more certainty' compared to 'life up here which is a roller-coaster'.

Since their decision to depart, Marissa has had two reactions. 'Some people have been affronted by us saying we don't want to live like this.' On the other hand, 'wives will come up to me and say, "I hate living here, you're so lucky. [My husband] won't leave – he's got family baggage." '

Marissa, whose main regret is that they didn't make their decision earlier, believes that anywhere they go now will be 'so much easier. It's been an incredible experience. Now we have wisdom. You can use failure either as a reason to continue to fail or as a reason to succeed. We're using it as a reason to succeed.'

Over at *Jandra*, Margaret and I saw the other side of the picture: that of continuity. Phillip Ridge has known the back country all his life, and we can see he's one of the stoics. Although he was brought up on another property, *Jandra* has been in the family since the 1870s, and he has the very strong sense of 'place' that researchers have found among those who've been bred to the West. The riverboat on which Bean travelled was named after this property; Phillip's grandfather, who was born on the dining-room table at the old homestead, was given 'Jandra' as his middle name.

When we visit in early 2003, Phillip tells us the family history, and shows us the small museum of station memorabilia that he is putting together. The river yields its treasure too; his sons have recently found an old riverboat anchor, which came to light because the river was so low in the drought. We walk around the sprawling weatherboard homestead that backs right onto the Darling's high bank; it is the oldest existing lived-in dwelling on the Darling, Phillip says.

The property is not mentioned in Bean's books, and we wonder whether Bean noticed it – or if not, how he missed it – either as the *Jandra* went past on its way to *Dunlop*, or at least on the return journey. I detect a sense of slight that Bean could have failed to spot the house high on the riverbank. 'Perhaps it was at night and there was no moon,' Phillip speculates. 'It seems extraordinary that he didn't recognise it in some way. There would have been 20 or 30 people there [these included a Chinese gardener and a blacksmith] and I imagine a heap of dogs.'

A few months after our visit, at the end of 2003, Phillip and Diana and their four boys shift from the cottage on the property to the big house, which had previously been occupied by Phillip's aunt Jacqueline, who was now living in Sydney because of ill-health. The family sees the move as something exciting and special; tightening their bonds to this land. There are three special ties, Phillip says.

'The first is the family heritage. I know it doesn't pay the bills but I feel a sense of history.' Both sides of his family have been in the West for several generations; on his mother's side Phillip is the fifth generation to own *Jandra*.

Secondly, 'I'm a great believer in Merino sheep and the wool and mutton industries, despite the hardships of the last 12 years. Wool as a product is a great article – that is why we persevere with it.

'And thirdly, to raise a family, it's the healthiest, happiest and best environment you can get. There are not the pressures and complications you get in the urban areas, or even the regional centres.'

Would he ever leave this country? I ask. No, says Phillip. 'I couldn't live in a climate where it rained all the time. I'm certainly in the right spot!'

Epilogue

The people of the outback would see their lives as ordinary. To the observer from the city, or from the 'inside' country, they are remarkable.

Bean found in the West a very special collection of Australians. And so, despite the great differences made by a century, did we. Sadly, the story of the sheep is much grimmer than 100 years ago. Wool growing is no longer a grand economic adventure with a great future. It has turned into the tale of struggle, with many uncertainties. But the wool men are as innovative and adaptive as before, and they have been joined in their businesses by many women. Even the great Merino is changing with the times, to become more suitable and competitive in the modern world.

Bean's critics are probably right when they argue that he over-stated the influence of the 'country' characteristics in Australia's Anzacs. Still, travelling the outback today, one does feel that these people have distinctive qualities which they bring to how they live their lives. The harsh land hones the people who must survive in it.

Our journeyings were finished before the rains came in

Queensland and a flow of water at last refreshed the Darling and provided much-needed relief for the irrigators at Bourke. Down at Menindee – where the great lake system had almost dried out and the people of Broken Hill had been buying water because the supply had become nearly undrinkable – expanses of water appeared again in one of the lakes.

The first drought of the new century had broken in parts of the West. Patches of country, however, remained as dry as the parched bones of its many victims. Those who live in such spots might question the arbitrariness of the rain pattern. And as I write this early in 2004, the pastoralists are again waiting anxiously for rain.

The West and its people, or some of them, have come through another cycle in the history of the plains country. It will be years before many get back on their feet economically, and a number have been driven out, defeated by forces beyond their control. Many, however, are regrouping, as they always have after difficult times. It takes a certain psychological toughness to accept that however good a particular season may be, in the next year, or the one after that, or certainly three or four years on, life is certain to become hell, when nature wreaks havoc. The people who stay in the West have an optimism in the face of an often discouraging reality that is among their enduring and endearing qualities. That optimism, and their resilience and open-heartedness, were captured by Bean, and will appeal just as much to the modern visitor to this distinctive part of Australia.

Notes on Sources

Bean's works used or consulted include:

On the Wool Track, Alston Rivers, London, 1912 (reprint of 1910 edition), and Angus and Robertson, Sydney, 1963.

The Dreadnought of the Darling, Alston Rivers, London, 1911, and Angus and Robertson, 1956.

With The Flagship of the South, William Brooks, Sydney, 1909.

Flagships Three, Alston Rivers, London, 1913.

Gallipoli Mission, Australian War Memorial, Canberra, 1948.

Official History of Australia in the War, Vol 1 (1921) and VI (1942) Angus and Robertson, Sydney.

Anzac to Amiens, Australian War Memorial, Canberra, 1968.

'Sidelights of the War on Australian Character', Royal Australian Historical Society, 1927.

'The Writing of the Australian Official History of the Great

War – Sources, Methods and Some Conclusions', *Royal Australian Historical Society*, 1938.

'The Technique of a Contemporary War Historian', *Historical Studies*, 1942.

'Australia' series, *Sydney Morning Herald*, June–July 1907 (published under the initials C.W.).

'The Barrier Railway' series, *Sydney Morning Herald*, May–June 1908.

'The Wool Land' series, *Sydney Morning Herald*, September–December 1909.

'The Dreadnought of the Darling' series, *Sydney Mail*, July–September, 1910.

'The Great Rivers' series, *Sydney Morning Herald*, May–June 1914.

Mostly, the early editions of *On the Wool Track* and *The Dreadnought of the Darling* are the ones quoted, although sometimes the later editions have been used when they provide extra information.

Chapter 1: 'The Finest Selector'

Information about the Leckie family came from Graham and Julie Leckie, at *The Avenue*.

Chapter 2–4: A Biographical Sketch

Sources (in addition to those cited above) that I have used for this biographical sketch include:

'Account for Effie', Bean's story of his early life handwritten for his wife, in the papers of Arthur Bazley, Australian War Memorial, Canberra. This is invaluable. See also Bean's letters to Tasker (October 18, 1930) and L.G. Wigmore (November 16, 1922) in the Bean papers, AWM.

Notebooks and family letters in the Bean papers, AWM.

W.A. Steel and J.M. Antill, *The History of All Saints' College Bathurst 1873–1963*, Angus and Robertson, Sydney, 1964.

G. Souter, *Company of Heralds*, Melbourne University Press, Carlton, 1981.

C.B. Fletcher, *The Great Wheel: An Editor's Adventures*, Angus and Robertson, Sydney, 1940.

E.H. Collis, *Lost Years: A Backward Glance at Australian Life and Manners*, Angus and Robertson, Sydney, 1948. (Collis quotes the Heney article 'A Darling Squatter').

K.S. Inglis, 'C.E.W. Bean, Australian Historian', in John Lack, *Anzac Remembered: Selected Writings by K.S. Inglis*, (ed.); University of Melbourne, Parkville, 1998.

D. McCarthy, *Gallipoli to the Somme*, Ferguson, Sydney, 1983.

S.C. Ellis, *C.E.W. Bean: A Study of his Life and Works*, MA thesis, University of New England, 1969.

M. Ball, *The Story of the Story of Anzac*, Ph.D. thesis, University of Tasmania, 2001. See also Ball, 'Re-Reading Bean's Last Paragraph', *Australian Historical Studies*, 2003.

Notes on Sources

D. Winter (ed.), *Making the Legend: The War Writings of C.E.W. Bean*, University of Queensland Press, St Lucia, 1992.

K. Fewster (ed.), *Gallipoli Correspondent: The Frontline Diary of C.E.W. Bean*, Allen & Unwin, Sydney, 1983.

E.M. Andrews, *The Anzac Illusion: Anglo-Australian Relations during World War I*, Cambridge University Press, Melbourne, 1993.

L. Carlyon, 'Charles Bean and the Gallipoli Journalists', Speech to Bean Foundation dinner, 2001.

L. Carlyon, *Gallipoli*, Macmillan, Sydney, 2001.

H.M. Green, *A History of Australian Literature*, Vol 1, Angus and Robertson, Sydney, 1961.

M. McKernan, *Here is their Spirit*, QUP/Australian War Memorial, St Lucia, 1991.

Reveille, 1 April, 1933.

A.W. Bazley, *Writing the Official History of World War I at Tuggeranong*, Canberra and District Historical Society Address, April 10, 1959.

L.L. Robson, 'The Origin and Character of the First A.I.F., 1914–18: Some Statistical Evidence', *Historical Studies*, October 1973.

For thumbnail sketches of A.B. Paterson and Henry Lawson see G. Davison, J. Hirst and S. Macintyre, *The Oxford Companion to Australian History*, Oxford University Press, Melbourne, 1998.

For a wonderful glimpse of the modern pilgrimage to Gallipoli, see T. Wright, *Turn Right at Istanbul: A Walk on the Gallipoli Peninsula*, Allen and Unwin, Sydney, 2003.

Members of the Bean family, granddaughter Anne Carroll and her husband Ian, and Phyllis Bauer were generous with both time and material; Peter Bazley, son of Arthur, shared memories and information; Michael McKernan, former director of the War Memorial, provided insights and read and supplemented the manuscript, as did Les Carlyon, Tony Stephens, Martin Ball and Peter Stanley.

Chapter 5: The Land That Never Leaves You

E.D. Millen, *Our Western Lands: A Vanishing Asset*, Sydney, 1900.

Before Millen, C.E. Lyne wrote articles for the *Sydney Morning Herald* under the title, 'The Industries of the Colony', after travelling the country; from them was published his 'The Industries of New South Wales', Government Printer, Sydney 1882.

L. Cronin (ed.), *A Camp-Fire Yarn: Henry Lawson, Complete Works 1885–1900*, Lansdowne, Sydney, 1984.

'Western Lands', Western Lands Commission, NSW Government, 1990.

B. Hardy, *West of the Darling*, Jacaranda Press, Milton, Qld, 1969.

W. Davis, *The Bush is Mine and Other Verse*, Bourke Historical Society, 1984.

Notes on Sources

Tom Griffiths's essay is in T. Bonyhady and T.Griffiths, *Words for Country: Landscape and Language in Australia*, UNSW Press, Sydney, 2002.

M. McInerney & C. Middleton, *Tilpa 1880–1980*, Tilpa Historical Committee, 2003. See also *Tilpa Vol II, 1857–1994* by the same authors.

Dick Condon, *Out of the West: Historical Perspectives on the Western Division of New South Wales*, Lower Murray Darling and Catchment Management Committees, 2002.

G. Main, *Gunderbooka: A 'Stone Country' Story*, Resource Policy and Management, Kingston, 2000. George Main also personally provided insights and lent me books.

M. Baines and G. Wise, *100 Years: Celebrating 100 Years of Natural Resource Progress in the Western Division of NSW*, NSW Department of Sustainable Natural Resources and West 2000 Plus, 2003.

Michael Pearson, 'Paroo Tracks: Water and Stock Routes in Arid Australia'. www.icomos.org/australia/tracks.htm

G. Brooke & L. McGarva, *The Glove Box Guide to Plants of the NSW Rangelands*, NSW Agriculture, Orange, 1998.

J. Woodford, *The Dog Fence: A Journey Across the Heart of Australia*, Text, Melbourne, 2003.

B. Mullins and M. Martin, *Western Parks of New South Wales*, A.H. & A.W Reed, Sydney, 1979.

Emily Ingram from NSW National Parks and Wildlife helped with information on national parks. Thanks to

Simon Hearn, M.D. of the Rural Industries Research and Development Corporation, for guiding me to helpful people and places.

Chapter 6: Adaptation and Change

J. Bowen, *Kidman: The Forgotten King*, Angus and Robertson, Sydney, 2000.

S. Muir, *Living Out Back: People of Western New South Wales*, NSW Agriculture, Orange, 2002.

Chapter 7: Fighting the Elements

For the modern face of drought, see L.C. Botterill and M. Fisher (eds.), *Beyond Drought . . . in Australia: People, Policy and Perspectives*, CSIRO Publishing, Collingwood, 2003 and M.Alston and J. Kent, 'Social Impacts of Drought: A Report to NSW Agriculture', 2004.

T. Webb, J. Cary and P. Geldens, *Leaving the Land: A Study of Western Division Grazing Families in Transition*, Rural Industries Research and Development Corporation, Barton, ACT, 2002.

Special thanks to Trevor Webb, for help and also providing the table in chapter 5, and Melanie Fisher.

K. Newman, several articles in *Sydney Morning Herald*, December 1944. See also *Country Life*, December 29, 1944 and T. Bonyhady, *Sydney Morning Herald*, December 24, 1994.

Chapter 8: Women of the West

M. Cannon, *Life in the Country*, Viking O'Neil, Ringwood, 1988.

B. Steven-Chambers, *The Many Hats of Country Women*, Country Women's Association of Australia, 1997.

M. Alston, *Breaking Through the Grass Ceiling: Women, Power and Leadership in Agricultural Organisations*, Harwood, Amsterdam, 2000.

Thanks also to Margaret Alston for her insights and getting material to me quickly.

E. Pownall, *Australian Pioneer Women*, Rigby, 1975.

R. Waterhouse, 'Rural Culture and Australian History: Myths and Realities', Arts, 2002.

H. Board, *Missed Opportunities: Harnessing the Potential of Women in Australian Agriculture*, Rural Industries Research and Development Corporation, Department of Primary Industries and Energy, Canberra, 1998.

The Real Matilda: Women of the West Video, Communications and Resources Project, to celebrate Australia's Bicentenary, Dubbo, 1988.

Thanks for assistance to Anna Cronin, of the National Farmers Federation.

Chapter 9: Falling off the Sheep's Back

R. Woldendorp, R. McDonald & A. Burdon, *Wool: The Australian Story*, Fremantle Arts Centre Press, Fremantle, 2003.

'Prospects for Further Wool Processing in Australia', Centre for International Economics Report, Canberra, 2002.

P. Cashin & C.J. McDermott, 'Riding on the Sheep's Back: Examining Australia's Dependence on Wool Exports', *The Economic Record*, September, 2002.

'Diversity and Innovation for Australian Wool', Report of the Wool Industry Future Directions Task Force, Commonwealth of Australia, Canberra, 1999.

C. Massy, *The Australian Merino*, Viking O'Neil, Ringwood, 1990.

S. Neller (ed.), *Wool in the Australian Imagination*, Historic Houses Trust of New South Wales, Glebe, 1994.

Thanks to Richard Hicks from the Department of Infrastructure Planning and Natural Resources, Far West Region NSW, for help with this chapter and much else.

Chapter 10: The New Merino

Charles Massy and Jim Watts were generous with time and information for this chapter.

Chapter 11: The Old Trade in a New World

D. B. Stuart et. al., 'Sheepshearing in Australia: Some Identified Problems with Practical Answers', University of South Australia, University of Ballarat and Wimmera Health Care Group. Presented to Infront Outback Conference, February, 2000.

Thanks to Bill Shorten of the Australian Workers' Union.

P. Adam-Smith, *The Shearers*, Nelson, Melbourne, 1982.

Chapter 12: The Start of Bean's Wool Track

J. Brunsdon (ed.), *I Love a Sunburnt Country: The Diaries of Dorothea Mackellar*, Angus and Roberston, North Ryde, 1990. Also thanks to Jyoti Brunsdon.

Dorothea Mackellar, *A Poet's Journey: Poems*, The Dorothea Mackellar Memorial Society and Triple D, Wagga Wagga, 2002.

Chapter 13: The Town with Iron Windows

History of Bourke, 13 Vols, Bourke Historical Society, Bourke Wool Press, Vol 1 (1964–66) to Vol 13 (1997).

W. J. Cameron, *Bourke: A Pictorial History*, Bourke Wool Press, Bourke, 1999.

Bourke: A Centenary of Local Government, Bourke Historical Society, 1978.

B. Hickson, A. McLachlan and H. Nicholls, *100 Lives of Bourke*, Bourke Shire Council, Bourke, 2003.

R.I. Jack, 'History of the Shire of Bourke', Report for the Bourke Shire Council, December 2000. And thanks to Ian Jack for material.

F. Hollows with P. Corris, *Fred Hollows: An Autobiography*, Kerr Publishing, 1993.

M. Kamien, *The Dark People of Bourke: A Study of Planned Social Change*, Australian Institute of Aboriginal Studies, Canberra, 1978.

Special thanks to librarian Ann McLachlan for making this project her own, and Paul Roe for help with this chapter and the next.

Chapter 14: A New Industry and a New 'Church'

See J. Yeomans, *The Scarce Australians*, Longmans, London, 1967 for the story of the early American cotton growers.

Information on the cotton industry can be found at www.cottonaustralia.com.au

Information on Cornerstone is available at www.cornerstone.edu.au, or from PO Box 1151, Dubbo, NSW 2830. Cornerstone's Email address is: national@cornerstone.edu.au

Chapter 15: The *Jandra* Sails Again

F.H. Brown, *Songs of the Plains*, compiled and illustrated by W.J. Cameron, Bourke Wool Press, Bourke, 1993.

Thanks to Barbara Hickson for showing us around the Browns' house, and assistance with other historical places.

Chapter 16: The Once Great *Dunlop*

P. McCaughey, *Samuel McCaughey*, Ure Smith, Sydney, 1955.

D.Wall, *The Other Side of Bourke*, published by D. Wall, Mona Vale, 1998. Also used for information on Louth.

R. McDonald, *Shearers' Motel*, Vintage, Sydney, 2001.

Chapter 17: The T on the Gum Tree

R. Burrows and A. Barton, *Henry Lawson: A Stranger on the Darling*, Angus and Robertson, Sydney, 1996.

Chapter 18: The Shearing at *Toorale*

See C. Lyne, *The Industries of New South Wales*, T. Richards, Sydney, 1882, for a description of *Toorale* in the early 1880s.

Chapter 19: Modern Bards Celebrate an Old Romance

H. Phillips, 'Investigation of Two Historic Monuments In Western New South Wales', student paper, University of Melbourne, 1998.

J. Huggins, *Mathews Family History: 1825–1985*, monograph, 1985.

A. Hull, 'Songs of the Bush', *Outback*, Feb/March, 2004.

Chapter 20: Sale of a Bride

References on Afghans are: C. Stevens, *Tin Mosques and Ghantowns: A History of Afghan Camel Drivers in Australia*, Oxford University Press, Melbourne, 1989; M. Cigler, *The Afghans in Australia*, AE Press, Melbourne, 1986.

Myrtle's granddaughter Marilyn and her husband John generously provided documents and photographs, and lent me Perooz's prayer books.

Chapter 21: A Garden in Need of Watering

T. McMillan (ed.), *The Wilcannia Historical Society Guidebook*, Wilcannia, 1987.

M. Lazarus, *A Tale of Two Brothers: Charles Dickens's Sons in Australia*, Angus and Robertson, Sydney, 1973.

B. Hardy, *Lament for the Barkindji: The Vanished Tribes of the Darling River Region*, Rigby, 1976.

Chapter 22: 'The Farthest Town'

G. Rowe, *Saltbush Rainbow: The Early Days at White Cliffs*, 1998.

O. Rogge, *Australia: A Visual Celebration*, New Holland, Sydney, 1997.

Chapter 23: 'A City Girl in Central Australia'

K.S. Prichard's series, 'A City Girl in Central Australia', appeared in *The New Idea*, May to October 1906.

D. Bird (ed.), *Katharine Susannah Prichard: Stories, Journalism and Essays*, University of Queensland Press, St Lucia, 2000. Thanks to Delys Bird for assistance.

K.S. Prichard, *Child of the Hurricane: an autobiography*, Angus and Robertson, Sydney, 1963.

Thanks to Wendy Brazil for chasing up articles.

R. Throssell, *Wild Weeds and Windflowers: The Life and Letters of Katharine Susannah Prichard*, Angus and Robertson, Sydney, 1990.

M.T. Shaw, *Yancannia Creek*, Melbourne University Press, Carlton, 1987, is a useful general reference on the area, and especially on the Quins of Tarella.

For the story of the coaches, see D. de St. Hilaire Simmonds, *Cobb & Co Heritage Trail Bathurst to Bourke*, Cobb & Co. Heritage Trail, Mudgee, 1999.

Chapter 24: Mining the Art Market

G. Blainey, *The Rise of Broken Hill*, Macmillan of Australia, Melbourne, 1968.

G. Blainey, *The Rush That Never Ended*, Melbourne University Press, Carlton, 2003.

R. J. Solomon, *The Richest Lode: Broken Hill 1883–1988*, Hale and Iremonger, Sydney, 1988.

L.S. Curtis, *The History of Broken Hill*, Adelaide, 1908.

R.H.B. Kearns, *Broken Hill 1894–1914*, Broken Hill Historical Society, Broken Hill, 2002.

J. Absalom (co-ordinator), *Art of Broken Hill*, Pitinjarra, 1999.

R.H.B. Kearns, *Silverton*, Broken Hill Historical Society, Broken Hill, 1992.

'Broken Hill and the West Darling', Regional Information Series, Research Publications Pty Ltd, 1980.

I.L.Idriess, *The Silver City*, Angus & Robertson, Sydney, 1956.

M. Twain, *Following the Equator: A Journey Around the World*, AMS, New York, 1971.

Chaper 25: The Maidens of Menindee

S.J. Maiden, *Menindee: First Town on the River Darling*, S. Maiden, Kelmscott, W.A., 2000.

Thanks to all the Maiden family.

For detailed information on Burke and Wills expedition, see T. Bonyhady, *Burke & Wills: From Melbourne to Myth*, David Ell Press, Balmain, 1991; A. Moorehead, *Cooper's Creek*, Hamish Hamilton Ltd., London, 1963; S. Murgatroyd, *The Dig Tree: The Story of Burke and Wills*, Text, Melbourne, 2002.

Chapter 26: The Secret of *Kilfera*

Chaper 27: Hospitality in a Western Town

H.M. (Noni) Glover, *A Town Called Ivanhoe*, H.M. Glover, Ashfield, 1989.

G. Twigg & Y. McBurney, *An Italian Heritage*, Educational Material Aid, Strathfield, 1985.

Sister Margaret McKay, school archivist, Kincoppal-Rose Bay School of the Sacred Heart, kindly looked at detailed Villa family records. The records have Elvira going home at the end of 1906, but I have accepted the family history version.

Chapter 28: The Mystery of Mossgiel

J. Ker Conway, *The Road from Coorain*, Heinemann, Richmond, 1989.

H. Walker, *Memories of the Past*.

H.D. Harris, *The Teams of the Blacksoil Plains*, Rohan Rivett, Camberwell, 1977.

Chapter 29: The End of the Line

B. McGowan, *Australian Ghost Towns*, Lothian, Melbourne, 2002. And thanks to Barry McGowan for assistance and access to unpublished material.

B. McGowan, 'Ringbarkers and Market Gardeners: The History and Archaeology of the Chinese in Rural and Regional Australia', unpublished paper presented at the Centre for Archaeological Research, ANU, Canberra, February, 2004.

D. Betts (ed.), *Our Outback Home: Memories of Nymagee*, Nymagee CWA, 2002.

Chapter 30: The Future of the Darling and its Land

Information on the fisheries from R.H. Mathews, 'The Aboriginal Fisheries at Brewarrina,' Journal and Proceedings of the Royal Society of New South Wales for 1903, published by the Society, Sydney, 1903.

C.J. Lloyd, 'Either Drought or Plenty: Water Development and Management in New South Wales', Department of Water Resources, NSW 1988.

R.M. Younger, *Australia's Great River*, Horizon Publishing, Swan Hill, 1976.

Acknowledgements

Many people helped in this book. It was a family affair: apart from Margaret Cerabona's unflagging assistance, special thanks are due to my uncle Ron Younger, who helped immeasurably in the final stage of writing, especially with the drafting of the prologue and some other sections, as well as bringing a wealth of knowledge of Australia to the project and a special interest in the journalists who covered Gallipoli.

I received extensive assistance with research from Gia Metherell (especially on Bean); Phil Dickie and Susan Brown (who drafted research briefs, found some people I later interviewed, and unearthed the story of the unusual Tilpa war memorial); Gillian Vale, who chased down material and straightened some tortured prose; Gabrielle Hooton, who coped patiently with searches through old newspapers and much checking, and Kerrie Arnett, Simon Holder, and Ron Cerabona for chasing, checking and proofreading.

Nadine Davidoff has, as always, been the best of editors, especially when the author flagged.

Acknowledgements

To all those we met on the 'track' who gave us time, information, recollections and often hospitality, and are quoted or mentioned in the text – please accept my thanks. Others who provided help are acknowledged in the notes to the relevant chapters, as are sources and further reading.